Gathered on the Road to Zion

Gathered on the Road to Zion

Toward a Free Church Ecclesio-Anthropology

DANIEL LEE HILL

Foreword by Marc Cortez

☙PICKWICK *Publications* · Eugene, Oregon

GATHERED ON THE ROAD TO ZION
Toward a Free Church Ecclesio-Anthropology

Copyright © 2021 Daniel Lee Hill. All rights reserved. Except for brief quotations in critical publications or reviews, no part of this book may be reproduced in any manner without prior written permission from the publisher. Write: Permissions, Wipf and Stock Publishers, 199 W. 8th Ave., Suite 3, Eugene, OR 97401.

Scripture quotations are from the ESV® Bible (The Holy Bible, English Standard Version®), copyright © 2001 by Crossway, a publishing ministry of Good News Publishers. Used by permission. All rights reserved.

Pickwick Publications
An Imprint of Wipf and Stock Publishers
199 W. 8th Ave., Suite 3
Eugene, OR 97401

www.wipfandstock.com

PAPERBACK ISBN: 978-1-7252-5077-2
HARDCOVER ISBN: 978-1-7252-5078-9
EBOOK ISBN: 978-1-7252-5079-6

Cataloguing-in-Publication data:

Names: Hill, Daniel Lee, author. | Cortez, Marc, 1972–, foreword.

Title: Gathered on the road to zion : toward a free church ecclesio-anthropology / Daniel Lee Hill ; foreword by Marc Cortez.

Description: Eugene, OR : Pickwick Publications, 2021 | Includes bibliographical references and index.

Identifiers: ISBN 978-1-7252-5077-2 (paperback) | ISBN 978-1-7252-5078-9 (hardcover) | ISBN 978-1-7252-5079-6 (ebook)

Subjects: LCSH: Church. | Free churches. | Zizioulas, Jean, 1931–. | Balthasar, Hans Urs von, 1905–1988. | Hauerwas, Stanley, 1940–.

Classification: BV600.2 .H50 2021 (paperback) | BV600.2 .H50 (ebook)

04/19/21

To Mr. Dr. Lloren A. Foster

Contents

Foreword by Marc Cortez — ix

Acknowledgments — xi

Abbreviations — xiii

1. Introduction — 1
2. The Ecclesio-Anthropology of John Zizioulas — 24
3. The Ecclesio-Anthropology of Hans Urs von Balthasar — 51
4. The Ecclesio-Anthropology of Stanley Hauerwas — 81
5. Zizioulas, Balthasar, and Hauerwas in Dialogue — 111
6. Gathered Under the Rule of Christ: A Free Church Ecclesio-Anthropology — 148
7. Conclusion — 202

Bibliography — 217

Topic Index — 235

Foreword

I grew up in the free church tradition, attending a variety of Baptist and baptistic churches. In those settings, I frequently heard about things like discipleship, maturity, spiritual growth and other terms related to developing as a Christian. However, in my experience relatively little was said about what the Church has to do with simply being *human*. We certainly would have recognized the anthropological significance of many cherished beliefs—the *imago Dei*, the morally responsible nature of the human person, the importance of community, and so forth. Yet I do not recall any extended reflection on how our understanding of what it means to be human might be shaped, not simply by those obviously anthropological commitments, but also by our vision of the Church itself. In other words, while we were well aware that everyone who gathered for worship on Sunday morning was in fact human, we spent relatively little time considering how the doctrine of the Church itself—its nature, purpose, and practices—might be shaping and forming our conception of what it means to be human.

That is tragic given that Christians have historically viewed the Church, even with all of its flaws and foibles, as the sphere within which people are freed to become fully and truly human. If the fundamental human vocation is about pursuing Christlikeness and all that this entails, and if the Church is the community of those brought into union with Christ through the power of the Spirit, then our vision of what it means to be human should be thoroughly shaped by the reality of what God is doing in and through the Church.

This fascinating intersection between ecclesiology and anthropology is precisely what Daniel Hill invites us to explore in this book, focusing specifically on what a free church ecclesiology has to offer for understanding the human person. Some might wonder whether this is an overly abstract way of approaching the study of humanity, particularly in a world wrestling with seemingly more pressing questions about things like the nature of human sexuality, race and racism, and the technological transformation of human bodies. Yet Hill argues convincingly that a Christian view of what it means to be human must be shaped ecclesiologically. And rather than resulting in an overly abstract of humanity, Hill demonstrates that delving deeply into the texture of a particular ecclesiology provides resources for understanding the concrete form of humanity in the world today.

Although Hill draws an array of dialog partners into the project—specifically Hans Urs von Balthasar, Stanley Hauerwas, and John Ziziouas—as a way of learning from other traditions, the real strength of this book lies in its decision to reflect deeply on the anthropological resources of the free church tradition. For those who wonder whether a free church ecclesiology has sufficient depth to fund a robust understanding of the human person, I can only invite you to continue reading. I think you will find, as I did, that those churches I attended as a kid said far more about what it means to be human than I realized.

MARC CORTEZ
Wheaton College and Graduate School

Acknowledgments

Writing projects are never created in isolation, nor are they the product of autonomous individuals. Having traipsed across the many hills and valleys of research, revisions, and rewrites, I am grateful for the many friends, family members, colleagues, mentors, and brothers and sisters who have made this project possible.

I am especially grateful to Dr. Marc Cortez. He has been an extreme help, both in teaching me how to think theologically and in helping me formulate my own ideas. Throughout the course of this project he consistently drove me to the biblical text and called me to clarify, explain, and expound my writing. I could not ask for a better advisor. I am also thankful to Dr. Daniel J. Treier, my second reader, who has spent countless hours sifting through every chapter before giving prompt feedback and helpful insight. Thank you both. I do not take your time for granted and my project is undeniably better as a result of your help.

I am also thankful for the other teachers and mentors who have both guided me to this point and helped me along the way. I am deeply grateful to Dr. Lloren Foster, to whom this project is dedicated, for first putting the tune of the academy in my ear ten years ago. I am thankful for Dr. Rodney Orr, under whose guidance I wrote my master's thesis, and Dr. Glen Kreider, who first pricked my heart with a love for theological theology. Dr. Paul Shockley has always encouraged me to keep an ear and eye toward the church. Additionally, Dr. Richard Schultz and Dr. Nicholas Perrin have been extremely helpful during my time at Wheaton. I am also thankful for all of the members of my PhD committee for their encouragement, support, prayers, and feedback during my proposal period.

I am also deeply grateful for the time I was able to spend in the Wheaton PhD program and with those who comprise its community. I am especially thankful for Ty Kieser, Daniel Lanz, and the members of my cohort, Benjamin Smith, Joshua Harris, Jeremy Lundgren, Jeremy Mann, and Nathan LeMahieu. They have all helped me grow as a scholar and follower of Christ. Ty in particular spent more time than I deserve debating my ideas, evaluating chapters, and giving encouragement and support. I am also incredibly grateful for Matthew Levering, whose course on Hans Urs von Balthasar proved to be immensely helpful and whose words of grace and kindness always seem to come at the right time. I am also thankful to the *Southeastern Theological Review* as portions of chapter 5 appeared in "'Breathe on Us, O Breath of God': The Pneumatological Grounding of Ecclesial Identity," *Southeastern Theological Review* 11.1 (Spring 2020) 79–98. The editors have kindly granted me permission to reproduce some of that material here.

Finally, I would not be here today without the help of my friends and family members who do the often-underappreciated and unforgiving work of bearing my burdens for me. Patricia and Elliot Hill, my parents, have sacrificed incredibly for my sake and have supported me through some rather difficult moments. My sister, Charis, has been a living demonstration of perseverance and lives up to her namesake. I am grateful to be able to call her both my sister and my friend. And while friendship is itself a gift of grace, I feel that I owe Joe Patz, Theon Hill, Mark Jeong, John Deng, Samuel Palacios, Colin Duff, and John Sampson a debt I can never hope to repay.

Abbreviations

CD	*Church Dogmatics*
LCC	Library of Christian Classics
LW	*Luther's Works.* Edited by J. Pelikan and H. T. Lehmann. 55 vols. St. Louis: Concordia, 1955–86
NPNF	*Nicene and Post-Nicene Fathers*
ST	*Summa Theologia*
TD	*Theo-Drama*
TGL	*The Glory of the Lord*
TL	*Theo-Logic*

1

Introduction

Churches are filled with human beings, or at least they ought to be. It is as a community of human creatures that the church gathers together on Sunday mornings to worship the Triune God. It is as a community of human creatures that the church celebrates baptism, receives the Lord's Supper, and hears the preached word. And it is human creatures that disperse from these gatherings back out into the world, fueled with an indefatigable hope, as witnesses to the redemptive work accomplished in Christ. It is enough to make one wonder: Does our life together as the body of Christ meaningfully contribute to our understanding of what it means to be human?

Merely knowing that the church is filled with human beings leaves the relationship between the ecclesial community and the human creatures who comprise it unresolved. While modern theology has demonstrated increased interest in theological anthropology as a distinct locus of theological inquiry,[1] articulating the relationship between these two loci remains an area ripe for theological exploration. In emphasizing the significance of the church as, hypothetically, the realm in which the ideal human community is realized, or the place where humanity is properly formed, an important

---

1. See e.g., Behr, *Becoming Human*; Shults, *Reforming Theological Anthropology*; Saracino, *Christian Anthropology*; Copeland, *Enfleshing Freedom*; Gandolfo, *Power and Vulnerability of Love*. In addition to the renewed interest in theological anthropology, there has been a resurgence in the study of ecclesiology. See e.g., Bray, *Church*; Liston, *Anointed Church*; Harper and Metzger, *Exploring Ecclesiology*; Gunton and Hardy, "Church on Earth"; Horton, *People and Place*.

anthropological query is raised: How *should* ecclesiology inform anthropology? Ecclesio-anthropology is a way of relating two theological loci, ecclesiology and anthropology, in order to understand how the former grants unique and significant insight into the latter.[2] More specifically, it asks the question, how do the nature, practices, mission, and *telos* of the church robustly inform our understanding of humanity? But even the posing of this question presupposes two others: Why think that ecclesiology might inform anthropology and not the other way around? Is ecclesio-anthropology exclusive, or are other approaches to theological anthropology legitimate? While I will return to each of these questions in my conclusion, it seems in undertaking such a project I may need help along the way. For that reason, I have chosen to work with three interlocutors, Hans Urs von Balthasar, Stanley Hauerwas, and John Zizioulas, in order to learn *how* to do ecclesio-anthropology before making my own attempt.

So what, then, is the church? And, to appropriate a phrase from Alasdair MacIntyre, whose church and which ecclesiology?[3] If we assume ecclesiology should in fact inform theological anthropology in unique ways, it stands to reason that different ecclesiologies will result in different anthropologies. Therefore, since this project seeks to articulate the manner in which ecclesiology should inform anthropology, it is important to identify which ecclesiological commitments are at work.

The goal of this project will be to develop a Free Church ecclesio-anthropology. While the Free Church is not typically understood as distinctive in its Christology or soteriology, it does present unique points of emphasis in its *ecclesiology*. With its traditional emphasis on congregationalism, the freedom of the church from state or provincial governance, voluntary adult membership, and the priesthood of all believers, Free Church ecclesiologies contain a broad range of commitments that have clear anthropological significance. I will seek to articulate these implications through the construction of a Free Church ecclesio-anthropology. However, before moving forward this introductory chapter must provide four important resources. First, I will offer a more expansive explanation of what is meant by the term

---

2. This statement does not deny the possibility that ecclesiology and theological anthropology exist in a dialogical relationship. Here, I am simply articulating the aim of this particular project. For a project that seeks to explicitly develop ecclesiology within the context of theological anthropology, see Franklin, *Being Human, Being Church*. Furthermore, I am not stating that ecclesiology *exclusively* informs theological anthropology. Christological or Trinitarian approaches to theological anthropology may in fact be viable options. My project will seek to discern how ecclesiology makes a unique contribution to our understanding of theological anthropology. This is not a claim regarding primacy, but a claim regarding uniqueness.

3. MacIntyre, *Whose Justice?*

"ecclesio-anthropology." Second, I will articulate an understanding of the expression "Free Church," highlighting central characteristics and points of emphasis within the movement. Third, I will give an overview of how contemporary scholars are connecting the two loci and identify why I have chosen Zizioulas, Balthasar, and Hauerwas as my interlocutors. Finally, I will close this chapter by providing a map of the work that lies ahead.

TOWARD A PRELIMINARY DEFINITION OF ECCLESIO-ANTHROPOLOGY

My first task is to provide greater clarity regarding what I intend to communicate with the term "ecclesio-anthropology." While greater precision must await this project's final chapters, a preliminary description will help provide context for my use of the term as we move forward. At minimum, an ecclesio-anthropology connects the two loci of ecclesiology and anthropology, arguing that the nature, mission, practices, and telos of the church play a distinctive and constitutive role in shaping anthropology. To a certain extent, the boundaries between these four categories overlap and are semi-permeable. Still, in this section I will briefly address each in turn and provide a preliminary description. Since my interlocutors use the concepts of nature, mission, practice, and telos in unique ways, this initial description will need to be broad enough in scope to incorporate their various differences. I will then revisit some of these categories in chapter 5.

The Nature and Identity of the Church

First, the church is a community whose origin and existence are predicated upon divine action. To inquire into the church's nature or identity is to ask about its *whatness*. Here, I am not necessitating a certain ontological or metaphysical approach to ecclesiology. Instead, I am asking the following questions: Who or what is this community? How did it come to be? And what organizes its life together? As will be demonstrated below, some of my interlocutors will answer these questions with strong metaphysical commitments while others will prefer an approach that avoids metaphysical concerns altogether, adopting a more pragmatic approach to ecclesial life. In either case, my interlocutors seem to agree that there is something about the church that distinguishes it from other communities and that inclusion into the ecclesial community entails a fundamental change in how we relate to God, to one another, and tothe world. This seems to imply that the very nature of this community significantly changes our understanding of the identity of its members.

The Mission of the Church

Second, the church is created for a specific purpose and is given a unique mission that participates in the larger *missio Dei*.[4] By mission, I am referring to the "being-sent-ness" of the church into the world for a particular task as they await the return of their Lord and the consummation of his kingdom. I will defer from making a decision on where to locate the church's mission until I have heard from each of my interlocutors. For now, mission provides us with an interpretive key for understanding the church's practical life, connecting the church's origin to its telos. The church is sent into the world and then is eventually brought into eternal fellowship with God. Mission helps us understand this overarching movement. Yet at the same time, mission provides the church with its *raison d'être*. In so doing, it gives us a lens for understanding the church's practical life and present existence. Liturgical practices such as corporate worship, baptism, and the celebration of the Lord's Supper are rightly understood in light of what God intends to do in and through the ecclesial community.[5] Chapters 5 and 6 will explore in greater detail how this missional task is to be understood. Minimally, the church's mission provides the interpretive arc that establishes the church's identity and describes the church's task in the present, a task that is concretized in liturgical practices. For example, if the church's mission is to bear witness to the revelation of God in Christ, then we can begin to delineate how particular practices are acts of bearing witness or forming community members into faithful witnesses.

The Liturgical Practices of the Church

Third, the mission of the church is concretized in specific church practices.[6] The practices of the church are intended to *do* something. Christians gather together to baptize initiates, celebrate the Eucharist, and sing songs of worship because they believe that these actions are both necessary and

---

4. Jenson and Wilhite, *Church*, 155.

5. Colwell, "Church as Sacrament," 59.

6. Since I have already articulated a theological approach to understanding the church in light of the *missio Dei*, I will approach the topic of church practices from a theological perspective. For a sociological and phenomenological approach to understanding of liturgical and ritualistic practices, see Bell, *Ritual Theory*.

fitting. Church practices give concrete shape to the church's mission. A robust discussion of liturgical action and practice is beyond the scope of this project. For our purposes, minimally, *a Christian practice is an action regularly performed by members of the ecclesial community in response to divine revelation that shapes and rightly forms its members for the purpose of attaining the community's telos.* A Christian practice finds its coherence within the Christian community's larger, overarching mission and is a response to divine revelation. In this definition, I seek to preserve the particularity of Christian practices and their relationship to divine revelation while also maintaining a level of breadth that incorporates the disparate approaches of my interlocutors.[7] Additionally, we will focus predominantly on liturgical practices.[8] A liturgical practice is a Christian practice that is performed when the ecclesial community gathers to worship and practiced by those "in covenant" with the church. Simon Chan notes that all worship is a divinely enabled response to God, ordered around Word and Sacrament.[9] More than just ritualistic actions, the ecclesial community's acts of gathering together in worship and performing liturgical practices must be understood in light of the living God. As James Smith notes, "The church's worship is a uniquely intense site of the Spirit's transformative presence. We must never lose sight of the changed nature of these practices. These are not just rituals that are unique because they are aimed at a different *telos*; they are also unique because they are practices that bring us face-to-face with the living God."[10] Throughout this book I will be using the term "liturgy" to describe specific practices that the church performs when it gathers together to worship God. Chan writes, "The liturgy may be described as embodied worship. It is worship expressed through a certain visible order or structure (thus

---

7. Here I am synthesizing aspects of both Alasdair MacIntyre's view of practice as rooted in communal notions of the good, as well as their inherently formative nature, with Dykstra and Bass's understanding of Christian practice as arenas in which "something is done to us, and through us that we could not of ourselves do" (Dykstra, *Growing in the Life of Faith*, 56; cf. Dykstra and Bass, "Theological Understanding of Christian Practices," 13–32; MacIntyre, *After Virtue*, 187). For a discussion of their unique contributions and differences, see Smith and Smith, "Introduction," 7–17.

8. As Ola Sigurdson observes, it seems that even practices done outside of the liturgical context are still informed by the liturgical gathering since liturgical practices change the way we see, understand, and experience the world (*Heavenly Bodies*, 276–85). For example, personal prayer is informed by the congregation's life together. In this setting, church members are reminded of God's promises in the preaching of the Scriptures and are confronted with their own shortcomings and failures. Additionally, they are made aware of the needs of their fellow members and can offer up prayer on their behalf.

9. Chan, *Liturgical Theology*, 48, 63.

10. Smith, *Desiring the Kingdom*, 150.

the phrase 'order of service')."[11] Additionally, the adjective liturgical will be used to refer to specific practices that are performed regularly and correctly by the covenanted members of the ecclesial community when they gather together for worship in response to divine revelation that shapes and rightly forms its members for the purpose of attaining the community's telos.[12] I do not deny that non-Christians will invariably partake of the Eucharist or hear the preached word. However, insofar as the non-Christian is not united to the ecclesial community, is seeking goods external to that practice, and fails to live up to the community's standard for that practice, they are not participating in these practices in the fullest sense.[13] Finally, whether it is realizing *theosis* or forming humans rightly, the end to which these practices are ultimately intended reveals something about the people who are being formed or molded through them.

The Telos of the Church

Fourth, the church is a community of the new creation, one that is destined for eternal life with God. When speaking of the *telos* of the church, I am referring to the church's destiny of eschatological fellowship with God following the resurrection of the body and the consummation of the kingdom. Yet this seems to necessarily entail that we view the individual members of the church as teleologically oriented as well. If the church's *telos* is holiness and eternal fellowship with God, it stands to reason that this holiness will

---

11. Chan, *Liturgical Theology*, 62.

12. The adverb "correctly" is attached to liturgical practices in order to appropriate Wolterstorff's notion of a liturgical script he views as the *sine qua non* of a liturgical act. He writes, "To participate in the enactment of a liturgy is thus to perform scripted, rule-governed, actions, just as to participate in the performance of some work of music is to perform scripted, rule-governed, actions" (*God We Worship*, 7; see also Cuneo, *Ritualized Faith*, 3–10). Appropriating the notion of "script" may seem odd for a Free Church account of church practices, but on closer inspection this need not be the case. For example, in celebrating the Lord's Supper there are certain ritual actions, such as the breaking and passing of the bread and cup as well as the reading of Scripture, that seem to be expected. Failing to pray over the elements might strike parishioners as odd, while choosing to read from another book instead of the Bible and refusing to allow any congregant to partake of the elements might be interpreted as a violation of the act itself. It seems these liturgical scripts are less static in the Free Church, but this does not make them any less concrete. Smith writes, "All Christian worship . . . is liturgical in the sense that it is governed by norms, draws on a tradition, includes bodily rituals and routines, and involves formative practices" (*Desiring the Kingdom*, 152). These liturgical scripts still exist on a conceptual level as the logic that governs appropriate performance and worship.

13. See MacIntyre, *After Virtue*, 188–90.

be realized in the lives of its individual members. But this seems to raise important anthropological questions. For example, what does the teleological nature of the members of the ecclesial community then entail about humanity in general? Are human creatures intrinsically teleological? Or is it something that is extrinsic and given to human beings from without? Although the Christian traditions differ vis-à-vis their conceptualization of what the eschatological state entails, the inauguration of the *eschaton* also seems to inform the church's self-understanding and the manner in which it exists in the world. Furthermore, while the church's *telos* is inaugurated within the ecclesial community, it also remains a future hope. This too seems to raise questions of how we should understand human action in the present.

DEFINING THE FREE CHURCH

Yet the goal of this project is not to engage in ecclesio-anthropology in general, although some helpful principles will be developed for guiding such an endeavor. Rather, the goal of my project is to develop an ecclesio-anthropology from a Free Church perspective. Consequently, it is necessary to clarify what is meant by the term "Free Church."[14] This is important if Free Church commitments are to then provide unique contributions to anthropology. Put differently, if the Free Church is unique in its ecclesiology, then it stands to reason that its anthropology will be informed in unique ways. Historically, there seem to be three predominant approaches to understanding Free Church identity: Free Church as the ecclesial prototype, Free Church as an ecclesial antitype, and Free Church ecclesiology as theologically rooted in a particular view of the ministry of Christ.

Free Church as the Prototype

Some view the Free Church form as the original ecclesial prototype that characterized the New Testament church. For these thinkers, Free Church ecclesiology is the recovery of that which had been lost. In contemporary theological discussions, James McClendon will serve as representative of this approach. He argues that the Free Church, at its most basic level, is characterized by a particular hermeneutical vision that emphasizes the continuity between the current ecclesial community and the New Testament

---

14. I am using the term "Free Church" to incorporate both the Baptist and Anabaptist traditions.

church.[15] He uses the phrases "then is now" and "this is that" to articulate this particular relationship, describing the Free Church vision as a "shared awareness of the *present Christian community as the primitive community and the eschatological community*."[16] He goes on to explain, "The church now is the primitive church and the church on the day of judgment is the church now; the obedience and liberty of the followers of Jesus of Nazareth is *our* liberty, *our* obedience."[17] While McClendon's vision argues for a certain approach to hermeneutics, it also gives a particular shape to his ecclesiology. For McClendon, the New Testament authors address particular, local congregations who are equipped by the Spirit and oriented toward mission.[18] According to McClendon, it is from here that Free Church distinctives emerge—namely, a commitment to congregational polity, regenerate membership, and freedom from provincial and governmental restraints vis-à-vis the local church's liturgy, confession, and prayer.[19]

---

15. McClendon uses the term "baptist" instead of "Free Church" to unite both Baptists and Anabaptists under one genus (*Ethics*, 1:19). Both Baptists and Anabaptists possess a unique story and understanding of the world that is informed by the death and resurrection of Christ. For McClendon, the Baptist vision contains two central motifs. First, it requires that Christians read the Bible in a manner consistent with the New Testament church's practice of reading Scripture. Second, it requires a "forward" and "endward" focus. By this McClendon calls the church to understand its identity in light of both the eschatological church and New Testament church (*Doctrine*, 2:343–44).

16. McClendon, *Ethics*, 1:31, italics his.

17. McClendon, *Ethics*, 1:31, italics his. For much of the nineteenth and early twentieth century, it was not uncommon for some Free Churches to view themselves as the original, ecclesiological prototype and attempt to draw continuity between their present, historical moment and the early church. Landmark Baptists viewed their church as the only true church, possessing the essential marks of the New Testament ecclesial community (Leonard, *Baptists in America*, 118–20). However, Landmarkism's interpretation of church history has fallen out of favor in recent years. I will not engage it substantively in this section for three primary reasons. First, such an approach does not adequately respond to the question of whether or not Free Church ecclesiology is a valid expression of ecclesiology. Second, it does not assist in delineating the distinctives of Free Church ecclesiology as its primary point of emphasis is credobaptism. Third, Landmarkism's interpretation of history has been largely contested even within Baptist circles. For discussion of the Landmark Baptist movement, see Tull, *High-Church Baptists in the South*.

18. McClendon Jr. writes, "[A church] is local, Spirit-filled, mission-oriented, its discipleship always shaped by a practice of discernment" (*Doctrine*, 2:343).

19. Cary provides a helpful overview of McClendon's view of ecclesial authority. He argues that for McClendon God is the only authority, with Scripture and the local church serving as proximate authorities. As a proximate authority, the church's primary task is to exercise communal discernment in order to determine how the Spirit is ordering the local community's life (*Free Churches and the Body of Christ*, 184–91).

Free Church as an Anti-Type

Typological approaches to Free Church identity typically describe the Free Church as a sect-type. As a sect-type, the Free Church emerges in response to corruption in the larger, established church.[20] Philip Bartholöma adopts this view and argues that the Free Church is primarily a reaction against other forms of ecclesiology. From this perspective, the Free Church is antitypical in nature, understanding itself in opposition to Catholic, Lutheran, Anglican, and Presbyterian forms of polity.[21] Niethammer writes, "The Free Church is primarily defined as an antitype. . . . As the church of the laity it differs from the church as an institution, as a voluntary church it is the opposite of the people's church."[22] Niethammer does not find theological approaches to Free Church identity particularly compelling. He argues that the Free Church's distinctions are predominantly sociological. Consequently, he avers that the Free Church is identified primarily by its alterity vis-à-vis its social praxis.[23] John Howard Yoder, a Christian ethicist whose abusive and destructive treatment of numerous women casts a significant shadow over any contributions he has made to the discipline of theology, follows a similar path in his work *Body Politics*. For Yoder, the Free Church is a protest against the coercive forces of Constantinianism.[24] Yoder identifies five practices that give the local church its visible shape and form in the world: communal discernment and church discipline, the Lord's Supper, baptism, charismatic ministry, and the open meeting.[25] These observable practices are vital to properly understanding the nature of ecclesial life. Yoder writes, "The free church vision is not satisfied with a renewal only of inwardness (mysticism) or of especially committed groups that let the rest of the body go its own way (monasticism); rather, it projects a visible, debatable, verifiable, attainable local shape."[26] Since the church is made visible through

---

20. See Wright, *Free Church, Free State*, 26–31.
21. Bartholömä, "Self and the Collapsed Other," 55–56.
22. Niethammer, *Kirchenmitgliedschaft in der Freikirche*, 40.
23. Niethammer, *Kirchenmitgliedschaft in der Freikirche*, 40.
24. Yoder argues that Constantinianism absolves the distinction between church and state, leading Christians to view the conversion of the world as their primary task. For Yoder, the duality of church and state must remain intact, as it creates a strict division between those who confess Jesus as Lord and those who do not. See Yoder, *Royal Priesthood*, 102–10.
25. Yoder, *Body Politics*.
26. Yoder, *Royal Priesthood*, 266. Yoder's legacy is a fraught one to say the least. His contributions to theological ethics and Free Church ecclesiology are difficult to overstate, which is the reason for his inclusion here. Many Free Church theologians, including Earl Zimmerman, Gerald Schlabach, and James McClendon, are deeply indebted to

these counterculturalpractices, Yoder encourages a sociological approach to understanding Free Church ecclesiology.

Free Church and the Ministry of Christ

A third way to identify the Free Church is by focusing on every members' participation in the *munus triplex* and the affirmation of Christ's direct rule over his gathered body. David Bebbington summarizes the thinking of Free Church Baptists as follows:

> Identification with Christ in baptism meant a participation in the roles of Christ as prophet, priest, and king. Every church member shared in the prophethood of Christ, and so was bound to bear public testimony; every member shared in his priesthood, and so enjoyed access to the Father; and equally every member shared in the kingship of Christ, and so was empowered to bear authority in his church.[27]

Here, it is argued that Free Church theological commitments give rise to a new form of church polity. The Spirit gathers the church under the direct rule of Christ and enables its members to discern his will for their lives,[28] a task that is given to the congregation as a whole.[29] Furthermore, the

---

his approach to church practices, pacifism, and the narrative of Jesus. However, Yoder's manipulative and sexually abusive practices toward women give significant pause to some who wish to resource his theological proposals, considering that Yoder saw such behavior as congruent with his ecclesiological program and resourced these judgments to resist the disciplinary efforts of the Mennonite institutions in which he participated. While some are hopeful that Yoder's project can be disassociated from his abusive actions, the sheer theological nature of his justifications leads others to suggest that his sexually predatory behavior is an extension of or intrinsic to his thought. What appears to be beyond dispute is the fact that Yoder himself saw his egregious behavior as contiguous with his theological ethics, especially the alterity of the church, his understanding of its authority to experiment with novel peacekeeping practices, and his interpretation and application of Matthew 18. This should serve as a serious warning to those striving to build with Yoder's architectonics, a task this project does not seek to do. Indeed, any Free Church theologian choosing to resource Yoder needs to do so with a careful and critical eye in order to ensure that they do not reify any authoritarian and coercive logics present therein. For further discussion of the complication of Yoder's legacy and abusive behavior, see Jamie Pitts, "Anabaptist Re-Vision," 153–70; Karen V. Guth, "Doing Justice to the Complex Legacy of John Howard Yoder," 119–39; Ted Grimsrud, "Reflections from a Chagrined 'Yoderian,'" 167–74; Isaac Samuel Villegas, "The Ecclesial Ethics of John Howard Yoder's Abuse," 191–213.

27. Bebbington, *Baptists through the Centuries*, 61–62.
28. Volf, *After Our Likeness*, 158.
29. Harmon, "Free Church Theology," 425–26.

Lord's will should not be imposed from without by provincial or parochial authorities since such structures would not be the church qua church.[30] Therefore, the church is free vis-à-vis its liturgy, worship, and confession.

Arriving at a Definition of the Free Church

However, while there are important differences to these various approaches to Free Church ecclesiology, all three articulate similarities vis-à-vis the marks and identity of the Free Church. For both Yoder (antitype) and McClendon (prototype), the shape of the ecclesial community and its practices are sourced in a particular claim the Free Church makes vis-à-vis the direct reign of Christ over the local congregation. Yoder writes, "The definition of the gathering of Christians is their confessing Jesus Christ as Lord. The definition of the whole of human society is the absence of that confession."[31] Yoder does believe that this confession of Christ's lordship gives a verifiable and visible form to the ecclesial community that can be approached sociologically. However, the church's particular shape is grounded in a *theological* commitment regarding who is the true ruler of heaven and earth. Similarly, for McClendon, "the rule of God requires church *members* subject to that very rule. The centrality of Jesus Christ demands church *leaders* led by Christ crucified and risen. The fellowship of the Spirit implies a *common life* whose practices suit, not this present age, but the age to come—a community at once redeemed and redemptive."[32] The church's practical life arises from a specific theological vision of the world understood in light of Christ's inaugurated reign.

Perhaps most importantly, all three approaches seem to identify the same primary characteristics, even if these characteristics are conceptually nuanced. For our present purposes, a church qualifies as a Free Church if it is marked by freedom of conscience, freedom of liturgy, voluntary and regenerate church membership, congregationalist polity, and an emphasis on every member's participation in the ministry of Christ.[33] Free Churches

---

30. Zimmerman, "Church and Empire," 477. This commitment to the freedom of the local church necessarily challenges the imposition of liturgical and confessional regulation from kings, bishops, and presbyters upon the local church. It would be anachronistic to draw a distinction between governmental and provincial rule since during John Smyth's and Thomas Helwys's lifetimes the bishops of the Anglican church also served under the authority of the state.

31. Yoder, *Royal Priesthood*, 108.

32. McClendon, *Doctrine*, 2:366, italics his.

33. See Freeman, "'To Feed Upon by Faith,'" 194; Littell, "Historical Free Church Defined," 59–63; Niethammer, *Kirchenmitgliedschaft in der Freikirche*, 31–43; Kirchner, "Einführung," 9–15; Wright, *Free Church, Free State*, 42–43.

have historically emphasized that Christ directly rules his local church, ordering its life and worship. Therefore, Christ's rule is not mediated by extrinsic governing bodies, but is discerned in the midst of the congregation as church members gather to seek his will. Furthermore, Free Churches place baptism logically subsequent to conversion and, since baptism is the means through which one is initiated into the local church, emphasize regenerate church membership. These baptized members are also all united to Christ and actively participate in his ministry.[34]

THE STATE OF THE QUESTION

While I have clarified my understanding of the terms "ecclesio-anthropology" and "Free Church," work remains to be done. If the goal of my project is to learn how to *do* ecclesio-anthropology from a Free Church perspective, it is important to study and learn from relevant examples. While historically many theologians have brought ecclesiological concerns to bear on their understanding of anthropology, few have made this relationship primary and explicit.[35] However, since it is necessary to delimit the scope of my research, I will now turn to briefly examine four figures who have begun to articulate the relationship between ecclesiology and anthropology: Stanley Grenz, Miroslav Volf, James K. A. Smith, and Patrick Franklin. I will focus here on why they do not serve as ideal dialogue partners for my particular project. I will then conclude this section with a discussion of why Zizioulas,

---

34. See Littell, "Historical Free Church Defined," 59–63; Yoder, "'Free Church' Perspective," 270; Holmes, *Baptist Theology*, 101; McClendon, "Concept of Authority," 2:123–25; Mead, *Lively Experiment*, 107–8.

35. For example, Athanasius of Alexandria argues that the work of Christ recreates human persons and centers their senses on himself, wrenching their heads upward so that they might once again worship God (*On the Incarnation of the Word*, 11.3–7; 14:8; 16:1 [NPNF 4:42–44]). Interwoven within this statement are a series of soteriological, christological, anthropological, and ecclesiological judgments. However, the primary purpose of Athanasius's work is to argue on behalf of the feasibility and necessity of the incarnation of the Son. He is not trying to delineate the relationship between ecclesiology and anthropology. Similarly, Martin Luther discusses anthropology and ecclesiology in conjunction with the concept of justification, defining human personhood in light of justification (Luther, *Luther's Works*, 34:139). In many ways, justification cannot be disassociated from ecclesiology. But Luther's anthropology, while containing several ecclesiological implications, seems to be more soteriological than ecclesiological. These two figures serve as examples, albeit separated by over a millennium, of ecclesiological and anthropological developments that are subsumed in other theological inquiries. Again, while numerous Christian thinkers have discussed these two theological loci, it appears the relationship between the two has only recently been made explicit.

Balthasar, and Hauerwas serve as key figures who are worth engaging on this topic.

Stanley Grenz and Communal Anthropology

Grenz appropriates modern theology's shift to social and relational understandings of the Trinity, granting ontological and epistemological priority to the individual triune persons.[36] He views the intra-Trinitarian relationships primarily through the lens of reciprocated divine love wherein the various members of the Godhead give themselves to one another.[37] For Grenz, "Love, therefore, that is, the reciprocal self-dedication of the trinitarian members, builds the unity of the one God."[38] For Grenz, God's being is constituted in loving relationships. These relationships provide the template that must govern our understanding of all being, especially human beings in particular.[39] "This understanding of God as persons-in-relationship informs our understanding of human personhood as intrinsically relational. Because God is the triune one, the three persons-in-relationship, the *imago dei* must in some sense entail humans in relationship as well, i.e., humans who through their relationships reflect the divine love."[40]

Grenz's relational account of the Trinity grounds his communal account of ecclesiology and anthropology. Understanding the *imago Dei* as both relational and communal, he argues that "the ultimate foundation for human relationships resides in the eternal dynamic of the triune God. Thus, humans fulfill their purpose as destined to be the *imago dei* by loving after the manner of the triune God."[41] Through the indwelling of the Spirit, one

---

36. Grenz, *Rediscovering the Triune God*, 222. Jason Sexton observes there appears to be a distinct shift that took place in Grenz's thought as he searched for a thoroughly Trinitarian ontology, arguing that Grenz followed and then departed from Pannenburg's project (Sexton, *Trinitarian Theology*, 184).

37. Grenz laments the deleterious effects that attempts to understand God under metaphysical categories had on Christian doctrine. He believes they presuppose a commitment to a prior knowledge of being which is then projected onto our understanding of the Triune God. He argues that in such accounts "God is made to fit within the concerns that motivated the discussion of classical ontology" (Grenz, *Named God*, 249). Instead, Grenz seeks to develop an account of divine being (and, by extension, all being) that is grounded in the Triune God. "A theo-ontology, in contrast, draws from the disclosure of the I AM name in a quite different manner. It views the narrative of the name of God as crucial to the ontological quest" (Grenz, *Named God*, 250).

38. Grenz, *Theology for the Community of God*, 71.

39. Grenz, *Named God*, 366.

40. Grenz, *Renewing the Center*, 330.

41. Grenz, *Social God and the Relational Self*, 320.

of the central marks in Grenz's ecclesiology, the individuals of the Christian community are united and established as church through divine love.[42] The Spirit "leads those who are in Christ to reflect through their communal life the kind of love that characterizes the triune God."[43] But this love is more than just an ethic that governs communal praxis; it involves a subsistence in perichoretic relationships. Moreover, "Spirit-evoked ecclesial solidarity entails living out the unity of the triune God. In this perichoretic in-one-another, 'traces' of the others are taken into oneself, and each participant finds (or 'refinds') one's self in the others."[44] Creaturely persons are constituted through a Spirit-empowered relationality wherein their affective interactions with one another enable a creaturely form of *perichoresis*. As a result, the church is a Trinitarian community. He writes, "The community that is ours is nothing less than a shared participation—a participation together—in the perichoretic community of Trinitarian persons."[45] A relational understanding of the Trinity robustly contributes to Grenz's understanding of the communal and relationship nature of anthropology.[46]

Grenz recognizes the importance of ecclesiology in our understanding of human identity and views the church as a prolepsis of the divine image. However, it appears that Trinitarianism is the primary lens through which Grenz develops his theological anthropology, and not ecclesiology. According to Grenz, the Trinity provides us with a lens for understanding humanity. The church is the realm in which this relational anthropology is realized. Grenz makes it clear that his project is aimed at "viewing all aspects of Christian doctrine in a trinitarian light."[47] Additionally, the practices and mission of the church do not play a fundamental role in shaping his understanding of the human person.

---

42. Grenz, *Revisioning Evangelical Theology*, 186.
43. Grenz, *Social God and the Relational Self*, 335.
44. Grenz, *Social God and the Relational Self*, 335.
45. Grenz, "Ecclesiology," 268.
46. Vanhoozer, "Three (or More) Ways of Triangulating Theology," 48.
47. Grenz, *Social God and the Relational Self*, x. Vanhoozer provides a helpful articulation of the differing roles Trinitarianism and community play in Grenz's theological approach. He writes, "In his mature works, Grenz made the Trinity the first of his three motifs that characterize Christian theology: the Trinity is the structural motif, the community the integrative motif, and eschatology the orienting motif" (Vanhoozer, "Three [or More] Ways of Triangulating Theology," 46). However, if Vanhoozer's analysis is correct, then the church, as an integrative motif, is the arena where the structure of the Trinity is realized in relational terms.

Miroslav Volf and the *imago Trinitatis*

Volf argues that the Godhead is an egalitarian community of free, self-giving love. "When gifts circulate within the Godhead, no rivalry happens; and hierarchy is not reaffirmed. The one who gives is not greater than the one who receives for all give and all receive. Each gives glory to the other with each gift given."[48] For Volf, God's unity is grounded in *perichoresis*, the mutual interiority and self-giving of Trinitarian persons,[49] and not in a divine nature.[50] Furthermore, each person of the Trinity is its own interdependent and mutually internal center of action.[51] He writes, "The structure of trinitarian relations is characterized neither by a pyramidal dominance of the one (so Ratzinger) nor by a hierarchical bipolarity between the one and the many (so Zizioulas), but rather by a polycentric and symmetrical reciprocity of the many."[52] For Volf, neither the particular persons of the Trinity nor the community has primacy, rather "persons and community are equiprimal in the Trinity."[53] Similar to Grenz, divine love emerges as an organizing principle and central motif for Volf's project.

Volf believes that the Trinity ought to inform our understandings of human personhood and ecclesiology. The church is a community that proleptically experiences communion with God.[54] One of Volf's primary goals is to advocate for the catholicity of Free Church ecclesiology. Consequently, he argues that the ecclesiality of independent and individual churches is rooted in the fact that "the church, both the universal *communio sanctorum* and the local church, is not a collective subject, but rather a communion of persons, though the latter are indeed not self-contained subjects, but rather are interdependent."[55] Here, significant similarities emerge between Volf's portrayal of the Godhead and his approach to ecclesiology. For Volf, the oneness of the Godhead ought to be understood as three interdependent centers of action that are unified perichoretically. Similarly, the church is one as multiple autonomous churches interdepend upon one another.

---

48. Volf, "Being as God is," 10.

49. Volf describes *perichoresis* as "the reciprocal *interiority* of the trinitarian persons: that in every divine person as a subject, the other persons also indwell; that all mutually permeate one another, though in so doing they do not cease to be distinct persons" ("Community Formation as an Image," 226, italics his).

50. Volf, *After Our Likeness*, 202–3.

51 Volf, *After Our Likeness*, 203, 220.

52. Volf, *After Our Likeness*, 217.

53. Volf, "'Trinity is Our Social Program,'" 409.

54. Volf, *After Our Likeness*, 129.

55. Volf, *After Our Likeness*, 145.

Human personhood is also described in perichoretic terms.⁵⁶ Individual persons do not exist in pure autonomy and isolation. Rather, human beings subsist in relationship to God and to other human persons.⁵⁷ Through the indwelling of the Holy Spirit, Christians are connected to one another and experience a "creative mutual giving and receiving, in which each grows in his or her own unique way and all have joy in one another."⁵⁸ Human creatures experience a Spirit-ed *perichoresis* in which they interpenetrate one another and participate in a communion of love.⁵⁹

Yet Volf, like Grenz, does not seem to make robust use of ecclesiology in his approach to theological anthropology. For Volf, the emphasis is placed firmly on humanity as *imago Trinitatis*. While Volf argues on behalf of Free Church forms of polity, his project is less interested on how this form of polity contributes to our understanding of the human creature or how the Spirit's work in the church's practical life contributes to our understanding of human nature and destiny. In other words, ecclesiological concerns do not appear to be driving his anthropological inquiry.

James K. A. Smith and Liturgical Anthropology

James K. A. Smith's liturgical anthropology strives to articulate how liturgy shapes human love, imagination, and identity. For Smith, human persons are beings whose identities are constituted by their deepest loves, loves that are formed through liturgical action. "To be human is to love, and it is what we love that defines who we are. Our (ultimate) love is constitutive of identity."⁶⁰ Liturgies, both secular and Christian, are formative of the human person, shaping how and what we love. Our loves are formed through liturgical action as we embody certain communities whose narratives shape us in accordance with certain visions of the good life.⁶¹ The

---

56. Volf is clear that human creatures are only capable of mirroring God's perichoretic life in creaturely ways. As corporeal beings and creatures we are inherently limited. "Since ontically human beings are manifestly not divine and since noetically human notions of the Triune God do not correspond exactly to who the Triune God is, Trinitarian concepts such as 'person,' 'relation,' or '*perichoresis*' can be applied to human community only in an analogous rather than a univocal way" (Volf, "Trinity is Our Social Program," 405).

57. Volf, *After Our Likeness*, 183.

58. Volf, *After Our Likeness*, 189.

59. Volf, "Trinity is Our Social Program," 410.

60. Smith, *Desiring the Kingdom*, 51.

61. Smith, *Imagining the Kingdom*, 109. Smith unpacks this predominantly through the concept of metaphor and narrative. Liturgies create "worlds" through a series of

church is fundamentally a worshipping community that provides an alternative liturgy. This alternative liturgy properly forms human persons in correspondence with the kingdom. Liturgical anthropology then seeks to explain how human persons, as imaginers and lovers, are shaped through the practice of worship. He writes, "A liturgical anthropology requires a Christian phenomenology of our embodiment (a kinaesthetics), which will then be the platform for a Christian phenomenology of our aesthetic nature (a poetics)."[62] In other words, Smith argues that a liturgical anthropology must account for how human embodiedness and situatedness in specific communities informs human imagination, love, and formation. If, as Smith avers, we are what we love and worship, Smith's project seeks to uncover how human identity is formed and fashioned through liturgical action. The church is then essential to our understanding of anthropology as it is only through the church's liturgical action that we can be properly formed.

However, despite the strong merits of Smith's proposal, I do not find him to be an ideal interlocutor for the learning how to go about *doing* ecclesio-anthropology. Smith, for his part, uses a phenomenological account of worship practices to elucidate their formative nature. Yet he seems to be more interested in exploring how the church shapes human loves and imaginations than he is in articulating how our understanding of the church fundamentally shapes our inquiry into anthropology. For that reason, I would not describe his project as ecclesio-anthropology per se.

Patrick Franklin and Anthro-Ecclesiology

Patrick Franklin's *Being Human, Being Church* is worth discussing since he explicitly seeks to explore the relationship between ecclesiology and theological anthropology. More specifically, Franklin's project attempts to

---

governing metaphors, some of which are hardwired into us through immersion into the various communities in which we exist (Smith, *Imagining the Kingdom*, 119–23). For Smith, Christian liturgies train us to adopt the right set of metaphors and, thus, become a people who habitually resist the alternative liturgies of the world. The church trains us for this lifestyle of resistance through its liturgical action. "Habits are inscribed in our heart through bodily practices and rituals that train the heart, as it were, to desire certain ends" (Smith, *Desiring the Kingdom*, 58). The task of the church is to cultivate the imagination of its parishioners, refashioning their vision of the "good life" so as to reorient their loves toward the k'ingdom. Smith writes, "If the practices of Christian formation are truly going to reform our manners and deflect our dispositions to be aimed at the kingdom of God, then such practices need to engender rightly ordered erotic comprehension by renewing and reorienting our imaginations" (Smith, *Imagining the Kingdom*, 159).

62. Smith, *Imagining the Kingdom*, 20.

demonstrate "how [theological anthropology] can help us better understand the nature and character of the church's (inner) sociality and its (outward) relation to the world, especially with respect to personal, social, and global ethics."[63] Franklin adopts three core motifs that structure his understanding of the human person: relationality, rationality, and eschatology. For Franklin, human creatures are relational in that their uniqueness emerges from the special ways that God relates to them.[64] The rational nature of human creatures "emphasizes the aspect of human purpose and destiny that concerns *knowing* God and other human beings and *understanding* God's created world."[65] Finally, the eschatological nature of humanity consists of the unique telos God has given to them to personally advance over time as beings and also care for and develop creation.

Franklin then uses these three guiding motifs to better understand the nature of the church.[66] For each of the three motifs, Franklin focuses on how it relates to the church's inner life as well as how it guides the church's interactions with the world. Regarding the relational nature of humanity, Franklin argues that the church is a community of love where members are united to one another in the Spirit and together participate in Trinitarian life.[67] The church seeks to engage the world by bringing "alienated human beings into life-giving relationships with God and other human beings by incorporating them into the Body of Christ."[68] Regarding the rational nature of humanity, Franklin describes the church as a community that cultivates wisdom and serves "as a social catalyst for wisdom and as leaven for godly social transformation."[69] Finally, the eschatological nature of humanity reveals that the church is "a kingdom community that forms kingdom disciples to become representatives and witnesses to God's present and coming reign" while engaging "the world by sharing in Christ's reign."[70]

Franklin intentionally seeks to discern how theological anthropology contributes to our study and understanding of ecclesiology. Yet this means

---

63. Franklin, *Being Human, Being Church*, 49.

64. Franklin, *Being Human, Being Church*, 84.

65. Franklin, *Being Human, Being Church*, 111, italics his.

66. It is worth noting that Franklin views these three components of the church through the lens of the *munus triplex*. The church's priestly task is to offer alienated people a relationship with God, its prophetic vocation involves proclaiming and demonstrating the truth, and its kingly calling is to influence the world by representing God's reign in Christ.

67. Franklin, *Being Human, Being Church*, 178–79.

68. Franklin, *Being Human, Being Church*, 206.

69. Franklin, *Being Human, Being Church*, 208.

70. Franklin, *Being Human, Being Church*, 237.

that he also cannot serve as an appropriate dialogue partner vis-à-vis exploring how to do ecclesio-anthropology since his project seeks to do the very opposite. While I do not deny that ecclesiology and theological anthropology may exist in a dialogical relationship, I am more interested in how ecclesiology is germane to our study of the human person.

Selecting Interlocutors

Instead, I will engage three figures as interlocutors, all of whom have served as significant voices of modern theology: John Zizioulas, Hans Urs von Balthasar, and Stanley Hauerwas. While not exhaustively indicative of their respective traditions,[71] each of these three figures have clearly connected the two loci of ecclesiology and anthropology, uniquely grounding the latter in the former. I have chosen these particular figures for three primary reasons. All three figures meet my basic criteria for my definition of ecclesio-anthropology, present clear articulations of ecclesio-anthropology in their respective proposals, and add a potential ecumenical gift to my project.

First, all three of these figures meet the basic definition for ecclesio-anthropology as I have outlined above. They view the church as a community created by God and journeying toward eternal fellowship with him, participating in his mission in the present. However, they also strive to articulate how each of these aspects of ecclesiology strongly contributes to our understanding of the human creature. Regarding liturgical action, for example, both Zizioulas and Balthasar argue that the church's liturgical life is vital to correctly understanding the human creature. Similarly, for Hauerwas it is through the church's concrete practices that human creatures are rightly shaped and formed. In so doing, these three figures articulate how the nature, practices, mission, and telos of the church inform our understanding of humanity.

Second, these three figures present clear articulations of ecclesio-anthropology. This is vital since my project seeks to learn how to go about the process of *doing* ecclesio-anthropology from a Free Church perspective. Zizioulas is clear that the *ordo cognescendi* for theology begins with the church's liturgical life. Similarly, Hauerwas has stated that all theology begins with ecclesiology and the church's practical life. If this is the case, a right understanding of theological anthropology would necessarily also be found in studying the church's life together. Balthasar emphasizes the

---

71. John Zizioulas is the Eastern Orthodox metropolitan of Pergamon, Hans Urs von Balthasar was a Catholic priest, and Stanley Hauerwas is a mainline Protestant theologian.

Marian shape of the church. And, when this is held in conjunction with his argument for the fundamentally feminine disposition of human creatures, it seems clear that ecclesiological considerations are fundamental to our understanding of the human subject. Additionally, both Zizioulas and Balthasar develop and employ the concept of "ecclesial persons"—that is, an understanding of personhood that emphasizes the ecclesial community as the place where human creatures are rightly formed (Balthasar), ontologically constituted (Zizioulas), and/or realized (both) within the church. Simply put, human personhood is tethered to ecclesiology. Hauerwas does not employ the concept of ecclesial persons per se. However, he still develops a strong ecclesio-anthropology. According to Hauerwas, a correct understanding of human vocation and teleology is revealed by the "story shaping practices" of the church. These ecclesiological points of emphasis are not over against the christological, Trinitarian, or narratival aspects of their theological anthropologies. Furthermore, I am not saying that ecclesiology is the exclusive dogmatic location for their theological anthropologies. Rather, I am arguing that all three figures view the church as an arena that both reveals and shapes our understanding of what it means to be human. Furthermore, in so doing, they seem to intimate that ecclesiology plays a constitutive role in our understanding of what it means to be human and what humans are meant to be.

Third, while I could choose to solely engage Free Church figures, I believe that engaging other voices within the Christian tradition will both challenge Free Church premises and broaden the potential ecumenical contributions of my project. Simply put, the Free Church has much to learn from the global church. Additionally, this may help prevent my project from being too insular as it seeks to go outside of the Free Church tradition in order to learn how to be more faithful followers of Christ. This will be evidenced in chapters 5 and 6 in particular. There, I will seek to learn from my interlocutors, place them in dialogue with one another, and critique them when necessary in order to become better equipped for the constructive work that lies ahead.

A MAP OF THE WAY FORWARD

While not denying that Trinitarian theology and Christology contribute vibrantly to our understanding of the human person, the goal of this project will be to connect the loci of ecclesiology and anthropology. Specifically, I will seek to answer the dogmatic question, how do the ecclesio-anthropologies of John Zizioulas, Hans Urs von Balthasar, and Stanley Hauerwas assist in the development of a Free Church ecclesio-anthropology? I will begin our project by engaging and analyzing the ecclesio-anthropologies of John Zizioulas, Hans Urs von Balthasar, and Stanley Hauerwas, three figures who have explicitly and robustly understood their anthropological conclusions in light of their respective ecclesiologies. These first three chapters will be primarily descriptive in nature. In each of them, I will begin by asking each interlocutor two questions: Who or what is the Church? What is the resulting relationship between ecclesiology and anthropology? The fifth chapter will then attempt to synthesize key themes that have arisen over the course of my project's descriptive work. The sixth chapter will then use the aforementioned dialogue for the construction of a Free Church ecclesio-anthropology.

In the first chapter, I will engage the ecclesio-anthropology of John Zizioulas. Beginning with a discussion of Zizioulas's ecclesiology, I will demonstrate that for Zizioulas the ecclesial community is primarily understood as a eucharistic community, experiencing a foretaste of eschatological *theosis*. Grounded in the Trinitarian life of God, human beings enter the ecclesial community through baptism where they are transformed from biological subjects into true, ecclesial persons. "The Church must cease to be looked upon primarily as an institution and be treated as *a way of being*. The Church is primarily *communion* i.e., a set of relationships making up a mode of being, exactly as is the case in the Trinitarian God."[72] I will then turn to demonstrate that Zizioulas's ecclesiology robustly informs his anthropology, particularly as it pertains to the sacramental and eschatological orientation of human personhood. There, I will demonstrate that four particular distinctives have emerged from the chapter's descriptive work. Zizioulas's ecclesio-anthropology is characterized by the constitutive nature of the church's liturgy, an eschatological orientation toward *theosis*, the punctiliar nature of personhood, and the ecstatic identity and vocation of human persons.

In the second chapter, I will turn my attention to the work of Hans Urs von Balthasar. There we will see that for Balthasar the church is a perpetuation of the mission of the incarnate Son who has poured himself out for the redemption of the world. Balthasar views Jesus as the theological person par excellence—that is, as the one whose self-perception corresponds perfectly to God's idea of him and as the one who understands his role entirely in light of God's mission for him.[73] The kenotic mission of Christ grounds Balthasar's ecclesiology. Beginning in the Godhead, this kenotic outpouring enters the world stage in the incarnation where it is ultimately received,

---

72. Zizioulas, *Being as Communion*, 15, italics his.
73. Balthasar, *Persons in Christ*, 3:166–68. Hereafter, it will be cited merely as *TD*.

embraced, and perpetuated by the church.[74] The ecclesial community is characterized by Mary's servant-like receptivity and openness to receive from God, enabling the church's members to receive Christ's mission and realize their identities in Christ. Consequently, Balthasar's ecclesio-anthropology has five predominating features: human personhood is ecclesially received, sacramentally formed, feminine in nature, vocationally shaped, and teleologically oriented toward self-surrender.

Next, in my third chapter, I will engage the ecclesio-anthropology of Stanley Hauerwas. For Hauerwas, the church is a community formed by the story of Jesus. Recognized predominantly through its practices, Hauerwas argues that the church is a political community that is shaped by the story of God's reign in Christ. The church's mission is then to be a community rightly formed by this story, existing as an alternative polis and community of witnesses.[75] The church is principally concerned with the moral life—that is, the training of its members to be a people of virtue who tell the Christian story rightly and whose lives demonstrate the truthfullness of the Christian narrative. Hauerwas writes, "As Christians, we are not, after all, called to be morally good but rather to be faithful to the story that we claim is truthful to the very character of reality—which is that we are creatures of a gracious God who asks nothing less of us than faithful service to God's Kingdom."[76] I will then argue that Hauerwas's ecclesio-anthropology contains four distinctives: the narrative shape of the self, the political nature of humanity, the eschatological orientation to human life, and the peaceable character of humanity's telos.

The fifth chapter will then place these three figures in dialogue with one another in order to identify helpful guardrails that should guide ecclesio-anthropology in general and my constructive work in particular. The dialogue will be organized around the articulation of four theses regarding the being, practices, mission, and telos of the church. In so doing, I will begin to question some aspects of the ecclesio-anthropologies of my interlocutors, highlighting necessary tensions that must be maintained, errors that must be avoided, and important questions that must be answered. Ultimately, these theses will play a vital role in the subsequent chapter where I will attempt to develop a Free Church ecclesio-anthropology.

My sixth chapter will seek to develop a Free Church ecclesio-anthropology. The first necessary step will be to articulate a particular form of ecclesiology. Consequently, I will claim that there are significant voices within the Free Church tradition who have viewed the immediate lordship

---

74. Balthasar, *Spirit and Institution*, 156.
75. Hauerwas, *In Good Company*, 6.
76. Hauerwas, *Christian Existence Today*, 102.

of Christ as the organizing principle for their ecclesiology and that this is a useful starting point. Next, I will turn to engage Ephesians 4–5, arguing that it is a key passage for exploring the importance of the gathered community's task of hearing the Lord's voice, growing in maturity together, and learning to live in ways that rightly reflect the confession that Jesus Christ is Lord. Gathered by the Spirit beneath its Lord, the church is a community that shares in a derivative form of his *munus triplex*, mediating God's word and presence through the agency of the Spirit while embodying the kingdom of God in the present. From there, I will explore how this particular ecclesiological commitment informs Free Church accounts of anthropology in distinct ways. I will identify four characteristics of Free Church ecclesio-anthropology: a Spirit-ed approach to identity, a Christotelic orientation, an interdependent and communal view of human nature, and the unique vocation of serving as the means through which God mediates his word and presence to the created world.

The Free Church has historically understood itself as a pilgrim people—that is, a community of regenerate believers, freely gathering together to discern their Lord's will as they journey toward future fellowship with him. Yet, as we have seen, this introduces important anthropological questions. The goal of this project is to articulate how Free Church distinctives provide unique or perhaps even necessary insight into theological anthropology per se. But before we can go about the process of *doing* Free Church ecclesio-anthropology, we must first learn *how to do so* from other members of the Christian community who have already walked this path. It is to this task that we now turn.

2

The Ecclesio-Anthropology of John Zizioulas

John Zizioulas, the Metropolitan of Pergamum, has emerged as a significant voice of modern theological inquiry. Believing that Western theologians have allowed substance ontology to alter their perception of God's being, Zizioulas returns to patristic sources—namely, the Cappadocian Fathers—in order to propose an understanding of the Trinity that rejects Western individualism and prioritizes the Triune God's communal nature.[1] While

---

1. It is beyond the scope of this project to engage in the veracity of Zizioulas's historical claims, particularly as they pertain to the Trinitarian divide between the East and West. Some have found Zizioulas's engagement with patristic sources to be less than satisfying: Ayres, *Nicaea and its Legacy*; Butner, "For and against de Régnon," 399–412; Loudovikos, "Person Instead of Grace," 684–99; Turcescu, "'Person' versus 'Individual,'" 527–39; Rostock, "Two Different Gods?," 321–34; Wilks, "Trinitarian Ontology of John Zizioulas," 63–88. For more sympathetic readings of Zizioulas's engagement with patristics, see Papanikolaou, "Is John Zizioulas an Existentialist?," 601–7; Brown, "On the Criticism of Being as Communion," 35–78.

However, Zizioulas's theological propositions still warrant consideration for a number of reasons. First, while he does depend upon the Cappadocian fathers, he attempts to root his argument in both existentialist claims and biblical passages. Even if Zizioulas's interpretation of the Cappadocians is incorrect, a premise in his larger argument, his conclusions could still be true. Second, there is also a degree of ambiguity and diversity in patristic sources. As Gijsbert van den Brink argues, "Social trinitarians do not need to denounce Augustine's views or uphold an over-simplified construction of Eastern versus Western accounts of the Trinity. It is enough for them to point to the

Zizioulas's work regarding Trinitarianism and theological anthropology has generated a considerable amount of interest in recent years, generally less attention has been paid to the manner in which his ecclesiology informs his anthropology.[2] This chapter will argue that for Zizioulas ecclesiology plays a pivotal role in his understanding of anthropology and human personhood. Beginning with a discussion of Zizioulas's understanding of the church as a community of persons, this chapter will proceed to explain the anthropological implications of his ecclesiology before delineating the distinctive elements of his ecclesio-anthropology. More specifically, I will argue that for Zizioulas the church possesses an eschatological mode of existence, one in which ecclesial persons subsist in Triune community. The event of the Eucharist historicizes the ecclesial community in the present.[3] Consequently, one of the significant aspects in Zizioulas's ecclesio-anthropology is that the church's liturgy, particularly the event of the Eucharist, actualizes human personhood by realizing the church's eschatological, theotic destiny. For Zizioulas, it is in that moment the members of the church are able to enjoy unhindered communion with God and, therefore, are most fully and truly human persons.

---

undeniable fact that the patristic sources contain a variety of trinitarian accounts, some of which may be more illuminating than others" (Brink, "Social Trinitarianism," 341). Third, there is always the possibility that the church fathers' conclusions, both those of Augustine and the Cappadocians, require modification. If Zizioulas can prove his readings of personhood and the Trinity are consistent with the judgments of the biblical text, they at least warrant consideration. Finally, Zizioulas's influence is quite pronounced, influencing the work of Miroslav Volf, Cornelius Plantinga, and, on a more popular level, Tim Keller. Suffice it to say, even if Zizioulas's historical conclusions are oversimplified or invalid, his theological positions must still be charitably engaged.

2. A few works have emerged that engage Zizioulas's ecclesiology and its relationship to both Trinitarianism and anthropology: Volf, *After Our Likeness*; Fox, *God as Communion*; MacDougall, *More than Communion*; Mong, "One and Many," 44–59. Yet, for the most part, each of these works focuses specifically on how Zizioulas's perception of the Trinity impacts his ecclesiology and anthropology. While Volf acknowledges Zizioulas's *ordo cognoscendi* begins with the life of the church before moving to discuss Trinitarianism and anthropology, he chooses to "begin with an examination of the ontology of person at the trinitarian and anthropological levels" before concluding "with an examination of the essence and structure of the ecclesial community" (Volf, *After Our Likeness*, 75). Each of these works is able to highlight the Trinitarian, relational, and eschatological emphases in Zizioulas's work, emphases that are undeniably present. However, while they provide helpful insights into Zizioulas's understanding of the nature of personhood, they do not focus primarily on how Zizioulas's anthropology is being informed by his ecclesiology, nor do they articulate particular themes that are present in his ecclesio-anthropology.

3. Zizioulas uses the verb "historicize" to refer to the Spirit's work of bringing the eternal kingdom of God into present history.

THE CHURCH AS A EUCHARISTIC COMMUNITY

For Zizioulas, true personhood and being are modeled after the Triune God. And since God's *tropos* of existence is in relationships, if the church, or human beings for that matter, is to possess true, authentic being as the image of God it must be modeled off God's way of being.[4] As Daniel Munteanu observes, "True being subsists in community."[5] For Zizioulas, "The Church is primarily *communion* i.e., a set of relationships making up a mode of being, exactly as is the case in the Trinitarian God."[6] Personhood is received and realized within the church through baptism where individuals are reconstituted in Christ and united with one another as persons in communion.[7] However, personhood remains an eschatological reality that is only fully realized in *theosis*. The liturgical practice of the Eucharist realizes this eschatological communion with God in the present. The Eucharist continuously grounds and regrounds the ecclesial community. Consequently, the church is a eucharistic community, one that models the life, love, and way of existence of the Triune God as persons in communion as they await the consummation of the kingdom of God.

The Triune, Communal God

The tension held between the "one" and the "many" is fundamental to Zizioulas's understanding of the church's being. For Zizioulas, a true understanding of being must be derived from the very life of God, a God who exists communally.[8] He writes, "The mystery of the church, even in its institutional dimension, is deeply bound to the being of man, to the being of the world and to the very being of God."[9] In fact, the being of God is archetypal for all being. If this is true, then the church's mode of being must mirror the

---

4. Zizioulas, *Being as Communion*, 15.

5. Munteanu, "Anthropologie der Freiheit," 72, my translation.

6. Zizioulas, *One and the Many*, 15, italics his.

7. Zizioulas claims to be agnostic regarding both the personhood and salvation of persons outside of the church. I will return to this below.

8. For Zizioulas, discussion of God must involve the totality of his relationships since he is intrinsically communal. As Luco J. van den Brom notes, "To speak of the Church means speaking at the same time of Christ in his togetherness with the community of believers and *vice versa*. And God is relational as well: to speak of Christ means speaking at the same time of the Father and the Holy Spirit and this implies, without the concept of communion we cannot speak of God's being" (Brom, "Church on its Way," 36, italics his).

9. Zizioulas, *Being as Communion*, 15.

intra-Trinitarian life of God.[10] This is especially true if, as Zizioulas argues, the church itself is the image of God, existing in the same mode of existence (*tropos hyparxeos*) in which God exists.[11] This way-of-being, for both God and the church, is in the event of communion, an event of subsisting in relationship with the other.

Rejecting what he identifies as an Augustinian revision to the doctrine of the Trinity, Zizioulas argues that the West has prioritized the oneness of God over against his Triune nature.[12] Zizioulas is unsatisfied with this understanding of the Trinity because he believes it elevates the substance of the divine being over against the persons of the Godhead, binding God's being to an impersonal nature. Accordingly, Zizioulas believes that Western approaches to the Trinity compromise God's absolute freedom to determine his own mode of existence.[13] Consequently, he views it as a departure from a traditional doctrine of the Trinity. Contra Augustine and other Western figures (according to his reading),[14] Zizioulas seeks to return to a Cappadocian understanding of the Trinity, one that adopts "an ontology which is based on personhood, that is, on a unity or otherness emerging from relationships, and not one of substance."[15] He claims that the intra-Trinitarian relationships obtain logical primacy in our understanding of being, an understanding that views being as inherently relational. The unity of the Godhead emerges through the loving relationships that constitute it.[16] Furthermore, each member of the Godhead is identified by the manner in which they relate to the other members of the Triune community. He writes, "If God exists, He exists because the Father exists, that is, He who out of love freely begets the Son and brings forth the Spirit. Thus God as person—as the hypostasis of the Father—makes the one divine substance to be that which it is: the one God."[17] For Zizioulas, the persons of the Trinity are

---

10. Zizioulas, *Communion and Otherness*, 4.
11. Zizioulas, *Communion and Otherness*, 42.
12. Zizioulas, *Being as Communion*, 44–46.
13. Fox, *God as Communion*, 40.
14. While it has been noted already that Zizioulas's reading of the Greek Fathers has been reexamined in recent years, it is also worth noting that his reading of Augustine has come under significant scrutiny, particularly its reliance on the *de Régnon* paradigm. As Butner argues, "Even granting [the de Régnon paradigm's] limited historical applicability, it bears little to no fruit in systematic theology. Beginning with the oneness of God simply does not lead inevitably to a theology in which persons are captive to substance ontology" (Butner, "For and against de Régnon," 237–50).
15. Zizioulas, *Being as Communion*, 159.
16. Zizioulas, *Communion and Otherness*, 9.
17. Zizioulas, *Being as Communion*, 41.

only conceivable in relationship to one another, as "'Father' has no meaning outside of a relationship with the Son and the Spirit, for he is the Father *of someone*."[18] And it is the Father, himself, who wills and causes God to exist as Trinity.

The Father wills and causes the Triune community, begetting the Son and sending forth the Holy Spirit. As Aristotle Papanikolaou summarizes, "Being, insofar as it is grounded in God, is grounded in the freedom and love of the person of the Father and, as such, is constituted as relational and personal in terms of its 'mode of existence' or *tropos hyparxeos*."[19] In other words, the Father grounds the ontology of Trinity, yet is inconceivable apart from the other members of the Trinity. As a result, God's being is fundamentally relational, existing in a nexus of personal relationships. It is this communion that accounts for the unity of the Godhead.[20] For Zizioulas, "The being of God is a relational being: without the concept of communion it would not be possible to speak of the being of God."[21] Neither the Father, the Son, nor the Spirit can be conceptualized apart from the event of communion and their relationship to one another. The existence of the other is the sine qua non of personhood because a person's identity emerges in communion with another person. "The person is an identity that emerges through relationship (*schesis*; in the terminology of the Greek Fathers); it is an 'I' that can exist only as long as it relates to a 'thou' which affirms its existence and its otherness."[22] But what characterizes this relationship? For Zizioulas this relationship is characterized by freedom and love *for* the other. Personhood, then, requires relationship, freedom, and love for the other. For example, the Father begets the Son and sends forth the Spirit. Without this process of begetting and/or sending forth, the concept of God as Father loses any meaning. God the Father exists as Father insofar as he freely begets the Son and sends forth the Spirit. The identity of each of these divine persons is constituted by the unique relationships in which they

---

18. Zizioulas, *Lectures in Christian Dogmatics*, 53, italics his.

19. Papanikolaou, *Being with God*, 87. Grounding the being of God in the person of the Father is a significant theological move for Zizioulas as he seeks to avoid substance ontology. Patricia Fox believes Zizioulas does this in order to emphasize "that the ontological principle of God is a person, that the being of God is identified with a person." She goes on to observe "the significance of this for Trinitarian theology is that God exists on account of a person, not on account of a substance" (Fox, *God as Communion*, 40). Zizioulas wants to give ontological priority to the person over against any substance ontology because he believes doing so compromises God's freedom, binding it to an impersonal substance.

20. Zizioulas, *Communion and Otherness*, 136.

21. Zizioulas, *Being as Communion*, 17.

22. Zizioulas, *Communion and Otherness*, 9.

subsist. Consequently, according to Zizioulas we are unable to conceive of the divine persons in isolation, but only in the event of communion.

Freedom and love, then, are what characterize the particular relationships between the three members of the Godhead. For Zizioulas, all three persons of the Trinity inhabit an ecstatic mode of existence. The Father *loves as* the person of Father and the Son *exists as* beloved by the Father. For Zizioulas, with this nexus of relationships between divine persons, the I-Thou of communion in otherness, the Father, Son, and Spirit subsist in a relationship of love. Each member of the Trinity freely moves toward the others and in so doing realizes the event of communion.[23] Miroslav Volf finds this to be intrinsic to Zizioulas's understanding of God as a person. "Personhood is God's essence and logically precedes God's characteristics; that *God's essence is person* means nothing other than that God *is* love."[24] The person freely moves toward the other and this movement of love is the heart of communion. Zizioulas describes love as the free choice on behalf of the other. It is "a *gift* coming from the 'other' as an affirmation of one's uniqueness in an indispensable relationship through which one's particularity is secured ontologically. Love is the assertion that one exists as 'other,' that is, particular and unique, *in relation to* some 'other' who affirms him or her as 'other.'"[25] For Zizioulas, love is the acceptance and affirmation of the other as a particular and the recognition of our own interdependence.[26] This is similar to how, in their perichoretic life together, the divine persons exist on behalf of one another. It is this mode of being, existence for the other, that is the *sine qua non* of loving community. He writes, "The phrase 'God is love' means that God is constituted by these personal relationships. God is communion: love is fundamental to his being, not an addition to it."[27] Love acknowledges otherness—that is, particularity—and moves toward the other in communion.

Zizioulas claims that God's mode of existence is such that his very being is identical with communion and that this mode of being is archetypal for the being and identity of the church.[28] He writes, "The genitive 'of God'

---

23. Zizioulas, *Communion and Otherness*, 72.
24. Volf, *After Our Likeness*, 78, italics his.
25. Zizioulas, *Communion and Otherness*, 55, italics his.
26. Zizioulas, *Communion and Otherness*, 55.
27. Zizioulas, *Lectures in Christian Dogmatics*, 53.
28. Zizioulas, *Being as Communion*, 44. Volf observes that for Zizioulas the church is ultimately best understood as *imago trinitatis* (Volf, *After Our Likeness*, 84–85). This is because the church reveals and "has its birth in the entire economy of the Trinity" (Zizioulas, *Being as Communion*, 112). Furthermore, the nature of the church in Zizioulas's ontology, as instituted by Christ and constituted by the work of the Holy Spirit,

shows clearly that the identity of the Church derives from her relation with the Triune God.... In the first place it means that the Church must reflect in her very being the way God exists, i.e. the way of personal communion."[29] He goes on to state, "When we say that the Church is *koinonia*, we mean no other kind of communion but the very personal communion between the Father, the Son and the Spirit. It implies also that the Church is *by definition incompatible with individualism*."[30] Thus, in order for individuals to become persons, since personhood is necessarily relational, they must be freed from what Zizioulas labels ontological necessity and be born again into communion, into the ecclesial community.[31] This seems to intimate that the church must be a *true* community of persons in communion—that is, a communion that mirrors and participates in the very Trinitarian life of God.

The Church as Community

For Zizioulas, the very being of the church is a reflection of the being of God. Just as God exists as persons in communion, so too does the church. In his own words, "Ecclesial being is bound to the very being of God. From the fact that a human being is a member of the Church, he becomes an 'image of God,' he exists as God Himself exists, he takes on God's 'way of being.'"[32] Zizioulas understands the church as a community whose very being is oriented in the same way as God's—that is, it recognizes and embraces particularity but rejects individualism through love. Entered through baptism, it is continually reconstituted by the Eucharist. Since the ecclesial community is

---

reveals the Trinity in history (Mong, "One and Many," 47). In other words, the Trinity is revealed within the life of the church.

29. Zizioulas, "Church as Communion," 7.

30. Zizioulas, "Church as Communion," 7, italics his.

31. For Zizioulas, ontological necessity describes how the individual human creature has no control over the fact that they exist and that their existence must be accepted as a statement of fact. Consequently, the human being cannot have freedom as they are bound and forced to subsist in necessity, an existence determined by the beings that preceded their own. And without freedom the individual cannot experience love (Zizioulas, *Being as Communion*, 51–52). This mode of existence, as Paul McPartlan notes, is "something to be overcome, and it is Christ who enables the overcoming" (McPartlan, *Eucharist Makes the Church*, 239). Not only does this mean that creatures qua creatures are intrinsically finite temporally, but it also means, as those predicated by the individualism of Adam's biological hypostasis, there is a relational finitude as well (Zizioulas, *Communion and Otherness*, 107). In contrast, ontological freedom is "an ability to choose and constitute one's own being" (Harrison, "Zizioulas on Communion and Otherness," 273).

32. Zizioulas, *Being as Communion*, 15.

constituted by the Holy Spirit and subsists in the Son-Father relationship, it is also an eschatological community of ecstatic love.[33]

As I have demonstrated above, Zizioulas views the being of God as archetypal for all true being. Similarly, personhood must be conceived in light of God's mode of existence. Zizioulas claims that the "ecclesial hypostasis, as a transcendence of the biological, draws its being from the being of God and from that which it will itself be at the end of the age."[34] It is a truer type of existence, one that conforms to and mirrors the *imago Dei*. As Cortez notes, this "ecclesial *hypostasis* comes only through Christ, who offers not just a *revelation* but the *realization* of true personhood in the world, and thus the possibility of *participation* in Christ's own hypostatic existence."[35] This new mode of existence does not erase the particular existence of the individual but rather reconstitutes it by grounding the individual in Christ and a relationship with God, more specifically, through participation in the filial Son-Father relationship. And if, as Zizioulas argues, true personhood is only correctly understood in light of God's existence as persons in communion, then in order for an individual to become a person their isolation must be overcome and reconstituted in God's mode of existence. Only then can the corporeal, relational, and temporal limitations of createdness be overcome as members of the ecclesial community pursue one another in love and participate in divine communion.[36] The ecclesial existence is one in which persons exist as only persons can: as communion in otherness. Furthermore, a fundamental characteristic of this community and this mode of existence is the capacity to love as God himself loves.[37]

As a community of ecclesial persons, the members of the church embody an ecstatic mode of existence, subsisting in the love of God while

---

33. Robert Turner argues that Zizioulas's ontology of being—that is, his understanding of being in light of divine being—and his view of the *eschaton* are foundational principles to Zizioulas's overall ecclesiology (Turner, "Eschatology and Truth," 15).

34. Zizioulas, *Being as Communion*, 62.

35. Cortez, *Christological Anthropology in Historical Perspective*, 182, italics his.

36. For Zizioulas, all of creation is bound by temporal and relational finitude. It is only through communion with God that this temporal, corporeal, and relational finitude is overcome. "It is such a particularity or *hypostasis* that the human being is called to be as an image of God, that is, a particularity that would be ontologically true by overcoming mortality, and at the same time capable of hypostasizing the rest of creation so that creation, too, may be saved through incorporation in the human being" (Zizioulas, *Being as Communion*, 67, italics his). As Papanikolaou observes, for Zizioulas, "personal existence . . . becomes a reality only in an *ekstatic* and *hypostatic* movement and communion with the uncreated, with that which does not die" (Papanikolaou, *Being with God*, 144, italics his).

37. Zizioulas, *Being as Communion*, 57–58.

offering this same love to one another. The church exists as God himself exists. If, as I have discussed above, for Zizioulas the statements "God is love" and "God is a person" are synonymous, then if the ecclesial community is to be comprised of ecclesial persons, it too must be a community of love. He writes,

> The Church, in her very way of being, is the truly erotic mode of existence. She is the place where God's love as the love of a particular and ontologically unique being (the love of the Father for his only-begotten, i.e., uniquely loved, Son) is freely offered to his creation in the person of Christ, so that every particular human being may freely obtain ontological otherness (i.e., true uniqueness not subject to annihilation by death) in him.[38]

The church mirrors God's personhood as *imago Dei*.[39] As a result, in order to obtain true personhood and to be conformed to the image of God, the individual being must be incorporated into the ecclesial community. For Zizioulas, personhood just is an ecclesial concept.

In essence, the ecclesial hypostasis is a theotic existence, one in which communion with God is unhindered and true being is realized. *Theosis* is the eschatological participation in the communion of Triune love and the acquisition of God's free mode of being.[40] Zizioulas understands this to be the primary characteristic of this new mode of existence as "the capacity of the person to love without exclusiveness, and to do this . . . out of the fact that his new birth from the womb of the Church has made him part of a network of relationships which transcends every exclusiveness."[41] The hypostasis of ecclesial existence involves a new way of relating to the Triune God and to the world. As a result of the fall, humanity is set on a descending path toward individualism and difference, one that distances human beings from one another and God. The work of redemption creates communion through the incarnation of Christ and the sending of the Holy Spirit. Christ, as both fully human and fully divine, overcomes this difference as the very embodiment of communion in otherness, the one and the many.[42] The Holy

---

38. Zizioulas, *Communion and Otherness*, 71.
39. Zizioulas, *Communion and Otherness*, 95.
40. Zizioulas, *One and the Many*, 12.
41. Zizioulas, *Being as Communion*, 57–58.
42. Zizioulas, *Communion and Otherness*, 241. We will discuss in greater detail below the difference between a biological and ecclesial hypostasis as it pertains to anthropology. However, it is important to note that Zizioulas views "otherness" and "difference" as different ideas. He writes, "Otherness and difference are often taken to mean the same thing in our minds. However, if we understand otherness as uniqueness, we must clearly distinguish it from the notion of *difference*" (Zizioulas, *Communion*

Spirit works in baptism to draw us into Christ's hypostatic existence and realizes the possibility of attaining communion with God.[43]

For Zizioulas, an ecclesial hypostasis is received through baptism wherein the individual becomes a member of the ecclesial community. In the event of baptism the human person is reconstituted so that they no longer subsist in the ontological necessity of Adam. Instead, they are freed to live for the other in Christ. He writes, "The *hypostasis of ecclesial existence* is constituted by the new birth of man, by baptism. Baptism as new birth is precisely an act constitutive of hypostasis. As the conception and birth of a man constitute his biological hypostasis, so baptism leads to a new mode of existence . . . to a new 'hypostasis.'"[44] The human creature is constituted as a biological hypostasis at conception and birth where they are ontologically and existentially bound to Adam. But this biological existence is marked by individualism and a spiraling descent toward isolation, culminating in death. For Zizioulas, individualism not only is the essence of sinfulness but leaves no room for love or freedom. And if the human creature is not free, they cannot be like or with God. Moreover, the impending reality of death is problematic as a temporal creature and relationship cannot adequately ground personhood. McPartlan recognizes that for Zizioulas, "I cannot be a person in relation to Adam because he is dead; his 'I' has expired."[45] As a result, the individual lacks the type of existence needed to truly ground their own identity. In order to be freed from ontological necessity and death, the human creature must be born again—that is, they must be reborn in the risen and living Christ. This ontological transformation occurs during the event of baptism where the individual is reconstituted by the Holy Spirit and reborn into the mode of existence that is characteristic of divine life.[46] In so doing, they are welcomed into the Christian community and given the gift of the ecclesial hypostasis. As MacDougall notes, "Incorporation into

---

and Otherness, 69, italics his). Otherness relates to both personhood and particularity, given that personhood is sourced in God. It describes the unique relationship that one particular has to another. Difference, on the other hand, relates to individuality—that is, what individuates me from the other. He goes on to say, "Difference does not involve uniqueness; it is not absolute or radical ontological otherness, since it does not require us to regard any 'other' as absolutely Other in relation to other others" (Zizioulas, *Communion and Otherness*, 69). As a result, difference, at least described this way, is inherently isolated from the other whereas otherness understands oneself in relationship to the other.

43. Zizioulas, *Eucharistic Communion and the World*, 74.

44. Zizioulas, *Being as Communion*, 53, italics his.

45. McPartlan, *Eucharist Makes the Church*, 177.

46. Zizioulas, *Eucharistic Communion and the World*, 114; cf. Turner, "Eschatology and Truth," 21.

the body of Christ, taking on the ecclesial hypostasis, is participation in the relational communion of Son to Father, which alone is *theosis*-salvation."[47] Baptism marks the initiation into the true, authentic mode of being: communion. It is the "adoption of man by God, the identification of his hypostasis with the hypostasis of the Son of God."[48]

Furthermore, baptism marks the individual's initiation into an eschatological community. For Zizioulas, the church can only subsist in the present temporarily through the work of the Spirit as the *eschaton* and history stand in contradistinction to one another.[49] "The Church is primarily a foretaste of the eschatological assembly of the Lord made present in the world. The Resurrection of Christ and Pentecost makes the Church and its worship the presence of the future."[50] This foretaste is of "the eschatological state of existence," one in which full communion and freedom are perfectly realized as all of creation is brought into relationship with Christ.[51] This full realization means that the church is not bound by history or even located within it. The church's true identity is eschatological. As Zizioulas sees it, "The reality of the Church comes to it from the eschaton. . . . The Church receives its identity from that which is to come, so that the Church is able to

---

47. MacDougall, *More than Communion*, 72.

48. Zizioulas, *Being as Communion*, 56.

49. I will discuss in greater detail how the Holy Spirit overcomes the "problem of history." For now, it is important to note that for Zizioulas the *eschaton* is not a future point in time but the end of time. In it, the redemptive plan of God is culminated and all of creation is brought into communion with God. MacDougall concludes that for Zizioulas "in the eschaton, the relationship between created and uncreated being will be transformed: created being will commune fully in God's own personal communion, thereby itself becoming fully personal and free for the first time" (MacDougall, *More than Communion*, 87). According to Zizioulas, time exists as it does today, fragmented between the past, present, and future, due to the fall and the presence of sin, a dissonance that culminates in death. But Zizioulas argues that the future, the *eschaton*, is not a distant point in future time, nor is it the culmination of history; rather it is the source from which present and past attain their significance and meaning. In the eschatological kingdom of God "the fragmentation and necessary sequence of the three elements of time (past, present, and future) have been healed" (Zizioulas, *Eucharistic Communion and the World*, 59). Furthermore, Zizioulas claims that in the *eschaton* we see true being. Papanikoloau comments that, for Zizioulas, "the 'eschaton' is nothing less than God's eternal life, and, as such, the eschaton is truth insofar as truth is God's being" (Papanikolaou, *Being with God*, 31). As a result, the *eschaton* serves as the basis of our epistemological understanding of truth and true being. Insofar as they are divinized and united with God in *theosis*, the temporal limitations of human persons will be transcended (cf. Munteanu, "Homo eucharisticus," 199).

50. Zizioulas, *Lectures in Christian Dogmatics*, 127.

51. Zizioulas, *Communion and Otherness*, 76.

make the future present to the world now."⁵² The reasoning for this is simple: it is only in the kingdom that death will be defeated and the people of God will experience true, unadulterated Trinitarian communion. He writes, "The trinitarian model of existence in which otherness and communion coincide can become an ontological reality for creation only when the 'last enemy' (1 Cor. 15:26), which separates and disintegrates beings, thereby generating individualism, self-love, and fear of the Other, is finally conquered in the Kingdom."⁵³ It is only in the *eschaton* that death will finally die. MacDougall observes that not only is the ecclesial community an eschatological reality, but that it is also the actualization of true ecclesial personhood as well. "The perfect attainment of the ecclesial hypostasis is only an eschatological reality, as communion is not a present reality for creation but is its eschatological destiny."⁵⁴ This will take place in the form of realized *theosis*, when the kingdom of God is fully instituted, the sequence of history ends, and communion with God is fully realized.

As an eschatological community, this community of ecclesial beings cannot exist fully in the present. Zizioulas is aware of the limitations of human sinfullness and the reality of death, an ontological reality that impinges on the attainment of true communion. In fact, it is for this reason that true communion and, by consequence, the attainment of ecclesial personhood and community, remains an eschatological destiny. It will only be achieved in the *eschaton* in *theosis*. So what then does this mean for the church as it exists today? For Zizioulas, it is the church's liturgy, through the work of the Holy Spirit, that bridges the gap between history and the *eschaton*. Particularly, this takes place through the Eucharist. It is through the practice of the Eucharist that the church becomes, again and again, the church. As a result, the church, as it exists in our experience, is also a eucharistic community.

The Church as a Eucharistic Community

As noted above, Zizioulas bases his ontology in his understanding of the Trinity as a community of persons. Since personhood is only experienced in communion with God, it is necessary for God to move toward us if we are to participate in the event of communion. In the Eucharist, the Spirit works through the church's liturgical action to realize the future reality of the *eschaton* in the present so that true and unhindered communion is experienced. In the liturgy, the Christian community receives divine communion

52. Zizioulas, *Lectures in Christian Dogmatics*, 129.
53. Zizioulas, *Communion and Otherness*, 88.
54. MacDougall, *More than Communion*, 68.

as a gift from God and participates in his ecstatic love. Consequently, for Zizioulas it is in the moment of communion that the church is most truly the church, as it is there that the ecclesial hypostasis is actualized.

For Zizioulas, the Eucharist is the liturgical event par excellence. It is essential to the very identity of the church. Zizioulas writes, "*The Church constitutes the Eucharist while being constituted by it.* Church and Eucharist are inter-dependent, they coincide, and are even in some sense identical."[55] While baptism involves an initiation into the ecclesial hypostatic mode of existence, in the celebration of the Eucharist, this eschatological, true mode of existence is realized in the present.[56] For Zizioulas, "What Baptism initiates, therefore, the Eucharist fulfills. Otherness as the emergence of a new particular being through Baptism is granted eternal being through communion in the Eucharist."[57] Baptism initiates an individual into personhood. The Eucharist continually regrounds personhood in its eschatological identity, wherein communion with God is fully and finally realized. As Dennis Doyle notes, the Eucharist "encompasses both history and its eschatological fulfillment; though performed in time, the ritual gives Christians a real foretaste of eternal divine love."[58] Through their participation in the liturgy, Christians are brought into communion with God and experience the reality of their ecclesial hypostasis through the work of the Holy Spirit.

An ontological transformation occurs in the event of the Eucharist that enables humanity to receive the love and communion of God. Zizioulas writes, "In the Eucharist we can find all the dimensions of communion: God communicates himself to us, we enter into communion with Him, the participants of the sacrament enter into communion with one another, and creation as a whole enters through man into communion with God."[59] Aristotle Papanikolaou identifies this understanding of the Eucharist as one of the distinct contributions of Zizioulas's project. He avers, "In the eucharist, the baptized faithful are constituted as the Body of Christ and, thus, as participants in the life of the triune God."[60] Furthermore, in the *anamnesis* of Christ within the event of the Eucharist, the church looks forward to the *eschaton* and remembers its true identity.

---

55. Zizioulas, *Eucharistic Communion and the World*, 105, italics his. This is especially important for Zizioulas in light of his understanding of what truth *is* and what the Eucharist *does*.

56. Zizioulas, *Eucharist, Bishop, Church*, 46.
57. Zizioulas, *Communion and Otherness*, 80.
58. Doyle, *Communion Ecclesiology*, 158.
59. Zizioulas, *Communion and Otherness*, 7.
60. Papanikolaou, *Being with God*, 31.

As the eucharistic community is a proleptic, historicized presence of the ecclesial community, mirroring a future union with God, it is also inherently eschatological. Zizioulas writes, "The people gathered by that Eucharist are an installment of that final assembly."[61] Rejecting a view of the Eucharist as a reenactment of the atonement, Zizioulas argues that "the truth of the Eucharist is that it does not take us to Calvary in order to leave us there, but brings us through it and beyond to the communion of the saints and the glory of the kingdom of God."[62] The celebration of the Eucharist takes the present Christian community into the *eschaton*, into the realization of communion with God and the truest, fullest experience of personhood as participation in the ecstatic life in God. As Gaëtan Baillargeon observes, for Zizioulas "the Eucharist is revealed to be the place where the mystery of the Church comes into history."[63] If the church as a community involves unhindered communion with God in the *eschaton* and this eschatological existence is the church in its truest sense, then during the event of the Eucharist the church is the church in its truest sense. In other words, the Eucharist realizes an experience of the still future *theosis*. McPartlan is helpful here as he notes, "Zizioulas wants to see each eucharistic assembly as the *bearer*, or *eikon*, of the eschatological assembly until the last day. Until then, the *one* eschatological assembly has its existence only in and as these *many* eucharistic assemblies, each of which is not part of the eschatological gathering, but that gathering in its fullness."[64] The eucharistic community is one that awaits its fulfillment when all of creation is transformed in the kingdom of God, fully transcending the limits of its createdness and achieving perfect communion with God.

Part of the church's eucharistic nature involves the vocation of offering creation back to God in order to give it true being and life. For Zizioulas, the finitude of the created world is something that must be overcome and transcended.[65] Creation, if left unattended, will eventually decay.[66] However, God's original goal for creation was that it would exist in communion with him. In the liturgy of the Eucharist, the church takes the elements of the created world and refers them back to God, offering the world up to him. He writes, "As images of God human beings are called to offer the rest

61. Zizioulas, *Lectures in Christian Dogmatics*, 129.
62. Zizioulas, *Lectures in Christian Dogmatics*, 134.
63. Baillargeon, *Perspectives orthodoxes sur l'Église-Communion*, 66, my translation.
64. McPartlan, *Eucharist Makes the Church*, 170, italics his.
65. Zizioulas, *Eucharistic Communion and the World*, 138.
66. Zizioulas, *Eucharistic Communion and the World*, 140. See Fox, *God as Communion*, 63–67.

of creation the possibility of overcoming mortality, that is, showing them to be truly hypostatic by hypostasizing their 'hypostasis' in a personal relationship with the immortal God so that they may obtain true hypostatic existence."[67] Zizioulas seems to intimate that those in the image of God (the church) possess the ability to transcend created finitude through their relationship with God as well as the ability to refer creation itself to God and thereby preserve it from destruction. More than that, the eucharistic ethos involves a commitment to cultivating and developing creation so that it becomes more than what it is by nature.

In conclusion, the church takes its very being from the being of God. Zizioulas's ecclesiology is communally, liturgically, and eschatologically oriented as he grounds the church's identity in its liturgy and in the very being of God. As God exists in communion and the person of Christ is inherently communal, the body of Christ, through the work of the Holy Spirit, is defined by communion in otherness, the unity of the "One" and the "Many." The mission of the church is then to extend this eucharistic fellowship to the rest of creation, bringing it into fellowship with God. The church's liturgical practices enable its members to experience true personhood. Human beings are only persons insofar as they become ecclesial persons, reborn and reconstituted in Christ through the work of the Spirit in the liturgy of the church.[68] The telos for humanity and all of creation is participation in the communal life of God. If this is the case, human personhood itself must be understood in terms of God's relational mode of existence and the ecclesial hypostasis. The church, as the body of Christ and the image of God, serves as the very basis for Zizioulas's understanding of human personhood and the only place where it is realized.

THE ECCLESIO-ANTHROPOLOGY OF JOHN ZIZIOULAS

In the introduction I argued that an ecclesio-anthropology must take into account how the nature, practices, mission and telos of the church inform our account of humanity. In this chapter I have demonstrated that for Zizioulas the church is a community that subsists in the Son-Father relationship,

---

67. Zizioulas, *Communion and Otherness*, 66–67.

68. Zizioulas is adamant that the church's liturgical action cannot be separated from the work of the Spirit. It is only through the work of the Spirit, as the one who is able to transcend history, that the *eschaton* can be brought into the present. Zizioulas argues "the Spirit is *beyond* history, and when he acts in history he does so in order to bring into history the last days, the *eschaton*" (Zizioulas, *Being as Communion*, 130, italics his). And if the church is an eschatological reality, then it is the Spirit who constitutes the church Christ has instituted (Zizioulas, *One and the Many*, 15).

thus existing as God himself exists. It is now time to examine how this particular understanding of the church informs Zizioulas's anthropology. Given Zizioulas's particular view of the church's nature, practices, mission, and telos, I will now proceed to identify four themes that are distinctive of Zizioulas's ecclesio-anthropology: it is liturgically realized, eschatologically oriented, intermittently experienced, and ecstatic in shape.

Liturgically Constituted Persons

Zizioulas's ecclesio-anthropology begins with the church's liturgy, particularly the Eucharist event, which actualizes human personhood. In the liturgy, the Spirit historicizes communion with God by allowing human creatures to obtain a foretaste of *theosis*. According to Zizioulas, "Man cannot realize his personhood outside the Church, or else the Church is ultimately irrelevant and should be made redundant. The Church must be conceived as the place where man can get a taste of his eternal eschatological destiny, which is communion in God's very life."[69] The liturgical action of the church through the work of the Spirit historicizes true being—that is, being as communion—resulting in an ontological change that enables human creatures to become persons. The Eucharist celebration is the moment in which individuals receive the communal life of God and, by consequence, experience true personhood. It grounds and regrounds ecclesial personhood as the Spirit brings the eschatological community into the present. However, participation in the event of the Eucharist is predicated upon baptism, which initiates human beings into the ecclesial community. These two liturgical actions together are ontologically and existentially constitutive of human personhood.

Baptism and Ecclesial Personhood

Baptism, for Zizioulas, initiates the human creature into the ecclesial mode of existence, reconstituting them as a person in Christ. As the Spirit baptizes an individual, they receive an ecclesial mode of existence and subsist in the Son-Father relationship.[70] For Zizioulas, a true person is a baptized person.[71] For Zizioulas, this involves both an ontological and an existential

69. Zizioulas, *One and the Many*, 15.
70. Zizioulas, *One and the Many*, 40; Zizioulas, *Lectures in Christian Dogmatics*, 150.
71. Zizioulas writes, "The agnosticism and uncertainty concern only those who do not believe in Christ and are not members of his Church. . . . As far as we know, the Church as the Body of Christ is the only sure and safe way to God" (Zizioulas, *One and*

claim. Regarding the existential shift that occurs in baptism, the identity of the baptized person changes from being grounded in Adam to being rooted in the Son-Father relationship. This new identity is received from God as a gift. Yet, baptism also involves an ontological transformation. As Munteanu and Russell observe, for Zizioulas baptism also imparts a new hypostasis, a new mode of existence, and a new identity to humanity.[72] In baptism, one is incorporated into the body of Christ and, as a result, acquires a new hypostasis, one that is no longer bound by the limits of ontological necessity. As Zizioulas argues, "Baptism in the Trinity means entering into a certain way of being which is that of the Trinitarian God."[73] In other words, baptism serves as the means, via the work of the Spirit, through which an individual receives personhood and participates in the life of God. And for Zizioulas this is an ontological transformation, not merely an ethical or existential one. Volf finds this to be an integral part of Zizioulas's understanding of personhood. "A human being can become a person only if her individualizing 'biological hypostasis' is altered in its inner constitution while not really being suspended as such; the change must be ontological and not merely moral."[74] For Zizioulas, a new (ontological) constitution is required in order to participate in the life of God and experience communion that results in a new existential understanding of the self. Baptism is the means through which the human creature is ontologically and existentially remade in the image of the Trinity. This seems to intimate that the liturgical action of the church is constitutive of human identity and ontology.

---

the Many, 397). Yet, he chooses to remain silent regarding the results of the last judgment. However, as Ciraulo notes, the exclusivity of personhood to Christians appears to be the logical conclusion of Zizioulas's theology if personhood is received through the Eucharist (Ciraulo, "Sacraments and Personhood," 996). Ciraulo posits that, while for Zizioulas baptism is the only revealed means of obtaining personhood for the Christian community, perhaps personhood can exist in degrees outside of the Christian community (Ciraulo, "Sacraments and Personhood," 997). But an understanding of degreed personhood or the suggestion that it is intrinsic to every human creature seems incompatible with Zizioulas's view of personhood. As Cortez notes, "Such a quantitative approach to personhood, though, suggests that personhood is at least partly an intrinsic capacity of the biological *hypostasis*, something Zizioulas explicitly rejects" (Cortez, *Christological Anthropology in Historical Perspective*, 185). In other words, to be a Christian is to be a person. It seems that, for Zizioulas, personhood must exist in varying degrees (an idea Zizioulas outright rejects), be extendable to those outside of the Christian community, or be received and experienced solely by Christians.

72. Munteanu, "Anthropologie der Freiheit," 75; cf. Russell, "Reconsidering Relational Anthropology," 174.

73. Zizioulas, *One and the Many*, 3.

74. Volf, *After Our Likeness*, 88.

Yet baptism not only marks an ontological transformation into a personal mode of existence, it also bestows a new telos upon human beings. It sets them on the road to communion. Whereas in Adam, finitude meant that they were destined for death and division, the baptized individual becomes a person in communion who finds their telos in *theosis*. Grigorije Durić summarizes this point aptly, noting that "otherness, for Zizioulas, implies the overcoming of a difference. . . . Only when the dialectic of created and uncreated is overcome by embracing the divine way of existence of the created, ontological limitations could be overcome."[75] The baptized are freed from the limitations of individualism and are set forth on the path toward eschatological communion with the Triune God. A foretaste of this eschatological mode of existence is experienced in the Eucharist celebration and, consequently, according to Zizioulas, baptism is done as an act of *"anticipatory* communion, calling for its fulfillment in the Eucharist."[76] Although this mode of existence ultimately awaits an eschatological fulfillment, it is through baptism that they are put on this path toward communion.[77] Ciraulo helpfully summarizes Zizioulas's thought: "The baptized person lives, as it were, in a paradoxical situation between his biological hypostasis and the transcendence of it."[78] While both biological and ecclesial hypostases are teleological, baptism reorients the human subject's telos. The baptized have begun to experience their eucharistic life as ecclesial persons, an existence that culminates in the event of the Eucharist as a foretaste of the *eschaton*.

The Eucharist Celebration and Ecclesial Personhood

If baptism marks one's initiation into the ecclesial community and reveals that identity is gifted, this "gifted identity" is sustained through the event of the Eucharist. Earlier, I discussed how the Eucharist is an event in which the Spirit historicizes the eschatological community, allowing the body of Christ to experience a foretaste of *theosis*.[79] As McPartlan argues, "The Eucharist . . . is the only occasion in history when the identification in Christ of the Church with the Son's hypostasis is a reality."[80] And if it is only through identification with the Son's hypostasis that communion with God is truly experienced, then the Eucharist is also the moment in which communion

---

75. Durić, "Constitutiveness of Otherness," 249.
76. Zizioulas, *One and the Many*, 59, italics his.
77. Zizioulas, *One and the Many*, 35.
78. Ciraulo, "Sacraments and Personhood," 996.
79. Zizioulas, *Communion and Otherness*, 85.
80. McPartlan, *Eucharist Makes the Church*, 269, italics his.

in otherness—that is, participation in the life of the Triune God—is realized within the ecclesial community.

Yet this emphasis on the Eucharist event as that moment in which communion with God is realized reinforces the *gifted* nature of human personhood. While God is able to determine his own mode of existence, human creatures must be freed from the limits of ontological necessity by God in order to experience true existence. True human identity does not emerge from within the human subject, but is extrinsic and is brought to them by the Spirit. It is in the epiclesis of the Eucharist that the Spirit historicizes the eschatological gift of *theosis* in the present. In essence, humanity receives its true, future self in the event of communion. Consequently, the church's celebration of the Eucharist, through the work of the Spirit, constitutes and actualizes human personhood during the moment of its celebration.[81] Particularly, it is through the Eucharist that the true telos of human beings is received and experienced. Papanikolaou is again helpful in summarizing that, for Zizioulas, "the person constitutes an eschatological reality, but within the Church man is able to *taste of* its truth even now."[82] Through the eucharistic liturgy of the church, the members of the body of Christ are brought again into communion with the Triune God and become persons. Personhood is actualized, realized, and experienced through the church's liturgy. As the church becomes the body of Christ and subsists in the Son-Father relationship, it and its members experience the event of personhood.

---

81. Alexis Torrance argues that Zizioulas's view of the Eucharist implies there is a quantitative difference of personhood experienced during the celebration of the Eucharist compared to the moments between celebrations. "The Eucharist is, for him, the foretaste of true personhood and the space in which the '*how*' of God's being (as absolute personal communion in absolute personal otherness) is most clearly articulated" (Torrance, "Personhood and Patristics in Orthodox Theology," 701, italics his). However, this statement does not seem to go far enough. Zizioulas constructs a view of personhood that is synonymous with his understanding of *theosis*, a *theosis* which is only experienced presently within the event of the Eucharist (Zizoulas, *Communion and Otherness*, 85). While some may argue baptism creates a measure of personhood, this is done in light of future participation in the communal event of the Eucharist. For Zizioulas, the Eucharist is "an *ecclesial reality* in which all that was individual in Baptism and Confirmation becomes *communal* by virtue of communion in the Body of Christ" (Zizioulas, *One and the Many*, 98–99, italics his). The Eucharist fulfills and completes all individual liturgical events and creates the communion and otherness required for personhood.

82. Papanikolaou, *Being with God*, 37, italics his.

The Distinct Role of the Liturgy

This marks a distinctive contribution of Zizioulas's ecclesio-anthropology. He views the church's liturgy, to a certain extent, as ontologically and existentially constitutive of human personhood. While this cannot be separated from Christology or pneumatology, for Zizioulas clearly sees both as inseparable from the life and practice of the church, it is in and through the liturgy of the church that personhood is realized and experienced. As Colin Gunton observes, for Zizioulas, "personal being can be received only sacramentally."[83] In other words, the liturgy of the church constitutes the human person in communion through the work of the Spirit. For Zizioulas, the church's liturgy, particularly the Eucharist celebration, realizes human personhood on both an ontological and existential level. It turns people into persons—that is, into a new type, a truer type, of being. It is through the church, a church that is grounded and re-grounded continuously in the Eucharist event, that the eschatological reality of ecclesial being is brought into the present and the eschatological hope of *theosis* is realized. As truth is realized eschatologically, the Eucharist's eschatological orientation historicizes the future reality of communion with God, a communion that defines what it means to be a person. And this ontological and existential realization of their identity comes as a gift from God. It is in the celebration of the Eucharist that human beings become fully and truly human persons.

Eschatologically Oriented Persons

Yet, given that the Eucharist realizes *theosis* in the present, to be a true being or a true person is to exist eschatologically. For Zizioulas, we are, in a sense, people who are waiting to become persons. It appears, then, that Zizioulas's ecclesio-anthropology is inherently eschatological as well. True personhood is eschatological and our access to it is contingent upon the historicizing work of the church's liturgy. For Zizioulas, as we have already noted, truth—that is, true being and true personhood—is derived from the *eschaton*. Consequently, "the Church is not the place where the Truth is contained or 'deposited,' but she is '*of* the Truth,' i.e., a real presence of Truth through her very being a communion and a community."[84] It is through the historicizing work of the Spirit that the truth of the *eschaton* is made accessible in the present as he transcends history.[85] The church becomes "both a presence

---

83. Gunton, "Persons and Particularity," 105.
84. Zizioulas, *One and the Many*, 85, italics his.
85. McPartlan, *Eucharist Makes the Church*, 167.

of the eschaton in history and a pointer beyond history."⁸⁶ This makes the Eucharist not only the epistemological ground by which we understand truth, but it also becomes the moment in which we see the eschatological reality of human personhood manifested.⁸⁷ If personhood is communion in otherness, the union of the "one" and the "many," it is only truly realized in *theosis*. As MacDougall observes, "Church, the entry point and site of this mode of authentic being, is construed not as 'here,' in the world, but 'there,' in divine communion, in 'heaven.'"⁸⁸ Becoming a member of the ecclesial community means becoming reconstituted in an eschatological community as persons. The reality of this personhood, while tasted and experienced in the Eucharist, is the breaking in of the *eschaton* into history through the Spirit's work in the church's liturgy. True communion and being, and as a result true personhood, will only be realized in the *eschaton*. As Ciraulo summarizes, "For Zizioulas, salvation, theosis, and the actualization of full personhood are synonymous terms."⁸⁹ For Zizioulas, we only become true persons in the theotic existence of the *eschaton*. Even in the present, personhood is eschatologically oriented, an experience realized and fulfilled in the kingdom of God that is only tasted in the present through the church's liturgy.

But since the *eschaton* is the source of truth and grounds our epistemology, the church's liturgy, through the process of anamnesis, remembers that its true being and identity is derived from its eschatological telos. Zizioulas writes, "The *anamnesis* of Christ is realized not as a mere re-enactment of a past event but as an *anamnesis of the future*, as an eschatological event. In the Eucharist the Church becomes a reflection of the eschatological community of Christ, the Messiah, an image of the Trinitarian life of God."⁹⁰ Remembering for Zizioulas is not simply the recollection of facts or a particular story in which the Christian happens to be a participant. Rather, it is an act of looking forward to the future kingdom of Christ and their position before the throne of God.⁹¹ From there, the people of God attempt to realize that erotic mode of existence and their true being as one people.⁹²

---

86. Zizioulas, *One and the Many*, 88.

87. Turner, "Eschatology and Truth," 26, 30.

88. MacDougall, *More than Communion*, 85, italics his.

89. Ciraulo, "Sacraments and Personhood," 995.

90. Zizioulas, *Being as Communion*, 254, italics his.

91. Zizioulas, *Eucharistic Communion and the World*, 41.

92. Zizioulas, *Eucharistic Communion and the World*, 45, italics his. Zizioulas argues that while the West has prioritized the historical continuity of the church, the Orthodox view the historical reality of the church in conjunction with the Eucharist and the *eschaton* (Zizoiulas, *Lectures in Christian Dogmatics*, 153). In the sacrament, the Holy Spirit "draws us and all our history into relationship with the end time" (Zizoiulas,

With its eschatological perspective the Eucharist heals us of self-love, the source of all the passions, shatters the very backbone of individualism and teaches us to exist in a gathering with others and with all the beings of God's creation. Thus the Eucharist ceases to be a "religious experience" or a means to individual salvation and becomes a *mode of being*, a way of life, illuminated by the vision and expectation of the future.[93]

And, as a result, the way the people of God live in the world should be indicative of this future reality, a reality in which they exist in perfect communion.[94] It seems, then, that anamnesis is an integral part of the liturgy of the Eucharist and that human persons are ultimately an *anamnetic* people—that is, a people who look forward with hope and live in light of their future communion with God. The liturgy of the Eucharist reorients the Christians' view of reality and truth, realigning it in light of the *eschaton* and kingdom to come. It grounds both our hope and our love, creating "the *eucharistic ethos*, the ethos of forgiveness, which is not merely an inner state but is experienced as *gathering* and *coexistence with the person who has hurt us*, in a future which we do not control and which has no end."[95] In the church, humanity becomes what it truly is intended to be: persons in communion with God who participate in his ecstatic mode of life.

Lectures in Christian Dogmatics, 153). Furthermore, it is important to recall that for Zizioulas anamnesis is a eucharistic experience. Zizioulas argues, "The Eucharist is the recapitulation of the entire economy of salvation, in which past, present, and future are united and in which communion with the Holy Trinity and the rest of the Church, as well as with creation, takes place" (Zizioulas, *One and the Many*, 59). If this is true, any act of remembrance necessarily involves looking forward. Additionally, he writes, "Remembrance does not mean recalling an event that is simply past, an event borne away from us by the stream of time. It requires a conceptual revolution to grasp that the liturgy is both an eschatological and historical event, and that it is a historical event because it is first the eschatological event in which all histories are called into being and gathered up into one" (Zizioulas, *Lectures in Dogmatics*, 153). But this is done only as the Spirit brings the *eschaton* into the present, creating communion and otherness. If the true identity of the church is eschatological, as I have argued above, then any remembrance of the work of Christ and coming of the Spirit must entail a looking forward to the church's true identity.

93. Zizioulas, *Eucharistic Communion and the World*, 82.

94. Zizioulas, *One and the Many*, 132.

95. Zizioulas, *Eucharistic Communion and the World*, 88–89, italics his. Zizioulas, for his part, is reluctant to embrace ethical or moral systems, instead preferring to prioritize the liturgy of the Eucharist as grounding and reorienting the church toward the future and its true existence as an ecclesial community. For a critique of Zizioulas on this point, see McPartlan, *Eucharist Makes the Church*, 297–305.

A Punctiliar Understanding of Personhood

With this emphasis on eschatology and the role of the church's liturgy in bringing this eschatological reality into the present, personhood appears to be a punctiliar existence. By describing Zizioulas's account of personhood as a "punctiliar experience" I am stating that it is not a capacity or property intrinsic to the human creature. Instead, it is a dynamic event the human creature is able to experience under specific conditions. This marks another distinctive aspect of Zizioulas's ecclesio-anthropology since this punctiliar experience is only possible in and through the church during the moment of the Eucharist. This can be summarized through the following argument:

1. True personhood is achieved in *theosis*—that is, in communion with God.

2. Communion with God is only realized in the *eschaton*.

3. The *eschaton* is only experienced in the present through the historicizing work of the Holy Spirit in the Eucharist.

4. True personhood—that is, *theosis*—is experienced in the present during the celebration of the Eucharist as a punctiliar reality.

While Zizioulas does not make this statement explicitly, it seems to logically follow his view of the Eucharist as historicizing communion with God. In other words, the eschatological reality of personhood and communion in otherness is only experienced momentarily in the Eucharist. In the Eucharist, human beings become what they will be, transforming into an ecclesial hypostasis that transcends their biological existence as it "draws its being from the being of God and from that which it *will* be at the end of the age."[96] Sergii Bortnyk observes that for Zizioulas the biological and ecclesial hypostases are different modes of existence that cannot coexist.[97] After the celebration has been completed, human beings are no longer able to taste of this communion and, reverting out of their ecclesial mode of being, are no longer identified as true persons because the historicizing work of the Holy Spirit only occurs in the moment of the Eucharist. For Zizioulas, "the Holy Spirit brings the future into history."[98] As a result, "what we experience in the Eucharist is the end times making itself present to us."[99] Therefore, as

---

96. Zizioulas, *Being as Communion*, 62, italics his.
97. Bortnyk, *Kommunion und Person*, 243.
98. Zizioulas, *Lectures in Christian Dogmatics*, 154.
99. Zizioulas, *Lectures in Christian Dogmatics*, 155.

Volf comments, personhood is only realized in the moment of the Eucharist. He concludes,

> If personhood is eucharistically determined, then personhood, like ecclesial being as well, is an event rather than a condition. In the act of baptismal rebirth, it is not continual life that is given pre-eschatologically to persons; rather, in baptism they become persons in a punctiliar fashion and at the same time are "admitted" to the eucharistically transpiring, acutalistic experience of personhood.[100]

As the Eucharist brings the entire Catholic Church into the one place, it is only here that the entire body of Christ is present and true communion with God is experienced. It is only in the celebration of the Eucharist that the church can "reflect in her very being the way God exists, i.e. the way of personal communion."[101] Since subsisting in God's mode of existence is the only way to experience true personhood, in the present it is exclusively during the celebration of the Eucharist that human personhood is realized.

Ecclesial Persons as Beloved Lovers

If the human person was designed for eschatological participation in the divine life and the Triune God exists freely and ecstatically, then freedom and love emerge as central traits of the ecclesial community and, by consequence, of personhood. This freedom is expressed as a pursuit of the other in love, recognizing and embracing their otherness in the realization of communion.[102] If God is most truly known as a community of persons and this means that God is love, then persons are fundamentally lovers.[103] The church's liturgy reorients the way we understand love and brings us into the ecstatic life of God. As a biological hypostasis, humanity is relegated to a life of self-love. But as a result of baptism, the ecclesial hypostasis "can love not because the laws of biology oblige him to do so—something which inevitably colors the love of one's own relations—but *unconstrained* by the

---

100. Volf, *After Our Likeness*, 105.
101. Zizioulas, *One and the Many*, 52.
102. Zizioulas, *Communion and Otherness*, 39–40.
103. Zizioulas argues that only persons can love and only persons can be the object of love, since love recognizes the uniqueness of a particular and freely moves toward them in relationship. This is derived fundamentally from our understanding of God and, additionally, from the relationships and unity of the church. As a result, love describes the types of beings we are, persons who move toward one another in mutual relationship for communion (cf. Zizioulas, *Lectures in Dogmatics*, 12–27).

natural laws."[104] Love, if it is to be a mirror of divine life, must be free and not dictated by biological constraints.[105] Consequently, as the only uncreated and uncaused being, it is the love of God that serves as the ground for true being.[106] He extends love to humanity who in receiving it also receives true personhood and a true identity as an ecclesial being, participating in the filial love between the Son and the Father. Incorporated into this community of divine love, human individuals transcend their biological hypostasis and receive an ecclesial hypostasis, as someone who is able "to love without exclusiveness . . . out of the fact that his new birth in the womb of the Church has made him part of a network of relationships which transcends every exclusiveness."[107] Humanity is then able to participate in the love of God and extend it to the other. Cortez comments on this concept, observing that "the fact that a person can only exist in the relationship between an *I* and a *Thou* means that persons are constituted only in a particular kind of relationship, one in which a being recognizes another as truly Other and reaches out to that Other in love."[108] But it is only within the church that this love of God is understood and realized, received and transformed. In baptism, this true being is received as a gift and the individual is re-identified as one who is beloved by God.[109] In the church, the believer possesses a unique identity

---

104. Zizioulas, *Being as Communion*, 57, italics his.

105. For Zizioulas, "Love is not simply a virtue; it is an ontological category" (Zizioulas, *Eucharistic Communion and the World*, 76). True erotic love is only possible within the event of communion, as only persons can function as loved and lovers. Furthermore, "love is that particular relationship that we may refer to as being 'in Christ,' within which we may acknowledge God as Father. We belong to the community and the body constituted by that relationship" (Zizioulas, *Lectures in Dogmatics*, 31). It seems then that biological hypostases, as isolated and individualistic, are incapable of love. They cannot freely choose the other. Furthermore, this experience of love is only possible within the punctiliar event of the Eucharist since outside the communion of love "the person loses its uniqueness and becomes a being like other beings, a 'thing' without absolute 'identity' and 'name,' without a face" (Zizioulas, *Being as Communion*, 49). Throughout this chapter, I will use the terms "erotic," which Zizioulas seems to prefer, and "ecstatic," a term he also uses, synonymously.

106. Zizioulas argues love "is about new birth, a 'call' giving someone a unique identity, totally incomparable to any other identity, a 'mode of being' distinguished and identifiable, after the model of the Holy Trinity, not by any natural or moral qualities, but by the sheer relations it has with the being who causes its identity to emerge." In other words, love is the basis for human identity, a gifted identity. We exist as true beings insofar as we are beings who have received true being from God, who gives it in an act of love. Our identity is then formed as one who is beloved by God (Zizioulas, *Communion and Otherness*, 89).

107. Zizioulas, *Being as Communion*, 57–58.

108. Cortez, *Christological Anthropology in Historical Perspective*, 168, italics his.

109. As we have noted before, for Zizioulas, the very nature of true being and

as beloved by God and receives an ecclesial hypostasis that subsists in the Son-Father relationship. Therefore, the community can together exclaim, "I *am loved*, therefore I am."[110]

But the ecclesial person does not exist for her own sake. In fact, no true being does. To be in communion is to recognize the other and reach out to offer them true communion. Extending the gift of communion to the created world is the vocation of every true person. As participants in the *ecstatic* love of God, the church is a community of persons who strive to bring the world into communion with God. More specifically, it is a community of priests who present the love of God to the created world. He writes, "Because the human being has this organic link with creation and at the same time the drive to unite creation and to be free from the laws of nature, he can act as the 'priest of creation.'"[111] Humanity, in becoming persons in communion, embraces God's telos to bring all of creation into transcendent participation within divine life. Knowing the love of God, the person seeks to extend it to the world around them. According to Zizioulas, humanity is hypostasized in the church in order to embrace the call of God and hypostatize the rest of creation and give it true being.[112] As the church takes up the elements of the bread and wine, all of creation is symbolically represented in those two elements.[113] Zizioulas goes on to argue that human persons then take "the world in [their] hands to refer it to God, and who, in return, bring God's blessing to what [they refer] to God. Through this act, creation is brought into communion with God himself."[114] In essence, the church, as persons subsisting in the love of God, endeavors to bring the world into participation in the life of God. The church moves toward the created world and offers it the hope and possibility of *theosis*.[115] This is the priestly characteristic of the ecclesial being and, consequently, a further demonstration of the central role that ecclesiology plays in Zizioulas's understanding of anthropology as this priestly nature is understood in the liturgy of the Eucharist.

---

ontology is derived from relationality. Existence, if it is to be true, must be derived from the *eschaton* and the life of God, a life characterized by perichoretic love. Hence, "to be *is to exist for the other*, not for the self, and to love is not to 'feel' something about the other, but to *let the other be and be other*" (Zizioulas, "Relational Ontology," 150, italics his). In other words, to exist, to be a true being and a true person, is to be loved and to love.

110. Zizioulas, *Communion and Otherness*, 89, italics his.
111. Zizioulas, *Eucharistic Communion and the World*, 137.
112. Zizioulas, *Communion and Otherness*, 67.
113. Bortnyk, *Kommunion und Person*, 171.
114. Zizioulas, *Eucharistic Communion and the World*, 137.
115. MacDougall, *More than Communion*, 84.

CONCLUSION

For Zizioulas, true being, true existence, and true personhood are derived from the very life of God. To truly be is to exist as God exists: as persons in communion. The church plays a fundamental role in shaping our understanding of human personhood. It is only within the church that true personhood is revealed. More specifically, the church informs our understanding of what type of beings we are: we are incomplete as individuals and in need of communion, in need of relationship with the other. Human individuals must become persons and this is only possible through the liturgy of the church and incorporation into the body of Christ. As the *imago Trinitatis*, the true church mirrors the ecstatic mode of divine existence and is fundamentally a way of being, a way of communion.[116] As Douglas Farrow observes, for Zizioulas, "personhood is a vocation, a process, a destiny. It is ecclesial in nature, liturgically accessed, and eschatologically consummated. Personhood, properly speaking, is the result of deification."[117]

Zizioulas's ecclesio-anthropology emerges with several distinctive characteristics: it is constituted and realized through the church's liturgy, oriented toward the eschatological expectation of *theosis*, punctiliar and ecstatic. Baptism reconstitutes the human person, transforming them from a biological hypostasis to an ecclesial hypostasis. In the celebration of the Eucharist, the Holy Spirit then brings the *eschaton* into the present, bringing a taste of true communion and *theosis*. As a result, Zizioulas articulates a punctiliar account of human personhood, one that views personhood as solely experienced in the present during participation in the event of the Eucharist. Personhood is ultimately, then, an eschatological reality realized in the ecclesial community as a life of communion with God.[118] And finally the person possesses an ecstatic vocation, one that is tasked with offering the gift of communion to the rest of the world and existing as God himself exists: in love.

---

116. Zizioulas, *One and the Many*, 15; cf. Zizioulas, *Communion and Otherness*, 88.
117. Farrow, "Person and Nature," 111.
118. Zizioulas, *One and the Many*, 37.

3

The Ecclesio-Anthropology of Hans Urs von Balthasar

Hans Urs von Balthasar was one of the leading voices in *nouvelle théologie* during the twentieth century, spearheading a return to patristic sources in the hopes of inspiring a resurgence in Catholic thought that would simultaneously resist the pull of modern liberalism and offer a corrective to the neo-Thomistic thought that dominated the academy. Balthasar viewed both approaches as forms of rationalism and sought to construct a project that articulated how "God's revelation is not an object to be looked at: it is his action in and upon the world, and the world can only respond, and hence 'understand,' through action on *its* part."[1] To know God is to be moved by him, enraptured and drawn into the arena of his dramatic action. For Balthasar, this means we can only understand what it means to be human in the sphere of God's dramatic action: the church. To see this, we will begin with an examination of Balthasar's understanding of the church as a kenotic community, receiving its being, identity, and mission from Christ as it perpetuates his incarnation in the world.[2] Consequently, for Balthasar,

---

1. Balthasar, *TD I*, 15, italics his. For a discussion of how Balthasar seeks to correct the errors he perceives in neo-Thomistic thought, see Sesboüé, "Comment sortir de la néo-scolastique?," 263–74. For an investigation into how Balthasar sought to respond to the questions posed by modernity, see Peterson, "Fortschritt und Untergang," 225–47.

2. It is important to note here that I am not arguing that Balthasar's kenotic

human persons are viewed primarily in light of the kenotic mission of Christ, a mission intrinsic to the church's identity as his body and bride. Balthasar's ecclesio-anthropology presents us with a view of human personhood that is vocationally embodied, liturgically formed, and epitomized in openness to the divine and kenotic, self-sacrificial love.

A KENOTIC ECCLESIOLOGY FOR THE WORLD'S REDEMPTION

For Balthasar, the church sacramentally perpetuates the mission of Christ, poured out eucharistically for the world's redemption. Receiving its being and identity from Christ, the church sacramentally continues his mission upon the earth as its particular members are equipped by the Spirit through the sacraments to participate in Christ's universal mission through their individual, personal missions. However, this identity must be received by the ecclesial community as epitomized in the Marian fiat.[3] The church is therefore christological and Marian in shape. As Nicholas Healy and David Schindler observe, "As sacrament of Christ's redemption of the world, the Church is both the abiding presence of the incarnate Christ and the continuation of his mission."[4] However, this implies that the mission, person, and work of Christ are essential to our understanding of the identity of the church. Balthasar writes, "Christology is the inner form of ecclesiology; it alone determines the nearness and distance that must obtain between the obedience of Christ the head and the obedience of the Church, his Body and members."[5] Elsewhere he writes, "Christology will have to be the touchstone of all statements about the stage of ecclesiology and of the individual Christian life."[6] Consequently, I must begin with Balthasar's Christology if we are to understand his ecclesiology. There I will demonstrate that, for Balthasar, Christ reveals the perfect embodiment of personhood as his "I" is identical

---

Christology or his resulting ecclesiology are indicative or representative of the larger, Roman Catholic tradition.

3. Mary's fiat is her "Yes" to the mission that God has given her to be God-bearer according to the flesh. Based on a reading of Luke 1:38, for Balthasar it is the moment when she receives the divine commissioning and says "Yes" on behalf of the church. Her cooperation and receptivity to God's call enables the incarnation to take place and, by extension, the redemptive mission of Christ (Balthasar, *Man is Created*, 179). I will return to the Marian shape of Balthasar's ecclesiology below.

4. Healy and Schindler, "For the Life of the World," 55.

5. Balthasar, *Spirit and Institution*, 139. See Körner, "Fundamentaltheologie bei Hans Urs von Balthasar," 138–40.

6. Balthasar, *TD II*, 185.

to his mission.⁷ Furthermore, the church, as a sacramental perpetuation of his presence in the world, is a community of persons whose lives are oriented, however imperfectly, by the mission of Christ. Entered through baptism, the church enables human beings to become theological persons—that is, those whose particular lives are "drawn into the Church's mission. . . . [It is] to be, together with Christ, the 'light of the world' and the 'city set on a hill.'"⁸ The sacramental life of the church builds up its members into their particular vocations, enabling them to truly embody the mission of Christ.

The Kenotic God

For Balthasar, *kenosis* begins in and constitutes the Godhead. Balthasar understands *kenosis* as the embodiment of selfless love.⁹ While many kenotic theorists argue that *kenosis* is a way of either accounting for the portrayals of the incarnate Son within the Gospels or reconciling the finitude of humanity with the infinitude of deity, Balthasar views *kenosis* as a primal, pre-temporal movement within God himself, an *Ur-kenosis*. For Balthasar, there is "a first 'kenosis' of the Father, expropriating himself by 'generating' the consubstantial Son. Almost automatically, this first kenosis expands to a kenosis involving the whole Trinity."¹⁰ As Helmut Dieser explains, for Balthasar, "the Son, in his generation from the Father, eternally kenotically receives the divine nature and its 'autonomy.'"¹¹ The Father's act of begetting the Son is itself kenotic.¹² In the begetting of the Son, God the Father "strips himself, without remainder, of his Godhead and hands it over to the Son. . . . [H]e lets go of his divinity and, in this sense, manifests a (divine)

---

7. Balthasar, *TD I*, 645.

8. Balthasar, *TD III*, 430–31; *TD IV*, 406.

9. Balthasar, *Mysterium Paschale*, 35. Matthew Moser is helpful here in providing a description of Balthasar's account of love. He notes, "Balthasar interprets love as a 'mode of being' or a 'form of life' rather than as an affective state. The description Balthasar commonly adopts is 'being-for-another.' Love is an ecstatic form of life, or what the classical tradition called *caritas* or charity" (Moser, *Love Itself is Understanding*, xix–xx). See also Martin, "'Whence' and the 'Whither,'" 217–21.

10. Balthasar, *TD IV*, 331. Georges de Schrijver is helpful here. He notes, "The inner trinitarian Ur-kenosis . . . is the basis, the precondition and condition of the possibility of the next three kenoses" (Schrijver, "Hans Urs von Balthasars Christologie," 147, my translation).

11. Dieser, *Der gottähnliche Mensch und die Gottlosigkeit der Sünde*, 196, my translation.

12. Dieser, *Der gottähnliche Mensch und die Gottlosigkeit der Sünde*, 196.

God-lessness (of love of course)."[13] In this sense, Balthasar seems to understand the self-giving, self-negating love that is displayed in *kenosis* as the very essence of God.[14] Papanikolaou avers that it is this kenotic act which constitutes God's very being. "Balthasar's trinitarian theology claims that being itself is a gifted event, even the being of the divine persons themselves. God's being is an event of communion of persons. This communion is freely constituted in relations that are kenotic, i.e., mutually self-giving and receptive."[15] God the Father pours his very self out into the Son who then perpetuates this movement by becoming godlessness and godforsakenness itself in his descent from heaven to hell.

The incarnation serves as a continuation of this kenotic movement within the Godhead as the Son pours himself upon the world for its redemption.[16] More specifically, the incarnation is the economic, historical enacting of the inner *processio* that constitutes the Son and Spirit.[17] In his *kenosis*, the Son embraces not only the self-abnegation of divine attributes, but also "in the *kenosis* of the Son . . . [the] innate 'form of God' stays back with the Father . . . as a pledge of his faithfullness to the will of God and as a 'reminder' to the Father of how much he himself is committed to the world adventure."[18] The Son limits himself and chooses to completely rely upon the Father so that he might reveal the love of God through absolute obedience. However, this self-limitation does not simply describe the earthly ministry of Christ. Rather it involves a continued trajectory of self-abnegation and godforsakenness to the point that the Son descends *ad infernem* and embodies perdition.[19] For Balthasar, no one has been as disowned and abandoned as the Son. This assumption of the guilt and penalty for every possible sin is the basis upon which Jesus is able to provide redemption for all of humanity. As Steffen Lösel explains, for Balthasar, "christological representation can and must be interpreted as the divine mediator assuming the sinner's situation. More importantly, Christ does so inwardly."[20] Christ's descent is an act of solidarity for all of humanity, assuming their guilt and

---

13. Balthasar, *TD IV*, 323–24.

14. Balthasar, *TD V*, 76.

15. Papanikolaou, "Person, Kenosis and Abuse," 48.

16. Oakes writes, "God the Father's love is so total that there is 'nothing left,' so to speak, when he generates his Son in love; and the Son returns that love so totally, also holding nothing back, that he too is totally 'emptied'" (*Pattern of Redemption*, 289). See also Holzer, "La kenose christologique," 212–22.

17. Balthasar, "On the Concept of Person," 25.

18. Balthasar, *Spirit and Institution*, 138.

19. Balthasar, *Word Made Flesh*, 265.

20. Lösel, "Plain Account of Christian Salvation?," 165.

expiating the penalty for their sin.²¹ Edward Oakes provides a helpful summary of Balthasar's view of *kenosis*: "By virtue of the Incarnation Jesus has assumed in his human nature godforsakenness and has incorporated it, by his descent into hell, into the nature of the Godhead itself."²² It is this mission, this descent, that then governs both the incarnation and the mission of the church, as both concepts are understood in light of God's redemptive, kenotic act.

Christology and Mission Consciousness

The kenotic life of the Triune God is then poured forth in the incarnation, in the *missio* of the Son. Mission, as Klaghofer-Treitler notes, is fundamental to Balthasar's understanding of Christ and his work of redemption.²³ The incarnate Son's kenotic mission governs his self-understanding. "Jesus always has and *is* his mission, he has utterly abandoned himself to the Father who guides him and in whom he has complete trust."²⁴ Arguing that philosophy and sociology cannot properly navigate the tension between the identity of the individual person and their role in society, Balthasar states that in Christ "the 'I' and the role become uniquely and ineffably one in the reality of his mission, far beyond anything attainable by earthly means."²⁵ Balthasar views the entirety of Jesus's self-consciousness and self-understanding through the lens of his mission of redemption. Identified as the Son of the Father, Jesus's self-identity is one of self-abnegation and complete obedience to the Father's will.²⁶ For Balthasar, "God's knowledge of a thing is absolutely archetypal

21. Balthasar, *Spouse of the Word*, 28. See also Pitstick, *Light in Darkness*, 109.
22. Oakes, "'He Descended into Hell,'" 239.
23. Klaghofer-Treitler, *Gotteswort im Menschenwort*, 159.
24. Balthasar, *TD III*, 170–71, italics his.
25. Balthasar, *TD I*, 645–46.
26. Donald MacKinnon argues that the concept of *kenosis* does not adequately encompass the entirety of the incarnate Son's mission. Instead, he finds that while *kenosis* certainly plays a prominent role in Balthasar's thought, mission is more central. He argues that while "*kenosis* remains profoundly significant for Balthasar; indeed it dominates his imagination in the many passages in which he gives free rein to his mastery of his own language and recaptures the emphases of the earlier monograph on the Paschal mystery," but that mission or *Sendung* is more central and guides Balthasar's ontology (MacKinnon, "Some Reflections," 168). Additionally, MacKinnon is critical of Balthasar's willingness to source this mission in the immanent Trinity, arguing that Balthasar's failure to delimit mission leads to a blurring of the distinctions between members of the Trinity (MacKinnon, "Some Reflections," 169–70). While MacKinnon's latter critique does seem to be valid, especially given the strong language Balthasar uses to describe the Father's self-gift to the Son, it seems he misunderstands Balthasar's use

and exemplary.... *Because* God sees things thus, they should be as he sees them. It is to this idea of things held by God's safekeeping that all of man's creative knowledge has to look."[27] As a result, if Jesus is to know himself rightly, he must know himself in light of God's idea of him. How then does the Father understand the incarnate Son's mission? At his baptism, Jesus is revealed as the beloved Son of God and commissioned as the Lord's Servant, the one born for redemption.[28] God the Father announces the "inner form" of the man Jesus, revealing his true identity as the Son of God.[29] Robert Koerpel writes, "Jesus' human consciousness is entirely under the auspice of his trinitarian mission, the mission commissioned by the Father and guided by the Holy Spirit to reveal the truth of both divinity and humanity to humanity."[30] This is important then for Jesus's self-understanding as the one being sent of the Father for the purpose of redemption.[31] As a result of this divine identification and commissioning, "in his mission, Christ knows

---

of *kenosis*. For Balthasar, Christ's incarnation is the appearance (and concealment) of the true nature of humanity and divinity (Balthasar, *Seeing the Form*, 513. Henceforth, it will be cited merely as *TGL*). In other words, the kenotic mission of Christ *is* the embodiment of the Triune love of God and self-abandonment in the form of self-gift (Balthasar, *Epilogue*, 93–94). Consequently, to say God is love is to say God is the self-surrendering and self-giving one precisely because love *is* self-surrender as demonstrated in the incarnation of Christ (Balthasar, *TGL I*, 477). In the kenotic mission of the Son, he hands himself over completely to the Father's abandonment and, in so doing, reveals the divine nature as one of kenotic self-gift (Balthasar, *Mysterium Paschale*, 29). As Rodney Howsare comments, "This law of self-surrender has its source in the Trinity: for Jesus does not come primarily to reveal the Son, but the Father. In Jesus' surrender of himself on the cross, then, we catch a glimpse of the Father's eternal surrender of himself to the Son" (Howsare, *Balthasar*, 137). It seems, then, that mission describes the kenotic action that begins in the Father who pours his own self out in begetting the Son, who then goes forth and pours himself out in the incarnation, atonement, and descent into hell. The Son's *missio* is a kenotic descent of self-surrender.

27. Balthasar, *Truth of the World*, 1:119–20, italics his. Henceforth, it will be cited merely as *TL*.

28. Balthasar, *TD III*, 154–55.

29. In *Theo-Logic*, Balthasar discusses how a being's "true identity" is latent within it but must be unveiled by the revelatory call of God. He elucidates this relationship between identity and divine address in the relationship between subject and object. He writes, "The object's immanence in the subject's consciousness is the prior condition for understanding its transcendence" (Balthasar, *TL I*, 67). Furthermore, "In the creative mirror of the subject, the object sees the image of what it is and of what it can be and what it is meant to be" (Balthasar, *TL I*, 78). In other words, it is only in the address of God that one is able see oneself truly. Therefore, if Jesus is to understand himself correctly it must be in light of God's commissioning.

30. Koerpel, "Form and Drama of the Church," 78.

31. Balthasar, *TD III*, 153.

that he is unique; he knows that he is fit for this task and dedicated to it."[32] Consequently, Jesus views his life entirely in light of his sense of mission and in so doing stands as the person par excellence. His identity and mission (role) cohere perfectly.[33]

But not only does mission inform Jesus's self-perception, it also constitutes his very existence. Balthasar writes, "Jesus is not a man who happens to find himself existing on earth and from that point gropes to find and do the will of God by reflecting on himself and asking about the purpose of his being here on earth. His existence is not a matter of chance. Rather his very existence itself is a result of his mission . . . and thus of his obedience."[34] Balthasar creates an inseparable connection between Christ's existence and his mission. Karen Kilby avers, "Balthasar does not, however, stop with the claim that Jesus has a very strong sense of mission, or that this sense of mission is particularly central to him, but wants rather to *identify* Jesus with his mission. Jesus does not just have a mission—he *is* the mission."[35] For Balthasar, the eternally begotten Son becomes incarnate so that he might empty himself of life to the point of death in order to experience solidarity with the lost and bear the sins of the world. By understanding his very existence in light of his divinely assigned mission, Christ is the person par excellence. As McIntosh observes, "Almost the entirety of Balthasar's Christology can be understood from this standpoint. Whereas other human beings are called into being to consummate their callings by sharing in the Word's mission, Jesus' humanity is called into being as the very expression in human historical terms of the Word's mission."[36] Jesus exists as the incarnate Son on account of his intrinsic mission as redeemer of the world.

Furthermore, Christ's mission is to reveal the Father to humanity and to uniquely represent humanity before God. Balthasar writes,

---

32. Balthasar, *TD III*, 163.

33. Oakes notes that because the world was made through and for the Logos, the incarnate Son is able to subvert the absorption of his "self" into the roles society attempts to bestow upon him. Human beings do not choose to exist but are "all *thrown* into existence." In contrast, the Logos voluntarily chooses "to become flesh and take on human form," altering the form of the world drama (Oakes, *Pattern of Redemption*, 223, italics his). This is similar to Zizioulas's view of the problem of ontological necessity, although Balthasar focuses predominantly on existential self-understandings and less on ontological categories.

34. Balthasar, *Spirit and Institution*, 141. Dieser notes that this is because the incarnate Son corresponds completely to the "mode of Son. As a result, there is no disconnect between the immanent Son's mission and the mission and identity of Jesus" (Dieser, *Der gottähnliche Mensch und die Gottlosigkeit der Sünde*, 190–91).

35. Kilby, *Balthasar*, 95–96, italics hers.

36. McIntosh, "Christology," 26–27.

[The Son] represents God to the world—but in the mode of the Son who regards the Father as "greater" and to whom he eternally owes all that he is—and he represents the world to God, by being, as man (or rather as the God-man), "humble, lowly, modest docile [*tapeinos*] of heart" (Mt 11:29). It is on the basis of these two aspects, united in an abiding analogy, that the Son can take up his *one*, unitary mission. This mission is to represent the Father's authority vis-à-vis men and to represent mankind's sin in the sight of God, the judge, achieving its atonement, together with his "brothers," before the Father.[37]

But this mission does not simply include his earthly ministry and death on the cross as an atoning sacrifice. According to Balthasar, the incarnation is intended to demonstrate the depths of divine love. As Klaghofer-Treitler notes, "There is a complete connection between the sonship of Christ and the mission of Jesus, so that all that Jesus Christ is, but also becomes, is the expression of his eternal Sonship and mission."[38] Ultimately, for Balthasar, Jesus's mission is one of kenotic self-surrender wherein he divests himself of the divine form in order to fully experience solidarity with humanity and demonstrate the depths of divine love. Yet in so doing the Son does not cease to be God. In order to experience solidarity with humanity, "Christ willed not only to die, but to go down, in his soul, *ad infernem*" since "only what has been endured is healed and saved."[39] Furthermore, he embarks

---

37. Balthasar, *TD III*, 230n68, italics his.

38. Klaghofer-Treitler, *Gotteswort im Menschenwort*, 160–61, my translation.

39. Balthasar, *Mysterium Paschale*, 164–65. Alyssa Pitstick, commenting on this passage, notes that Balthasar credits Irenaeus for the statement "only what has been endured is healed and saved," but that the cited text does not contain the adage. She goes on to observe that this substitution of terminology is extremely vital to accurately understanding Balthasar's thought on the redemptive mission of Christ. "The importance of the substitution of *endured* for *assumed* cannot be overestimated. Balthasar's principle takes suffering as the *formal* principle of Christ's redemptive work: Christ's experience in Sheol must be like the suffering unredeemed man deserved to experience there and His endurance of this state is expiatory" (Pitstick, *Light in Darkness*, 96, italics hers). Here, Pitstick alludes to the role that solidarity plays in Balthasar's soteriology. Balthasar writes, "The Church community is the true product of the solitude of Christ, his solitude on the Cross, his solitude as the incomparable God-man, which is, in turn, the manifestation of his trinitarian solitude and ultimately the primordial solitude of the Father in the generation of the Son" (Balthasar, *Spouse of the Word*, 28). The eternal Son experiences complete Godforesakenness in his descent from heaven to hell, becoming the embodiment of sin and experiencing the greatest separation from God imaginable as a consequence of sin. Balthasar writes, "The Crucified Son does not simply suffer the hell deserved by sinners; he suffers something below and beyond this, namely, being forsaken by God in the pure obedience of love. Only he, as Son, is capable of this, and it is qualitatively deeper than any possible hell" (Balthasar, *TD V*, 277).

on a trajectory of self-surrender and complete obedience to the will of the Father, becoming sin and perdition itself so that, in becoming the object of the Father's wrath, those trapped in sin might be redeemed.[40]

The Marian Shape of Ecclesiology

Balthasar is quick to point out that there is also a great dissimilarity between Christology, ecclesiology, and anthropology.[41] Mariology serves as the bridge between the three loci as she demonstrates creatureliness in its most faithful form. For Balthasar, Mary serves as a type of the church in that her "Yes" to the divine call brings forth redemption in the person of the Redeemer. Unprovoked and uncoerced, she freely and willingly disposes of herself to be used for the purposes of the Creator and freely surrenders her son, a willingness that culminates in fruitfullness (e.g., the birth of the Savior and the creation of his body, the church). "She is not the Word but the adequate response awaited by God from the created sphere and produced in it by grace through the Word."[42] As Lüning observes, Balthasar "makes Mary the 'prototype' of redeemed humanity, but above all her kenotic 'disempowerment' under the cross evokes the response of the church as the embodiment of the Marian 'Fiat.'"[43] Consequently, "the Marian response of faith [is the] principle and exemplar of the response of the entire Church."[44] Mary serves as the archetype of the ecclesial community in two important

---

40. Pascal Ide argues that Balthasar's view of Christ's redemptive work is best encapsulated in the Germanic term *Stellvertretung*, one that loses some of its meaning in translation. Christ, in the atonement and descent, acts in the place of others. He writes, "On the Cross, Christ, whose whole being is *pro nobis*, takes the place of the sinner: he suffers what [the sinner] ought to suffer. This substitution becomes more radical during the descent into hell: Holy Saturday adds to the suffering and to the incredible agony of the Passion, the trial without any consolation from the separation from the Father, lived as definitive, in the absolute darkness of hell" (Ide, *Une théologie de l'amour*, 55, my translation).

41. Here, it appears Balthasar creates a little more space between Christology and ecclesiology than is typical in some Catholic understandings of *totus Christus*. While Balthasar does affirm that the church is the continuation of the presence of Christ in the world, he also stresses it is in a state of *becoming* his body through its members' acts of self-surrender. He writes, "This violent, this often 'crucifying' sacrifice of the pious subject to the ecclesial object (that is what Schleiermacher and Hegel call 'community-conciousness') is ultimately one of the conditions for the presence of the Eucharistic Lord" (Balthasar, *Church and World*, 32).

42. Balthasar, *Spouse of the Word*, 161.

43. Lüning, *Der Mensch im Angesicht des Gekreuzigten*, 350, my translation.

44. Lüning, *Der Mensch im Angesicht des Gekreuzigten*, 350.

ways.⁴⁵ First, she embodies readiness and openness to divine vocation, passively receiving a unique mission from God. Balthasar writes, "Her mission, in the feminine and creaturely mode, is to let things happen; as such it is perfectly congruent with the masculine and divine mission of the Son."⁴⁶ Second, in embracing the unique vocation that God assigns her to be the bearer of the Redeemer, she appropriates his kenotic act, de-privatizing and de-personalizing herself for the mission of God. Thus, Mary is not only an exemplar of the creature's proper disposition before the Creator, she is also the type of the church.⁴⁷ As the embodiment of Christian obedience and selflessness, she freely chooses to make herself available to the call of God. John Saward writes, "Mary's *fiat*, through the grace which filled her from conception, is an anticipated participation in Christ's obedience and the perfect model of obedience of every Christian."⁴⁸

Mary's disposition of perfect obedience is the ideal form of the church. Consequently, the church must mirror her disposition and share in her fiat, existing in a state of constant readiness and receptivity, receiving its mission and form from its Lord.⁴⁹ Christ's *kenosis* is the origin of the church who receives and becomes "the pure outpouring of the Lord."⁵⁰ In so doing the church perpetuates his kenotic work of self-surrender on the world stage.⁵¹

---

45. Lucy Gardner writes, "The Church Fathers understood the patriarch to be types of Christ, prefiguring him for us; so Balthasar understands Mary to be a type of the Church and of the individual Christian, prefiguring us for us.... Mary's archetypicality is figured precisely in her being uniquely, personally, and historically ordered to Christ as his Mother and as his spouse or helpmate" (Gardner, "Balthasar and the Figure of Mary," 68).

46. Balthasar, *TD III*, 352.

47. Balthasar, *TD III*, 325.

48. Saward, "Mary and Peter in the Christological Constellation," 105–6.

49. Balthasar, *New Elucidations*, 103.

50. Balthasar, *Spouse of the Word*, 28

51. It is worth noting that Balthasar does advocate for a "Petrine" or "Institutional" structure of the church as one of its essential pillars, arguing that it is the objective form of the church given by Christ. He writes, "The Church is the 'Bride' of Christ, and at the same time [it] is equipped with an official and institutional side" (Balthasar, *TD III*, 357–58). Additionally, he discusses the role of ordination within the Christian community, particularly focusing on the distinctions that exist between priests and laity, as well as the need (and beauty) of the laity's submission to her divinely ordained structure. In fact, this submission to the ecclesial structure is an act of self-surrender for the sake of unity (*TL I*, 129). He writes, "This Church office of reminding, recalling and admonishing, the official Church receives authority from the unity of Christ to feed his sheep, to strengthen the brethren and to make decisions that bind in heaven. And then office becomes not only a sign but an effective, confirmed and sacramental sign" (Balthasar, *Spirit and Institution*, 158). Yet, Balthasar seems to indicate there is a kind of preeminence to the nuptial nature that supersedes and transcends that of the Petrine

Balthasar writes, "The Church as holy is essentially bound up with Christ's work of redemption, she 'makes up for what is lacking in his suffering' (Col 1:24)."[52] Fergus Kerr observes that for Balthasar, the church is essentially feminine. "Ultimately, fundamentally, Balthasar insists, the Church is feminine, receptive, nurturing; giving birth to what she receives from Christ."[53] In other words, the church receives and only then continues the redemptive work. In fact, for Balthasar this is the only way that the church can be christological in its orientation since the church is only kenotic in a derivative sense. The church receives its mission and identity from the Son in order to offer a redeemed world back to the Father, completing Christ's eucharistic action. "Where the divine decision has been made known to the creature in Christian revelation, the perfect attitude of the creature will be handing over to God; in other words, this attitude can assume the form of *offering* to be taken along the way of Christ's *kenosis*."[54] The church therefore receives and then perpetuates Christ's *kenosis*, demonstrating the depths of divine love.[55] "Just as God so loved the world that he completely handed over his Son for its sake, so too the one whom God has loved will want to save himself only in conjunction with those who have been created with him, and he will not reject the share of penitential suffering that has been given him for the sake of the whole."[56]

Ecclesial Identity and Mission

The church's mission then is an extension of the *missio* of the eternal Son as it bears within itself the imprint of the Word and is a free yet required

---

structure, as the latter only exists due to the persistence of sin (Balthasar, *Spirit and Institution*, 157; cf. Oakes, *Pattern of Redemption*, 261). Additionally, it is Mary, after all, not Peter, who is the church *imaculatta*, just as it is love that serves as the origin and ground of truth, that which enables it to be (Balthasar, *TL I*, 112).

52. Balthasar, *Spirit and Institution*, 202.
53. Kerr, *Twentieth-Century Catholic Theologians*, 139.
54. Balthasar, *Spirit and Institution*, 134, italics his.
55. Balthasar, *Spirit and Institution*, 135. Johann Roten, in explaining the relationship between Balthasar's view of Mary's vocation and his ecclesiology, notes, "Mary is pictured as the model of theo-dramatic existence, the archetype of creaturely *kenosis*. In Mary, there is no rupture or opposition between *exstasis* and *kenosis*.... Her Self, which contained the word of God (*ecstasis*), gradually and irresistibly grew to be contained, remodeled and active in the service of God's own Word (*kenosis*)" (Roten, "Marian Light on Our Human Mystery," 131). In other words, Mary is a type of the church and the individual Christian in that she illustrates how reception of the Word calls the Christian to kenotic action upon the world stage, into a life of self-surrender.
56. Balthasar, *Love Alone is Credible*, 97.

response to him.[57] For Balthsar, nuptial imagery plays a governing role in his understanding of the church and its relationship to Christ. In contrast to some traditional Catholic emphases on the church as the body of Christ, as Aurica Nutt observes, "Balthasar barely elaborates on his understanding of the Church as the Body of Christ, in contrast to the metaphor of the Church as the Bride of Christ."[58] For Balthasar, "The Church, therefore, is Christ's fellow servant in his task of liberating the world. She shares with God in his work of sharing himself in Christ with the world."[59] But in order to share in Christ's work, the church must embrace his call to kenotic, self-surrender and costly love. It is only in appropriating the mission of Christ that the church can truly be what God has called and created it to be.[60] As Healy and Schindler rightly observe, "If the mission of the Son is to redeem creatures by means of an exchange (*admirablile commercium*) in which he offers himself eucharistically to the world and receives the world as gift from the Father, then the Church is called to enter into Christ's life and mission *by eucharistically receiving creation in its entirety as a gift that mediates and expresses triune life.*"[61] The church, mirroring the actions of its Lord and Archetype, is selflessly, kenotically and eucharistically poured out upon the world for its redemption. Roch Kereszty avers, "The liturgy of the Eucharist consists precisely in Jesus' bestowal of his sacrifice upon the Church, in order that the Church may offer it as her own."[62] This mission then spreads to the particular members of the Christian community who perpetuate Christ's redemptive work in their individual vocations. "This special vocation of Christians is explicitly to adopt his standpoint (Mk 3:14) and to receive the fullness of his powers so that they can continue his work in the world."[63] Not only does Balthasar view the church as receiving and perpetuating Christ's mission, but he also argues that the particular members of the

---

57. Balthasar, *TGL III*, 175.

58. Nutt, "Das 'Leib Christi,'" 144, my translation. Nutt notes that while Balthasar does not deny that the church is Christ's mystical body, he emphasizes the idea that the church is Christ's bride. Here, in alluding to the traditional Catholic emphases on the church as the body of Christ, I am specifically thinking of the doctrine of *totus Christus*. *Totus Christus* refers to the belief that "Christ and his Church thus together make up 'the whole Christ' (*Christus totus*). The Church is one with Christ" (Catholic Church, *Catechism of the Catholic Church*, 795). For a discussion of the idea of *totus Christus* in the thought of Augustine, see Baker, "Augustine's Doctrine of *Totus Christus*," 7–24; Durand, "La variété des langues," 1–25.

59. Balthasar, *Engagement with God*, 33.

60 Balthasar, *Engagement with God*, 34.

61. Healy and Schindler, "For the Life of the World," 51, italics original.

62. Kereszty, "Eucharist and Mission," 7.

63. Balthasar, *TD III*, 282.

Christian community find their true selves as ecclesial persons insofar as they receive Christ and surrender to the task of selflessly embodying their unique vocations. Since all vocations are "summed up" in the mission of Christ and, similar to Christ's mission-consciousness, serve as the Father's designation of the individual's true identity, each individual Christian act is to be "eucharistic" and "kenotic" wherein "we have been emptied of ourselves to serve God and his loving freedom—and to find ourselves in such service and only in such service."[64] But in order to do this effectively and consistently, the Christian community must be grounded in its sacramental and liturgical life, as it is here that they receive and are nourished anew by Christ's mission.[65]

The Sacramental Life of a Dramatic Church

For Balthasar, baptism marks one's entrance into the ecclesial community as the first act of kenotic self-surrender.[66] In baptism, the individual is constituted as a "dramatic person." Balthasar uses the term "dramatic person" to describe someone who has been chosen, called, and sent forth in Christ to participate in the love and mission of God.[67] The baptized freely renounce any attempts at autonomous self-determination and receive their identity in light of divine calling, beginning the process of a life of self-surrender.[68] As David Crawford helpfully summarizes, "The basic state of life, membership in the Body of Christ, is brought about by baptismal vows."[69] For Balthasar, baptism awakens the individual to their inner identity and imparts divine life to them as they surrender and passively receive the work of Christ.[70] He writes, "In this sacrament, the Church in Christ takes over the believer,

---

64. Balthasar, *Spirit and Institution*, 147.

65. Koerpel, "Form and Drama of the Church," 91. Again, it is important to note that Balthasar's point of emphasis seems to differ from traditional Catholic doctrine. While not denying the church is a perpetuation of the incarnation, he places greater emphasis on the church as a continuation of the Son's *missio*. This mission necessarily involves historical, physical, and bodily modes of existence, but the emphasis is on action. Consequently, the church continually receives the mission of Christ and seems to exist in a state of becoming.

66. Balthasar, *Spirit and Institution*, 249.

67. Balthasar, *TD III*, 448.

68. Balthasar, *Christian State of Life*, 39; Balthasar, *TGL VII*, 405–6. For Balthasar, the ecclesial community can engage in this act of renunciation in baptism on behalf of the candidate if the candidate is unable to do so on their own (Balthasar, *TL III*, 335).

69. Crawford, "Love, Action, and Vows," 254.

70. Balthasar, *Spouse of the Word*, 161; Balthasar, *TGL VII*, 308–11.

who as such recognizes the priority of Christ as 'Head and Body.' Baptism both meets the believer from the outside, as it were, but also constitutes the believer in his true reality."[71] In baptism, the individual is reconstituted both ontologically and existentially, finding their true identity "with an act that is both an act of obedient faith as well as an act of self-surrender in faith."[72] As we have seen with both Christology and Mariology, for Balthasar, the individual's inner form is innate but requires a revelatory divine address. Baptism then illuminates the individual to their inner form and, in their baptismal vows, they are bound to their beloved.

While the ecclesial community is entered through the practice of baptism, for Balthasar the Eucharist stands at the center of the ecclesial life. "Since the Eucharist expressly includes the utmost suffering . . . which released the Son to suffer and raised him from the dead, every possible detail of the believer's life is caught up, supported and simultaneously enclosed in the Eucharist as an ecclesial, sacramental act."[73] In the Eucharist, Christ actively re-presents himself to the Christian community as their sacrifice, further pouring himself out in redemptive love and draws them into his sacrificial work.[74] Koerpel writes, "When the Church celebrates the Eucharist it does not offer Christ's sacrifice as a new or foreign sacrifice but is itself drawn into Christ's original sacrifice to the Father."[75] For Balthasar,

> To receive into me the One who was sacrificed for me means to grant him space in, and power of disposition over, my whole existence, both spiritual and physical, and thereby to follow him—at a distance, since it is he (in a masculine fashion) who decides, whilst I (in a feminine fashion) let him act, but also in unity, since, through letting him act, he will decide in me only in accordance with the meaning of his own *disponibilité*.[76]

---

71. Balthasar, *Spirit and Institution*, 150.

72. Balthasar, *Spirit and Institution*, 150.

73. Balthasar, *New Elucidations*, 120.

74. Balthasar, *TD IV*, 398. Alyssa Pitstick is helpful here, arguing that, for Balthasar, Christ's kenotic work is still present as the Holy Spirit universalizes it across time. In fact, it is only in the eucharistic participation of the human person in the life of God that the incarnation reaches its intended *telos*. She writes, "The Eucharist is effectively the sacrament of Holy Saturday, signifying and continuing the utter self-gift of Jesus, and causes a like selflessness in the communicant. . . . When the Eucharist is received by the believer, the Son's kenosis attains its intended end of including man in the Trinitarian life, which occurs through configuration to Christ in the self-abandonment of faith" (Pitstick, *Light in Darkness*, 249–50).

75. Koerpel, "Form and Drama of the Church," 90.

76. Balthasar, *Mysterium Paschale*, 99. In recent years, many feminist theologians have questioned Balthasar's portrayal of the sexes and his project's reliance on nuptial

THE ECCLESIO-ANTHROPOLOGY OF HANS URS VON BALTHASAR 65

By partaking of the Eucharist, the church opens itself up with a readiness for the Father's will, participating in Christ's own availability and is built up into its true form, the body of Christ.[77] But again, for Balthasar, if the church is truly to become the body of Christ it must receive his mission and thereby be conformed to his cruciform mode-of-life. As Kereszty rightly observes, "As we are drawn into the unfathomable depth of Christ's love, we become conformed to Him so that we can empty ourselves of our own self-centered existence and learn to love our fellow human beings with the very love of Christ. In this way we share in the life-giving and life-nourishing mission of the Word made flesh."[78] Therefore, the Eucharist is to be understood in light of the mission and vocation of Christ.

As the "inner form" of a Christian has been revealed in their initiation into the body of Christ, the Eucharist imparts divine life, life that enables them to better embody their vocation as participants in the mission of Christ. For Balthasar, "Reception of the Eucharist ought to have equipped all the members to go out and personally radiate what they have received, not as single individuals but as 'ecclesial souls' (*animae ecclesiasticae*), either by an express proclamation or in the tacit preaching of their entire conduct."[79] By receiving the Eucharist, the individual members of the ecclesial community receive divine life. But this reception of divine life is not an end to itself, but a means of offering the world back to the Father. In the Eucharist, the church becomes grounded in Christ's *pro nobis* and its members are equipped for participation in his mission. In so doing, the reception of the Eucharist enables the church, as a community of members, to embody and become its mission. Healy and Schindler rightly argue that, for Balthasar, "the Church is both the body and blood of Christ poured out for the salvation of the world and the bride who, in receiving the substance of Christ's life in the Eucharist, brings new life to the world."[80]

Yet while the Eucharist stands as the Sacrament of ecclesial life, the other sacraments enable the Christian community to inactively realize its true form—that is, a life of self-surrender. The church's sacramental life is the means through which human identity and vocation find coherence.[81] The members of the church, in partaking of the various sacraments, are

---

imagery. Balthasar appears to portray femininity in a way that correlates it strongly with passivity and turns their bodies into instruments of male personalization. I will return to this in greater detail in chapter 5.

77. Balthasar, *TGL I*, 574.
78. Kereszty, "Eucharist and Mission," 9.
79. Balthasar, *New Elucidations*, 105.
80. Healy and Schindler, "For the Life of the World," 57.
81. Balthasar, *TD III*, 432.

formed into persons and a community, wherein they acquire an ecclesial quality and are enabled to serve, suffer, love, and give themselves to one another.[82] Here, Balthasar seems to have appropriated aspects of traditional Thomistic views of the sacraments as instrumental means of grace, enabling individuals to reach their telos. However, he appears to have repurposed this traditional understanding in terms of mission and identity. In other words, the grace communicated through the sacraments enables one to receive anew the mission and redeeming act of Christ's *kenosis*. And since the descent is the apex of the kenotic mission of Christ, for Balthasar the sacraments cause a participation in the *kenosis* of Christ. Healy provides further clarity on this point. He writes, "In the gift of the Eucharist, Christ communicates his own life and mission, including his descent into hell. . . . The Christian is nonetheless one who, in the following of Christ, forgets his own salvation in order to be disponible, in flesh and blood, for God's universal saving will."[83] In the sacraments, God "imparts his life-giving love to us; and this love flows through the Church and out into the world."[84] The church is then able to offer the world back to God, extending and completing the mission of Christ.

For Balthasar, the church's identity and mission is grounded in the kenotic mission and work of Christ. Balthasar views the incarnation of the Son as the embodiment of divine love, wherein the Son hands himself completely over to the will of the Father, embracing godforsakenness and perdition so that humanity might be redeemed. This *kenosis* is then perpetuated in the ecclesial community. The church receives Christ's mission of self-surrender, embraces godforsakenness, and embarks on a journey of self-abnegation and surrender, as it seeks to offer the world back to the Father. Entered through baptism, the sacraments are viewed as the impartation of divine life and enable ecclesial persons to actualize their identity, discovering it within the kenotic mission of Christ. In a sense, this completes the eucharistic mission and it is in this participation in the mission of Christ that the ecclesial community experiences union with God.

THE ECCLESIO-ANTHROPOLOGY OF HANS URS VON BALTHASAR

Having outlined the central aspects of Balthasar's ecclesiology, I will now move to the central task of this chapter: to identify the essential tenets of

82. Balthasar, *TD III*, 282.
83. Healy, *Eschatology of Hans Urs von Balthasar*, 208.
84. Balthasar, *Engagement with God*, 34.

Balthasar's ecclesio-anthropology. For Balthasar, the church is a kenotic community, grounded in the redemptive mission that it receives from Christ. Mission and identity are tightly bound together and Christ stands as the person par excellence, the only one in whom mission and identity cohere completely. An individual only becomes a person wherein they understand their identity in light of their revealed mission. Consequently, humanity was made for a relationship with God that is constituted within the ecclesial community wherein God reveals their true self and enables them to serve in the midst of others. From here, we begin to see several distinctives of Balthasar's ecclesio-anthropology. For Balthasar, it is only within the church that one can recognize and realize their true self. Through the formative work of the sacraments, human creatures are formed into true, theological and ecclesial persons whose identities cohere with their assigned roles in the mission of Christ. Therefore, according to Balthasar's ecclesio-anthropology, personhood is received through the church, sacramentally formed, and embodied in ecclesial vocation, culminating in a disposition of receptivity and kenotic, self-giving love.[85]

True Personhood Received within the Church

For Balthasar, human beings were created for fellowship with God and are oriented toward a supernatural end. Therefore, human identity is dependent upon God and divine address. When God addresses the individual, he reveals their true self (form) and calls them to a task (vocation).[86] In accepting this revealed form, human beings become persons. "If man freely affirms and accepts the election, vocation and mission which God, in sovereign freedom, offers him, he has the greatest possible chance of becoming a person, of laying hold of his own substance, of grasping that most intimate idea of his own self—which otherwise would remain undiscoverable."[87] Through

85. It is worth noting that this summary may sound very similar to my discussion of Zizioulas's ecclesio-anthropology. However, while there certainly are similarities between the two figures, there are also some key differences. The distinctions and similarities between their two proposals will be described with greater clarity in chapter 5.

86. Raymond Gawronski provides a helpful summary, writing, "The meeting of the I and the Thou is the heart of Balthasar's theology, for it is at the heart of being human—and divine. Indeed, the human comes to self-consciousness itself first by being addressed by another" (Gawronski, *Word and Silence*, 81).

87. Balthasar, *TD III*, 263. Here we see that personhood, for Balthasar, is something progressively attained—that is, we are built up into persons. This differs from Zizioulas, who views personhood as something we experience only during the historicization of *theosis* in the Eucharist. In contrast, for Balthasar it seems each individual has a latent identity within them that must be revealed by God. It is only as they progressively

the impartation of the Spirit, the individual is shown the uniqueness of the incarnate Son.[88] As Dominic Robinson notes, it is only in perceiving and being enraptured by Christ, the *Gestalt* of God, that humanity can see the truth about itself.[89] But more than that, the Spirit enables human beings "to participate in the divine realm of Father-Son relationship . . . and to participate in the Incarnation."[90] However, it is important to remember that for Balthasar this participation in the incarnation is not individual, but social. In other words, God calls the individual to a community and to a participation in the divine relationships that constitute that community.

Where then does the church come in? For Balthasar, the church *is* the "Yes," the response to God's call, and it *is* the perpetuation of the incarnation.[91] Therefore, God calls an individual into a community, a community that perpetuates the mission of Christ.[92] Human beings obtain personhood in a derivative sense in that they are only true persons insofar as they participate within his mission, a mission embodied (in a very literal sense) in the ecclesial community. Therefore, any consideration of human beings as persons qua persons must take place within the church as it participates in the mission of Christ.[93] For Balthasar, "The call of the individual Christian always takes place within the context of the community of those who are in Christ, that is, in the Church, the individual cannot in any way reflect upon himself . . . without encountering the Church as his fellowship in her with

---

attain a coherence between their perceived identity and vocation that they will be able to become persons qua persons. John O'Donnell is helpful here. He writes, "Man is created with the faculties of intellect and will but he becomes a person only through the dialogical relation" (O'Donnell, "Hans Urs von Balthasar," 220). Put simply, while both Balthasar and Zizioulas understand personhood in eschatological terms, for Balthasar it is progressively received while for Zizioulas it is experienced in a punctiliar fashion during the Eucharist.

88. Balthasar, *TL III*, 60.
89. Robinson, *Understanding the "imago Dei,"* 84.
90. Balthasar, *TL III*, 75.
91. Oakes, *Pattern of Redemption*, 224.
92. Balthasar, *TD I*, 645.
93. Balthasar, "On the Concept of Person," 25. Balthasar uses phrases such as "individual conscious subject" to describe human beings that have either responded negatively to God's call or have not fully realized a coherence between their identity and vocation. In contrast, personhood is something we receive from God. He writes, "*In Christo*, however, every man can cherish the hope of not remaining a merely individual conscious subject but of receiving personhood from God, becoming a person, with a mission that is likewise defined *in Christo*" (Balthasar, *TD III*, 220). In other words, the dichotomy is not between "true persons" and "individual conscious subjects." Those who are truly persons are those who have received the call to participate in the mission of Christ and have found their identity completely in their vocation.

others."⁹⁴ Through the church, the individual is socialized and personalized. It is only through the church that the individual is able to become whole, as receiving the call of God enables them to uniquely become themselves.⁹⁵ The church personalizes the individual and reconstitutes them as a theological person. Within the church, they receive and "find themselves" within the mission of Christ.⁹⁶ As an ecclesial person, the individual is socialized within the church—that is, they are given a unique and specific role that participates in its mission of eucharistically engaging the world for the purpose of redemption. Balthasar writes, "The man who receives faith is never a mere individual cut off in isolation from the rest of mankind. He must become for the world around him a credible sign of the love of God that has been revealed to him in the Church."⁹⁷ Consequently, "the Christian is never a private person. . . . Rather, he is always part of the Mystical Body of Christ, and it is also in this Body—and in each of its members—that Christ lays down his life for the world as a whole."⁹⁸

Human conscious subjects are re-constituted as persons within the body of Christ wherein their individual, particular identities are incorporated within the greater identity of Christ. Since only the incarnate Son fully realizes his identity in his vocation and thus is a true person, all those who are received into his body are able to realize their own, respective identities in relationship to him and his mission. As a result, personhood is only visible and attainable within the body of Christ as true personhood is both a theological and ecclesial reality. While Balthasar is clear that the church is an instrumental means of salvation, the church appears to be essential to the attainment of personhood in the same way that Mary is essential to the incarnation. An ecclesial person is one who eucharistically serves the world, offering their very self in sacrificial love so that a redeemed world might be offered back up to God. For Balthasar, the individual becomes "a dramatic 'person' in Christ; he is constituted as a Christian individual through being chosen, called and sent forth, in and through Christ."⁹⁹ As I will demonstrate below, this corresponds closely with Balthasar's understanding of the human person as embodied in vocation. However, for the present moment, it is important to note that personhood is expressed and actualized as an ecclesial reality. In contrast to the world where an individual's role

94. Balthasar, *TD I*, 647.
95. Balthasar, *TD II*, 408–9.
96. Balthasar, *TD III*, 269.
97. Balthasar, *Man is Created*, 190.
98. Balthasar, *Man is Created*, 191.
99. Balthasar, *TD III*, 448–49.

and identity are disharmonious, it is only within the church, a community whose mission and identity comes from God, that humans are able to attain personhood and truly become themselves.[100]

Sacramentally Formed Persons

If personhood is uniquely received and experienced through the church, for Balthasar it is through the sacramental life of the church that human persons are progressively formed into their true selves. The sacraments impart divine life, enabling the individual to truly participate in the mission of Christ and forming them in accordance with their respective missions. Here, Balthasar appears to take a traditional Catholic understanding of the sacraments as a means of God's grace and reorients it around mission. As I have argued above, baptism provides entrance into the ecclesial community. He writes, "Baptism is a participation both in Jesus' birth (eternally from his Father, temporally from his Mother) and in his death (lived toward the Father and toward the world) and, so, in the whole of his personal form of existence as well."[101] Baptism incorporates the individual into the mission of Christ as the first act of self-surrender. In so doing, the church instrumentally provides the grace required to reveal the individual's intrinsic vocation and true self.[102] Similarly, as I have outlined above, the Eucharist imparts divine life into the individual and further forms them into the image of Christ—that is, into the one who fully embodies his mission.[103] For Balthasar, partaking of the Eucharist enables the ecclesial community "to receive the fullness of his powers so that they can continue his work in the world."[104] And this is necessary given the manner in which Balthasar connects mission to the telos of particular human subjects. "Vocation to the Church and within the Church is both personalizing and socializing. The human conscious subject becomes a person in the theological sense through the unique way in which he is addressed by God and taken into his service, which always takes place within the Christological framework. Thus, the Church is the genuine interpersonal community."[105] If the church

---

100. Balthasar, *TD II*, 14.
101. Balthasar, *Man is Created*, 159–60.
102. Balthasar, *Christian State of Life*, 82.
103. Balthasar, *New Elucidations*, 211.
104. Balthasar, *TD III*, 282.
105. Balthasar, *TD III*, 427–28.

personalizes and socializes the individual, it appears that the sacraments are the primary means through which this personlization occurs.[106]

Therefore, for Balthasar, the liturgical and sacramental life of the church is essential to human formation and "becoming" as the life and practices of the church train the individual in the way of self-service. While Zizioulas viewed the sacraments as ontologically constitutive of human personhood, for Balthasar the sacraments properly form ecclesial members in light of Christ's mission. And since, according to Balthasar, personhood is intricately linked to kenotic, sacrificial love, the sacramental life of the church becomes necessary for the formation of the individual into full personhood. He writes, "The Church fastens the believer—who as a man of the earth would just as well creep along the ground—to the espalier of her objective order, and on this trellis he can grow and bear fruit according to his gifts."[107] Additionally, as true life is realized in communion with God, the sacraments enable the individual member of the ecclesial community to participate in Trinitarian life. "Since the incarnate Word is always the Word of the Father in the Spirit, that is, a trinitarian Word, the reception of any sacrament within the Church always imparts trinitarian life to the Church's members. . . . Every sacrament received with a lively faith, clarifies and deepens the grace of sonship vis-à-vis the eternal Father and stirs up God's spirit in the believer."[108] Participation in the sacramental life of the church draws the church's members into the life of Christ.[109] In so doing, it enables the church and its members to truly realize their divine identity in the *missio* of the Son and become true, authentic persons as they find their identity in Christ.[110] When viewed in light of Balthasar's emphasis on the "missioned" nature of personhood, the sacramental life of the church enables the church's members to realize their true identities in the mission of Christ. In other words, the individual members of the church can only become true persons through the sacramental life of the church wherein they are progressively built up into their missioned-identity.

---

106. Balthasar holds out the hope that God will extend the blessing of salvation to all of humanity since Christ has suffered on their behalf. In fact, he argues that Christians must hold to this hope since God himself hopes all will be saved (see Balthasar, *Dare We Hope?*).

107. Balthasar, *Spirit and Institution*, 240.

108. Balthasar, *TD III*, 432.

109. Balthasar, *New Elucidations*, 98.

110. Balthasar, *TD III*, 232.

The Feminine Nature of Human Creatures

For Balthasar, the true nature of the human creature is understood in light of their "feminine" nature in relationship to God—that is, their passivity and receptivity. This emerges in part from his view of the church. For Balthasar, the church receives its identity and mission from Christ. He frequently revisits nuptial imagery in order to elucidate the relationship between Christ and the church wherein a husband and wife become one and he imparts life to her in the conjugal act.[111] As I have noted, the church's *kenosis* is a received *kenosis*, one it takes from its Lord and pours out through its members. But this also requires a certain disposition within the Christian, one exemplified in Mary: *indiferencia*.[112] In fact, this is the only appropriate disposition of the creature before their Creator. Fergus Kerr notes, "The world's response to God in Jesus Christ takes the feminine form of Mary-Church; a culture, which would be Christian and fully human, would be 'Marian,' primarily 'feminine.'"[113] I have discussed above how the church's feminine, Marian form is articulated in two distinct themes: a readiness for the divine will and pure selfless, self-abnegation both as exemplified in the fiat. The sacramental life of the church forms the individual members of the church into their missions and, by extension, into the truest expression of themselves. Additionally, it also places them in a position of constant readiness for the divine. Balthasar writes, "The 'indelible character' that every baptized person receives . . . guarantees that the Christian remains potentially open to every new encounter with the Lord."[114] The same holds true for the Eucharist. "In the eucharistic event, however—if the symbol of eating and drinking is to be a fulfilled sign—it is the believer who offers the whole sphere of his life to the Lord who knocks, and places it at his disposal."[115] In other words, the whole of the Christian life is to be one of openness to

---

111. Robert Zwank illustrates the central role that the polarity of gender difference plays in Balthasar's project; see Zwank, *Geschlechteranthropologie in theologischer Perspektive?*, 136–43.

112. Balthasar builds off the concept of "Ignatian Indifference," which David Crawford defines as the "sense of complete disponibility to God's will" (Crawford, "Love, Action, and Vows," 247). Crawford goes on to note that while Balthasar uses the concept of indifference in two different senses, "Balthasar draws on the idea of 'Ignatian indifference' to indicate the basic Christian stance of readiness for God's call and initiative, particularly as this readiness is manifested in relation to a potential vocation to the consecrated life. For Balthasar, this sort of indifference correlates with love" (Crawford, "Love, Action, and Vows," 247n10).

113. Kerr, *Twentieth-Century Catholic Theologians*, 137–38.

114. Balthasar, *TD III*, 356.

115. Balthasar, *New Elucidations*, 120–21.

the divine because the Church receives its very being and identity from the Lord. With Balthasar's emphasis on the feminine nature of the church as well as the foundational role that receptivity, surrender, and openness play in the Christian life it seems that in his framework true, creaturely personhood is inherently feminine.[116] Kilby writes, "We must all become more 'female' to be authentic Christians."[117] Kerr makes a similar observation, arguing that for Balthasar "all created being, we might say, is feminine in relation to the creator God."[118] The Christian life is to be one in which the community is constantly preparing themselves to receive and respond to God's call, reorienting our affections and desires around God's purposes for our lives.[119] And since the individual's true form is intrinsic, within the Christian community this "feminine" form is made visible. Here we find that Balthasar's ecclesiology, particularly its reliance on nuptial imagery and the Marian type, plays a constitutive role in his anthropology, as the fulfillment of human personhood is a reflection of the openness and readiness of Mary. As McIntosh articulates, "*Christian* love is always a response to the drawing near of God in Christ and is marked chiefly by a readiness for service."[120] And if, as I have argued above, the church is the instrumental means of personalization, then true personhood is found in a feminine, Marian *disponsibilité*, in readiness to hear and respond to the divine will.

Personhood Embodied in Ecclesial Vocation

While personhood is received through the church and the individual is formed into their true identity through participation in the sacraments, Balthasar's ecclesiology is grounded in the mission of Christ. Insofar as the

---

116. Karen Kilby is helpful here in clarifying Balthasar's thought. She writes, "To be woman is to be open, receptive, surrendering, passive, to be characterized by weakness and dependence, to be contemplative" (Kilby, *Balthasar*, 129). Similarly, Crammer observes, "For Balthasar, the feminine is characterized by receptivity (*Empfanglichkeit*), obedience, disponsiblity, and willing consent to the action of another, or letting be (*Gelassenheit*)" (Crammer, "One Sex or Two?," 98). Aidan Nichols argues that from Balthasar's standpoint this is because creation and the church are made in the image of the Word, not the image of the Father. "Creaturehood has an archetypally feminine quality. Because the creature is not made in the image of the Father but in the image of the Word, humanity is more primordially receptive than it is creative—just as in the eternal Trinity the Son is primarily receptivity, sheer reception of the Father's life" (Nichols, "Marian Co-Redemption," 255).

117. Kilby, *Balthasar*, 125.

118. Kerr, *Twentieth-Century Catholic Theologians*, 140.

119. Balthasar, *Man is Created*, 40.

120. McIntosh, *Christology from Within*, 115, italics his.

human creature is welcomed into the ecclesial community, they receive a new identity, one that illuminates their intrinsic mission. Human identity is rightly formed in the church as their divinely revealed identity and role in Christ's mission find coherence. It is this mission that not only grants them salvation from the deleterious effects of sin, but also gives them the ability to participate in the mission of God.[121] Balthasar writes,

> Grace brings man a task, opens upon for him a field of activity, bestows upon him the joy of accomplishment, so that he can identify with his mission and discover in it the true meaning of his existence. Grace gives man a center of gravity that, like a magnet, draws all the forces of his nature into a clear and definite pattern that is neither foreign nor cumbersome to the patterns already formed in his nature, but engages them, like idle laborers, in a task that is both pleasant and rewarding. This is the power of the grace of mission.[122]

Here we see that Balthasar understands grace as illuminating the individual to the true shape of their nature and, consequently, enabling them to understand their mission and vocation. Grace is essentially linked to mission as grace reveals and enables one to participate in the mission of Christ. As Roten rightly comments, "The theo-dramatic person lives in a constant tension between his identity as creature and the God-offered challenge to mature into a new personality grounded in mission."[123] And since mission lies intrinsic to the creature, grace reveals humanity's telos: ecclesial vocation. For Balthasar, "The concept of mission suffices to express the full measure of what man is; fulfillment of mission encompasses the whole concept of human perfection. It even replaces it, since human perfection is not in itself self-sufficient and purposeful."[124] Howsare provides a helpful summary: "Our humanity, far from being threatened by being taken into God's service, finds its proper expression only there."[125] It is within the church that mission is revealed and expressed as the grace of Christ. It is here that the grace of God is received. For Balthasar, one's initiation into the church results in the reception and illumination of one's true identity and mission. Moreover, the church does not receive its own mission but rather the mission of Christ. For the human creature, true identity is only found within the church wherein we are commissioned and enabled to serve in

---

121. Balthasar, *Engagement with God*, 53; Balthasar, *TL III*, 270.
122. Balthasar, *Christian State of Life*, 74.
123. Roten, "Marian Light on Our Human Mystery," 129.
124. Balthasar, *Christian State of Life*, 82.
125. Howsare, *Hans Urs von Balthasar and Protestantism*, 115.

Christ's redemptive mission for the sake of the world's salvation.[126] Mark McIntosh writes, "Mission fulfills, even in a sense creates, identity."[127] Humanity finds its true identity and reaches its telos through participation in ecclesial vocation.

And what is true of the whole is true of the parts—that is, every particular member of the ecclesial community is personalized through participation in the mission of Christ. "It is when God addresses a conscious subject, tells him who he is and what he means to the eternal God of truth and shows him the purpose of his existence—that is, imparts a distinctive and divinely authorized mission—that we can say of a conscious subject that he is a 'person.'"[128] Gawroski writes, "For Balthasar, Jesus Christ addresses each human being (*Geitsubjekt*) individually; each must decide if he will bear the Name of Christ and accept the unique mission that God has for each, within the mission of His Son. It is only by identifying with this mission that we become persons in the deepest, theological sense."[129] The individual is able to truly become a person—that is, a co-actor with Christ—when they truly identify with their unique mission. As Cyrus Olsen observes, "Our participation in Christ is a participation in the activity of divine condescending in the mode of self-communication."[130] In other words, to participate in Christ as a member of the ecclesial community is to participate in the action of the theo-drama and to become one's identity. For Balthasar, "The identification of one's own self with the mission received from God is an act of perfect faith and, as such, is the union of our work with the work of God in us."[131] The individual must surrender their freedom and any presuppositions regarding their identity, fully finding themselves in the commission of God. This is the

---

126. Balthasar, *TD III*, 429.

127. McIntosh, *Christology from Within*, 44.

128. Balthasar, *TD III*, 207. Balthasar emphasizes the distinction between humans as persons and humans as rational, conscious subjects. Human persons are those who have responded to God's revelation. Balthasar's understanding of human rational subjects, while stressing humanity's latent capacity to see and respond to God's revelatory address, must be nuanced by Balthasar's approach to epistemology as outlined in *Theo-Logic*. A subject must appropriate a stance of vulnerability wherein they grant an object access to its "inner spirit" and transform the way the subject understands the world (Balthasar, *TL I*, 166–69). Knowledge itself is an act of self-surrender (Balthasar, *TL I*, 119–20). It is, after all, love that forms the basis of knowledge in Balthasar's taxonomy. In other words, "rational subjects" is not used to communicate that human creatures are primarily "thinking" things, but rather that they have the capacity to engage in vulnerable, sacrificial love.

129. Gawronski, *Word and Silence*, 84.

130. Olsen, "Act and Event in Rahner and von Balthasar," 10.

131. Balthasar, *Christian State of Life*, 400.

only way for a human being to become a true person. As Kereszty writes, "Mission thus makes persons out of those who, before accepting their mission in Christ, were mere individual rational subjects (*Geistessubjekte*)."[132] If this is true, mission is fundamental to our understanding of personhood. But more than that, for Balthasar, embodying Christ's mission within the church simply *is* what it means to be a person in the most meaningful sense. The church becomes, in a sense, a means of personalization as its practices, particularly baptism and the Eucharist, serve as the means through which the individual can hear and receive God's word. As Dominic Robinson observes, "Above all Balthasar's new dramatic picture of human identity is vocational. To be created in God's image is expressed above all in Christ's call to each one of us."[133] But this is not a call to individuals in isolation, but it is a call to individuals within the life of the church and is an invitation into relationship with God. As McIntosh observes, "Unity with God is attained not by an identification of essences but by a fusion of the divine choice of mission for a person and that person's own free choosing and enactment of the same mission."[134]

Humans as Kenotic Lovers

Additionally, it must be remembered that the mission of Christ and, by extension, the mission of the church is one of kenotic, self-surrendering love.[135] If true personhood is only revealed in divine address and if, in so doing, God reveals the individual's missioned-identity as participating in Christ's kenotic mission, then, at least in a sense, personhood is kenotic. To be a person is to be an actor, a participant in *the* action. "Since the new theological name always implies the social dimension of service on behalf of others, it is precisely by forgetting his private subjectivity and becoming one with his function that he grows into what is most distinctive and personal to him."[136] Johann Roten helpfully summarizes Balthasar's view of human personhood as entailing both an ecstatic and kenotic existence. He writes,

---

132. Kereszty, "Eucharist and Mission," 9.

133. Robinson, *Understanding the "Imago Dei,"* 119.

134. McIntosh, *Christology from Within*, 43.

135. This differs significantly from our observation that, for Zizioulas, true human personhood is necessarily participatory in the love of God in that Zizioulas and Balthasar define this love differently. While both see the Christian community and individual appropriating a life of love, one that is consistent with the intra-Trinitarian life, for Balthasar this is strictly understood in terms of self-sacrifice and self-gift. In fact, for him, love *is* self-sacrifice.

136. Balthasar, *TD III*, 267.

"Each in its own way, *ecstasis* and *kenosis* testify to the eccentric disposition and vocation of the human person. In *ecstasis* we are decentered by God's loving glory, only to be re-centered in the mission of the kenotic Christ."[137] As we have outlined above, the church obtains its being, identity, and mission by receiving Christ's mission. Similarly, the individual member of the church becomes whole by appropriating the church's mission and realizing their inbuilt vocation. He writes,

> The formal sharing in Christ's sacrifice on the Cross that is the sine qua non of the Christian state as such is not to be divorced from one's personal sharing in the mind of Christ. The *kenosis* of the Christian who is daily being separated from the "outer man [that] is decaying" (2 Cor 4:16) so that he may become "a new creature" (2 Cor 5:17) in Christ is not something that can find its ultimate explanation either in himself or in his own conversion. It is a sharing of the *kenosis* of Christ himself.[138]

For Balthasar, to be a person is to participate in the kenotic life of Christ through and within the life of the church. As Aristotle Papanikolaou observes, "In Balthasar's trinitarian theological anthropology, personhood is not defined in terms of a quality possessed, but as a gifted event. One is a person only in *kenotic* relations of freedom as love."[139] For Balthasar, "The surrender of man's will to God's elective will means the sacrifice of his personal freedom insofar as it is regarded or exists as an entity distinct from the divine will."[140] Identity and personhood are actualized through a kenotic disposition. And if personhood is the telos for which God created humanity, then human persons were designed for a life of kenotic, self-sacrificial love.

Additionally, since to be human is to be finite and since incorporation into the mission of Christ and the being of the church enables the individual to transcend the limitations of their finitude through inclusion into the redemptive work of Christ, in Balthasar's ecclesio-anthropology we see that true personhood is found in the surrendering of our human freedom, identity, and very self in openness to the divine. He writes, "No single man can attain his true freedom unless he is borne by the power of men's openness to one another in love; if this is true of the sphere of the human mind, then it is naturally even truer of the man raised to loving communion with God."[141] The kenotic, ecclesial life then becomes the only

---

137. Roten, "Marian Light on Our Human Mystery," 127.
138. Balthasar, *Christian State of Life*, 219.
139. Papanikolaou, "Person, Kenosis and Abuse," 52.
140. Balthasar, *Christian State of Life*, 400.
141. Balthasar, *Theological Anthropology*, 88.

way to both self-actualization and self-transcendence, to the realization of an individual's "actual" identity.[142] Human freedom ultimately is to be laid down as an act of self-surrender, embracing divine vocation and a life of self-surrender. And it is only along the path of self-abnegation that humanity can experience communion with God. "Man will not be admitted to the kingdom of heaven until he has learned in the anteroom of heaven to renounce every will of his own, every desire, all personal autonomy that would oppose itself to the will of God as an independent authority."[143] In other words, the human person must transcend their personal finitude by surrendering their personal freedom if they are to participate in the kenotic life of the Trinitarian God himself.[144] Nicholas Healy helpfully explains that, for Balthasar, knowledge is communion, involving an act of self-disclosure and self-surrender in which God receives his creatures as they offer their very selves up to him, finding themselves in him—that is, in a communion of love.[145] For Balthasar, this abnegation of freedom is just a further insight into the nature of love. "For the sake of the beloved, love would gladly renounce all its possessions if it knew the beloved would find happiness in the act of giving. For love, even receiving is a form of self-giving."[146] This life of kenotic, self-gift perpetuates into the eschatological state wherein members of the ecclesial community freely give themselves to one another in love. It is only in appropriating God's kenotic mode of existence that the members of the ecclesial community can participate in the life of God.

This process of self-surrender continues even after the individual's death in purgatory. There, the individual is remade and reformed in accordance with their true form in Christ. Balthasar writes, "On earth the individual can strive for this Idea; but if we reflect upon the purification that

---

142. Balthasar will go so far as to apply this concept of self-surrender as a means of transcendence to the physical finitude embodied in death. For Balthasar, the person and work of Christ "revises" death so that it no longer becomes the symbol of human finitude but rather becomes an expression of the Father's love. He writes, "In the Incarnation of the eternal Son, death is already taken up as the expression of God's love for the creature, especially the sinner" (Balthasar, *Epilogue*, 107). As a result, incorporation into the body of Christ enables the individual to commit their very lives to the Father and, in so doing, appropriate Christ's perspective of death. He writes, "After him those who believe in him can adopt such an understanding of death. Henceforward, dying can now be seen—beyond being our naturally constrained end—to be the perfect surrender of oneself into the hands of the Father; death is now an opportunity for letting everything go and being free in God" (Balthasar, *Epilogue*, 107–8).

143. Balthasar, *Christian State of Life*, 128.

144. Balthasar, *Spirit and Institution*, 202–3.

145. Healy, *Eschatology of Hans Urs von Balthasar*, 181–85.

146. Balthasar, *Christian State of Life*, 29.

takes place after death, it emerges that the definitive recasting of the I is carried out in the divine fire. The pattern for this is the total self-surrender of Christ: those who are waiting to enter heaven contemplate this self-surrender and are transformed into it."[147] Balthasar's allusion to "divine fire" here is a reference to purgatory, the final discipleship wherein the individual is made aware of the world's sin and the depths of divine love.[148] For Balthasar, purgatory is the last step in which the individual becomes who God has created them to be in Christ.

CONCLUSION

In chapter 2, we examined the manner in which John Zizioulas's ecclesiology plays a constitutive role in his anthropology and understanding of human personhood. Similarly, within Balthasar's framework, we see that personhood and anthropology are both grounded in ecclesial being and mission. Since, for Balthasar, the church is a perpetuation of the mission of the Son, continuing the historicization of his kenotic procession from the Father, the church is both an institution and sacramental community that communicates Christ to the world. Marian in shape and type, the church receives its identity from the Son and is characterized by its self-abnegation and readiness to do the Father's will. Just as the incarnate Son is wholly constituted by his mission, so too is the ecclesial community constituted by its participation in his mission for the sake of the world's redemption. He writes, "Christianity is the community of those whom God, by his loving choice, has allowed to participate in the redemptive work and suffering of his Son. The company of Christ consists of those who have been redeemed by Christ, but the redeemed, at the same time, also those who, having been initiated into Christ's redemptive act, become sharers in his work of redemption."[149] Entered through baptism, the ecclesial community is a missioned community tasked with perpetuating the action of its Lord upon the cosmic stage for the sake of the world's redemption.

Balthasar's articulation of the church as a missioned community illustrates that his ecclesiology is robustly informing his anthropology. Indeed, five particular characteristics have emerged that are indicative of Balthasar's ecclesio-anthropology: it is ecclesially received, sacramentally formed, vocationally embodied, and culminates in kenotic, sacrificial love and openness to the divine. Through baptism, the individual is personalized

147. Balthasar, *TD V*, 391–92.
148. Balthasar, *TD V*, 369.
149. Balthasar, *Christian State of Life*, 219.

and socialized as they receive and respond to God's address. The ecclesial community is necessary for an individual's personalization. Similarly, the sacramental life of the church forms its members, enabling them to better correspond to God's divine idea as they become their missions. Participation in ecclesial vocation is essential to the obtainment of personhood. For Balthasar, human rational subjects can only become persons insofar as they find their identity completely grounded in the church's participation in Christ's mission. Since Christ's mission is one of *kenosis*, one that we must receive and fully identify with, the telos of human existence is one of self-abnegation and openness to the divine wherein we find our very selves in the communion of Trinitarian love. In the end, for Balthasar, ecclesiology reveals that human persons were made for perfect love—that is, "the unconditional surrender of self, in the *donum Dei*."[150]

---

150. Balthasar, *Christian State of Life*, 59.

4

The Ecclesio-Anthropology of Stanley Hauerwas

Stanley Hauerwas, a theologian at Duke University,[1] has gained significant notoriety in recent years for his contributions to the fields of theological ethics and theological politics.[2] Borrowing and adapting Barthian themes, Hauerwas critically rejects many of the tenets of Christian liberalism. Instead, he promotes a narrative approach to theology that prioritizes

---

1. Although he feels indebted to his Methodist upbringing and shares many affinities for the Catholic tradition, Hauerwas has described his ecclesial identity "as being a high-church Mennonite" (Hauerwas, *Work of Theology*, 53). Russell Reno comments that Hauerwas's ecclesial identity is notoriously difficult to identify: "Born hardscrabble Methodist, socialized into mainline Protestant intellectual life at Yale, a sometime communicant at Catholic Masses during his Notre Dame years, a Mennonite fellow traveler, and presently worshipping among Episcopalians, for all his emphasis on the church, Hauerwas' church can be hard to pin down" (Reno, "Stanley Hauerwas and the Liberal Protestant Project," 320).

2. Hauerwas, for his part, has repeatedly resisted the label of "ethicist," arguing it fails to account for the theological nature of his project. It is true he possesses a substantial background in ethics. However, Hauerwas views theological ethics as the practical outworking of Christian convictions. In other words, ethics describes the manner in which Christian communities live in harmony with their narrative. He writes, "I understand myself as a theologian and my work is theology proper. I have accepted the current academic designation of 'ethics' only because as a theologian I am convinced that the intelligibility and truthfullness of Christian convictions reside in their practical force" (Hauerwas, *Character and the Christian Life*, 1).

the church as a community of truthful witnesses to the story of Jesus Christ and the kingdom of God.[3] While much of Hauerwas's work has revolved around the church's role in the world, the centrality of the story of Jesus, theological politics, and character formation, his commitment to beginning theological inquiry with the church has led to the formulation of a rather robust ecclesio-anthropology. This chapter will argue that ecclesiology plays an essential role in Hauerwas's understanding of humanity.[4] I will begin with an examination of Hauerwas's articulation of the church as an alternative polis and school of virtue that is formed by the story of Jesus. I will then close with a discussion of the specific characteristics of Hauerwas's ecclesio-anthropology. For Hauerwas, the church is a political community whose mission primarily consists of bearing witness to the story of God's peaceful rule in Christ. The liturgical life of the church is itself an act of witness while also serving as a means of forming its members so that their lives bear witness to the kingdom of God.[5] It is only within the church that the individual is gathered into a community that rightly accords with the revelation of God's rule in Christ, thereby enabling them to attain their eschatological *telos* as a people of peace.

THE CHURCH AS AN ALTERNATIVE POLIS, A COMMUNITY OF WITNESSES

For Hauerwas, the life of the church is the starting point for all theological inquiry. As Arne Rasmusson observes, for Hauerwas, "theology has its base

---

3. See Dermange, "Église et communautarisme," 99–102. Particularly, Hauerwas is critical of Christian liberalism's confidence in the ability of political systems to embody principles abstracted from Christian doctrine and the ability of the church to Christianize the world. Instead, Hauerwas argues the church is simply a witness to the truth. Insofar as it pertains to the world, the church's role is to be the church, remain faithful to their witness, provide a foretaste of the kingdom, and demonstrate to the world its true identity as belonging to God (Hauerwas, *Peaceable Kingdom*, 100).

4. Throughout this chapter, I will use the terms "humanity," "human creatures," and "human beings" synonymously. Hauerwas has objected to appealing to the term "person" as a universally accessible category for Christian ethics because he believes that making such a move isolates human creatures from their situatedness in their particular narratives (Hauerwas, "Must a Patient?," 598–601). However, I would submit that both Balthasar and Zizioulas use "person" in a way that is theologically informed, thus avoiding Hauerwas's critique. With that being said, Hauerwas frequently uses the term in his writing but does not clarify the specific theological connotations he is bringing to bear on it (See, e.g., Brock and Hauerwas, *Beginnings*, 10; Hauerwas, *Approaching the End*, 161; Hauerwas, *Against the Nations*, 131; Hauerwas, *Better Hope*, 180–84).

5. Hauerwas, *Peaceable Kingdom*, 26.

in ecclesiology."[6] Hauerwas's ecclesio-centric approach prioritizes the stories, liturgy, and practical lives of the members of the Christian community. For Hauerwas, the church is an alternative polis that bears witness to the gospel of the kingdom, inaugurated and embodied in the life of Christ.[7] Furthermore, the church is a community that hears the truth of God's inaugurated reign and lives accordingly as faithful, virtuous witnesses.[8] As Ariaan Bann notes, "Though witness may not be the most remarkable term in Hauerwas's oeuvre, *With the Grain of the Universe* reveals that the idea and practice of the church as a community of witnesses is *the* basic and leading idea in all of Hauerwas's ethics and theology."[9] Entered through baptism, the church trains its members by retelling and remembering its story in order to form them into a "peaceable people" who live rightly. As I will demonstrate below, since it is only within the church that the narrative of God is properly told, received, and heard in a transformative manner, it is only within the church that the individual is able to rightly understand what it means to be human. Additionally, it is exclusively within the church that human beings can be rightly formed as creatures in God's world.

---

6. Rasmusson, *Church as Polis*, 189.

7. Hauerwas seems to use the term "alternative polis" to articulate the church's identity as a community that recognizes God's rule. He will contrast it with a world that does not. Part of this, as we will see below, has to do with Hauerwas's belief that the church provides a foretaste of the inaugurated "new creation" in the present. Adopting aspects of Aristotle's polis, for Hauerwas the church is a political community committed to the task of bearing witness to the rule of Christ (Hauerwas, *Matthew*, 68). Consequently, this means they live in conflict with other political leaders and rulers who seek to solidify their existence through violence as they are fundamentally a community of peace. He writes, "The Gospel seems to pose an alternative: those who wield power must either comprehend that God is the Lord of our lives or resort to violence as a means for denying that God is the Lord of our lives" (Hauerwas, *Christian Existence Today*, 214). In other words, the ecclesial community is an alternative polis in that they recognize the rule of God and are shaped by the declaration that Jesus is Lord, seeing and living in the new creation constituted by the person and work of Jesus Christ.

8. Hauerwas, *Christian Existence Today*, 102. According to Peter Ochs, Hauerwas does not understand truth as "a predicate of our immediate intuitions of the world, but only of the temporally extended relationship that we have with the world. This means that truth is a predicate of our behavior in the world, which means the way that life in the world shapes us, over time" (Ochs, "On Hauerwas' *With the Grain of the Universe*," 78). Hauerwas, for his part, agrees with Ochs's identification of what is essentially a pragmatic approach to truth (Hauerwas, "Hooks," 91).

9. Baan, *Necessity of Witness*, 51, italics his.

The Church, Jesus Christ, and the Kingdom of God

Hauerwas views the church as an alternative polis grounded in the story of Jesus. The church is an alternative polis in that it is a community constituted by the reality of the kingdom of God as revealed in the life, death, and resurrection of Jesus Christ.[10] It tells and embodies a different type of story,[11] one unconcerned with the pursuit of political power or the Christianization of the world. For Hauerwas, the church is a people formed and constituted by the story of Jesus. Mark Gingerich rightly recognizes that Hauerwas views the life of Jesus as essential to comprehending the identity of the church and the kingdom of God. He concludes that the church is seen "as the embodiment of God's rule on earth, a necessary response rooted in the eschatological hope of the God who brought about this Kingdom in the suffering of Christ."[12] God's rule is inaugurated, declared, and embodied in the life of Jesus Christ since "what Jesus came to proclaim, the kingdom of God as a present and future reality, could be grasped only by recognizing how Jesus exemplified in his life the standards of that kingdom."[13] Yet, the story of Jesus is made visible in the life of the community that bears witness

---

10. Hauerwas, *In Good Company*, 6. Hauerwas will go on to note that Christianity is formally a matter of politics. By this he means it is rightly oriented around the fact that God is the Creator and Lord of the cosmos, and that his kingdom will not be established through coercion but rather through peace. For this reason, the church is fundamentally a political reality as it stands in defiance of the present world political systems that advance their causes through violence. As Hauerwas argues, "We would like a church that again asserts that God, not nations, rules the world, that the boundaries of God's kingdom transcend those of Caesar, and that the main political task of the church is the formation of people who see clearly the cost of discipleship and are willing to pay the price" (Hauerwas and Willimon, *Resident Aliens*, 47).

11. The terms "story" and "narrative" refer to the historical, communally dependent, and temporal nature of human existence. For Hauerwas, all human persons are born in time, communities, and traditions that are formative to our understanding of reality. Samuel Wells notes, "Narrative conveys the particular, historical, temporal, contingent nature of human existence" (Wells, *Transforming Fate into Destiny*, 34). But, as Wells goes on to describe, for Hauerwas, narrative also refers to the received traditions and practices that a community has embodied over time. "It is in many ways a shorthand term to denote the ethical method of a tradition that tries to regulate character according to the character of God as found in Scripture" (Wells, *Transforming Fate into Destiny*, 63).

12. Gingerich, "Church as Kingdom," 129.

13. Hauerwas, *Peaceable Kingdom*, 74.

to it.[14] Jesus is only known through his followers.[15] As a result, the church, the kingdom, and the life of Jesus Christ are invariably linked together. Jesus is the very embodiment of the kingdom as he reveals its peaceful and nonviolent nature. The church is a community whose practical life together is the concrete, visible manifestation of this confession, bearing witness to this revelation and faithfully following in the way of Jesus. In Hauerwas's own words, "Discipleship and witness together constitute Christology; Jesus cannot be known without witnesses who follow him."[16] The church tells, passes on, and embodies the story of Jesus Christ—the embodiment and inaugurator of the kingdom of God.

Because the life of Jesus reveals the nature of God's rule, the Gospels are central in Hauerwas's project. If the church is a community of witnesses to the reign of God as exemplified in the story of Jesus, Christology becomes essential to our understanding of the church. Hauerwas believes that Jesus's incarnate life demonstrates "that Jesus's person and work cannot be separated because Jesus saves by making us participants in a new way of life."[17] For Hauerwas, Christian practice is the embodiment of Christian convictions. If Christ came to reveal a new way of life, then Christian theology is less about propositional knowledge and more about participating in the life that Christ makes possible. Therefore, what Christians believe about Christ and his kingdom is visible in the practical life of the church. Three particular emphases emerge in Hauerwas's Christology: Christ as *exemplar, autobasileia,* and *victor.* As *Christus exemplar,* Jesus provides a living illustration of

14. Hauerwas believes witnessing to God's truth is one of the fundamental tasks of the Christian community. It is "to speak the truth about the world as God's" (Hauerwas, *Approaching the End*, 42). This "speech" about the world involves both a way of living in the world as well as a telling and retelling of the story of God's reign (Hauerwas, *Christian Existence Today*, 40). Baan writes, "Hauerwas uses the *word* 'witness' to understand what's going on in the Christian *life*" (Baan, *Necessity of Witness*, 217, italics his). For Hauerwas, "witness" is a term used to describe the church's social life together. Hauerwas has written repeatedly on the manner in which Christians living Christianly both supports and serves medical, legal, Jewish communities, justice, and the elderly as well as describing charity as an obligation for the Christian (see, e.g., Hauerwas, *Suffering Presence*; Hauerwas, "On Surviving Justly," 132–59; Hauerwas, "How to 'Remember the Poor,'" 208–28).

15. Hauerwas, *Peaceable Kingdom*, 73.

16. Hauerwas, *Approaching the End*, 44.

17. Hauerwas, *Matthew*, 30. He argues, "What is asked by Jesus of the disciples reflects his identity as the Son of God. The 'what' that is Christ is inseparable from the 'how' of following him" (Hauerwas, *Work of Theology*, 270). In other words, any claims regarding Christ's nature and work cannot be separated from the manner in which the disciples followed him. For a further discussion of the relationship between ecclesiology and Christology in Hauerwas's theology, see Lorrimar, "Church and Christ in the Work of Stanley Hauerwas," 306–26.

what it means to be a witness to the rule of God. Arne Rasmusson observes that for Hauerwas Jesus's life is oriented around proclaiming and witnessing to the kingdom of God.[18] Hauerwas argues that Jesus shows us a life shaped by the story of God and the content of the kingdom that "turns out to be nothing more or less than learning to imitate Jesus' life through taking on the task of being his disciple."[19] As *autobasileia*, Jesus is the perfect embodiment of the peaceable kingdom as he continually refuses to exercise power through violence.[20] "Scripture refuses to separate the Kingdom from the one who is the proclaimer of the Kingdom. . . . Jesus is the *autobasileia*—the Kingdom in person."[21] Victoria Lorrimar writes, "As the inaugurator of the kingdom, Christ is the manifestation of the peaceableness that characterizes the kingdom, setting the example of nonviolent living which the Christian community must imitate."[22] God intrudes into this world to empower a people to live in light of his eschatological reign—that is, to live as a community that acknowledges his lordship and subverts the power of violence by living peaceably. Jesus is ultimately the one who proclaims and grounds the kingdom of God by revealing its true nature. For Hauerwas, "Jesus is he who comes to initiate and make present the kingdom of God."[23] Finally, Christ's work and resurrection, as *Christus victor*, triumphantly denounce and defeat the powers of this world,[24] revealing that "God's eschatological kingdom is genuinely one of peace."[25] While the complete realization of this kingdom ultimately remains eschatological, Christ's life demonstrates that it is possible to live "kingdomly" in the present.[26] In fact, the Christian community sees the present in a different manner, as they now know the direction in which all of creation is headed.

However, while the kingdom is inaugurated in Jesus, its consummation remains in the future. Consequently, the kingdom of God is a proleptic reality, simultaneously existing in the present while ultimately awaiting full realization in the *eschaton*. Reluctant to equate it with any ethical ideal, Hauerwas argues that it is exemplified and embodied in the life of Jesus.[27]

---

18. Rasmusson, *Church as Polis*, 183.
19. Hauerwas, *Peaceable Kingdom*, 80.
20. Hauerwas, *Against the Nations*, 117.
21. Hauerwas, *Community of Character*, 45.
22. Lorrimar, "Church and Christ in the Work of Stanley Hauerwas," 308.
23. Hauerwas, *Peaceable Kingdom*, 74.
24. Hauerwas, *Without Apology*, 89.
25. Hauerwas, *In Good Company*, 113.
26. Hauerwas, *Peaceable Kingdom*, 83.
27. Hauerwas, *Peaceable Kingdom*, 74.

The kingdom is a present reality in that Jesus's "life reveals the effective power of God to create a transformed people capable of living peaceably in a violent world."[28] As an eschatological reality, the kingdom breaks into the present in the political form of the church.[29] He writes, "Apocalyptic means that there is another world, another time, than the one in which we live; but it turns out to be the same world in which we live."[30] Christians believe that the eternal is present in present time and are empowered to live "eschatologically" as they await the kingdom's consummation.[31] As a result, Christians can live as a people whose lives are constituted by the present foretaste of the kingdom. As Nathan Kerr writes, for Hauerwas, "the importance and meaning of God's apocalyptic action for history lies in the manner in which Jesus' death and resurrection is constitutive of a people whose lives are formed by the 'irruption into history' of God's Kingdom as a distinct political reality."[32] The eschatological kingdom is experienced in the present in the Christian community. Ultimately, for Hauerwas, the kingdom of God is "a category which presumes and creates a new people."[33] For, "without the kingdom ideal, the church loses its identity-forming hope; without the church, the kingdom ideal loses its concrete character."[34]

It is against this backdrop that the church emerges as a central starting point for Hauerwas's theological project. Hauerwas has famously stated that "all theology must begin and end with ecclesiology."[35] Christian thinking about God begins in those communities that are shaped by the story of Christ. As a community formed by the revelation of God's reign, the church is a present foretaste of the eschatological kingdom of God. The ecclesial community bears witness to the way of Christ. The church's "task as followers of Christ is not to rule, but to be a people capable of witnessing to the One who rules through love, truth, and submission to the Father's will."[36] The concept of witness is central in Hauerwas's articulation of the church's mission and praxis. He writes, "To witness is to speak the truth about the world as God's, that is, the God of Israel, the same God who raised Christ from the

28. Hauerwas, *Peaceable Kingdom*, 83.
29. Kerr, *Christ, History and Apocalyptic*, 102.
30. Hauerwas, *Matthew*, 24.
31. Hauerwas, *Work of Theology*, 100.
32. Kerr, *Christ, History and Apocalyptic*, 102.
33. Hauerwas, *Against the Nations*, 115.
34. Hauerwas, *Against the Nations*, 112.
35. Hauerwas, *In Good Company*, 58.
36. Hauerwas, *Without Apology*, 61. Hauerwas's understanding of the church's task of bearing witness is a development of Barth's articulation of ethics as *Zeugnis*. See Ulrich, "Ethos als Zeugnis," 56–57.

dead—of which we are witnesses."[37] He frequently switches between using the term "witness" as a verb and as a noun.[38] The church is a community of witnesses whose central task is to bear witness. For the Christian community, the task of bearing witness involves pointing to the story of Jesus as that which shapes their lives. In spite of its evangelistic connotations, Hauerwas seems to use the concept of witness to communicate the church's task of reflecting the kingdom of God in its life and speech. He writes, "Witness requires the faithful display of Christian speech sufficient to test what is said in the light of how it is said. Such a testing, moreover, cannot be separated from the character of those who speak. Indeed, to speak Christianly means that the speakers' lives must correspond to what they say."[39] In this quote, Hauerwas makes a clear connection between speech and action. His descriptions of the church as a manifestation or foretaste of the kingdom along with his claims that the church exemplifies or embodies the story of Jesus all seem to communicate this central articulation of the church's mission: it is through the church and its practices that the individual is able to know, follow, and be formed by the story of Jesus. The church's liturgical practices, then, are formative, crafting lives that adequately correspond to the reality of the kingdom.[40] For, "it is in the church that the narrative of God is lived in a way that makes the kingdom visible."[41] In fact, it seems that for Hauerwas the very christological claims that seem to define the Christian community are attempts to assert plot points of the story of God's rule. Nathan Kerr

---

37. Hauerwas, *Approaching the End*, 42. In the paragraph immediately preceding this citation, Hauerwas explicitly identifies his own understanding of witness as a concept that is indebted to Wittgenstein's account of language. See also Baan, *Necessity of Witness*, 84–86.

38. For examples of Hauerwas's use of "witness" as a noun, see, e.g., Hauerwas, *Peaceable Kingdom*, 14–15; Hauerwas, *Christian Existence Today*, 11, 40; Hauerwas, *Matthew*, 25; Hauerwas, *With the Grain of the Universe*, 212; Hauerwas, *Working with Words*, 51. For examples of Hauerwas's use of "witness" as a verb, see, e.g., Hauerwas, *In Good Company*, 181; Hauerwas, *With the Grain of the Universe*, 207; Hauerwas, *Working with Words*, 51; Hauerwas, *Peaceable Kingdom*, 102; Hauerwas, *Approaching the End*, 53, 109.

39. Hauerwas, *Approaching the End*, 42. Hauerwas also uses locutions such as the church "exemplifies," "serves as a foretaste of," "embodies," or "manifests" the kingdom. Each of these expressions seems to communicate this same concept of "witness" wherein the church makes visible what it believes in its daily life. Hauerwas also uses the phrases "to bear witness" or "to be a witness." However, if there is a conceptual distinction between these words, Hauerwas does not elucidate it. Suffice it to say that when the Christian community confesses "Jesus is Lord" truthfully, their lives are shaped in a particular and distinctive way that manifests its truthfullness. This then underscores Hauerwas's conviction that theology and ethics cannot be separated from one another as the former is an articulation of the church's belief in the latter.

40. Hauerwas, *Sanctify Them in the Truth*, 79.

41. Hauerwas, *Peaceable Kingdom*, 97.

summarizes this point well: the "apocalyptic *work* of Jesus determines the kingdom by creating a new socio-political reality defined by conformity to the way of the cross that is the life of this singular human being."[42] Framed by the ethos of the kingdom, the church is a community of witnesses, testifying to this story, the story of Jesus, and the in-breaking of his kingdom into the present.

The Church as an Alternative Polis

For Hauerwas, the life of Jesus is inherently political—that is, it defies the authoritative claims of false regimes that rely upon power and violence to sustain their existence. It then follows that those constituted by his work and bearing witness to his life must be a political community. As has been noted above, for Hauerwas the church is an alternative polis, "an alternative politics to the politics of the world."[43] While the politics of the world seeks to establish power and control through violence, the church, as an alternative polis, rejects this notion by rightly recognizing the peaceful rule of God that has been revealed in Christ. It refuses to resort to coercion and violence, instead revealing "the insufficiency of all politics based on coercion and falsehood and finds the true source of power in servanthood rather than dominion."[44] It is in Jesus's person and work that such a people is constituted, a people who have been so formed by the truthfullness of God's story that they can live peaceably in a world of violence.[45] As Joel Lehenbauer notes, for Hauerwas, "the church bears witness to the world by serving as a contrasting model to the world's way of 'doing politics' on the basis of power and pressure, preference and violence."[46] It is for this reason that nonviolence stands as one of the central characteristics of the Christian community. Lehenbauer goes on to observe that "there is simply no way, according to Hauerwas, that the church can bear witness authentically and meaningfully to the world and at the same time make use of aspects of

---

42. Kerr, *Christ, History and Apocalyptic*, 105, italics his.

43. Hauerwas, *Matthew*, 29. For a discussion of how Hauerwas develops Yoder's critique of Constantinianism and attempts to maintain a distinction between the church and the world, see Materne, *La condition du disciple*, 190–202.

44. Hauerwas, *Peaceable Kingdom*, 102.

45. Hauerwas, *Peaceable Kingdom*, 83.

46. Lehenbauer, "Theology of Stanley Hauerwas," 164. We will return shortly to a discussion of peace as one of the central characteristics of the Christian life, but for now, suffice it to say that for Hauerwas peace is also a fundamental aspect of the life of Christ, the kingdom of God, and Christian community, whose central task is to bear witness of these realities to the watching world.

the politics of the world that compromise the clear words and example of Christ."[47] The Christian community is one that rightly recognizes the sovereign, peaceful rule of God and embodies an ethos indicative of his reign in their communal life.

As an alternative polis, the church exists in the world in a fundamentally different manner, a way constituted by the example and work of Jesus Christ. The life of Jesus provides a vivid illustration of what the kingdom looks like and a life that corresponds appropriately to it. For Hauerwas, as Mark Gingerich notes, Jesus's "life is the very witness of the kingdom, it is what the kingdom looks like. It can then be seen that Jesus' ministry is the embodiment of God's kingdom: not simply ideals to be followed, but the concrete announcement of what God's reign looks like."[48] Jesus is both the embodiment of the kingdom and its *exemplar*. Consequently, as a community of witnesses to this story, the church is marked by the manner in which it faithfully accords to the kingdom. In other words, the church is identified by its life. Rejecting deontological and consequentialist theories for ethics, Hauerwas understands Christian ethics as more than a way of living morally in the world.[49] Rather, ethics is primarily a learned way of seeing the world

---

47. Lehenbauer, "Theology of Stanley Hauerwas," 166.

48. Gingerich, "Church as Kingdom," 130.

49. Hauerwas is unconvinced of the usefullness of deontological and consequentialist theories of ethics because, in his estimation, they fail to account for the importance of a rightly formed self. As Sean Larsen articulates, Hauerwas appears to have two problems with these ethical approaches. First, they are foundationalist and presuppose an elevated view of practical reason that Hauerwas finds incoherent with Christian claims regarding the nature of reality. He writes, "They presume a theoretical structure accessible to all right-thinking people and then derive judgments from that structure" (Larsen, "How I Think Hauerwas Thinks about Theology," 28). But these judgments are based upon preconceived ideas of goodness or justice, which are then imported into Christianity in order to govern ethical decisions. Second, according to Hauerwas, these approaches to ethics fail to adequately account for the importance of character and virtue as it pertains to the reasoning process. As Sean Larsen observes, "One can only practically reason in order to evaluate decisions retrospectively in light of who one has become and who one wants to be" (Larsen, "How I Think Hauerwas Thinks about Theology," 28). Thus, Christian ethics must be fundamentally Christian. For Hauerwas, this means ethics is not a matter of simply making the right judgments, but of being the type of people who seek to live in a manner that is consistent with their narrative. "His overall concern is to shift the focus of ethical reflection from the individual in a crisis to the Church in its faithfullness. The purpose of theological ethics, for him, is not to make quandaries easier, but to build up the Church" (Wells, *Transforming Fate into Destiny*, 61). Mark Ryan helpfully connects this back to Hauerwas's understanding of the narrative the church has received and embodied. He comments, "Through the stories of Israel and Jesus Christians learn to be a community that strives to become like their God (*imitatio Dei*) in its ways of life" (Ryan, *Politics of Practical Reason*, 114).

in light of the story of Jesus.[50] "We simply must learn to see the world in which we live as the world that the Father created and redeemed through the Son."[51] Yet this new way of perceiving the world cannot be divorced from performance. If the world is truly redeemed by the Son and if the way of peace has truly triumphed over violence, Christian practice must embody this kingdom reality, a way of life made possible by the reign of Christ. He writes, "The church is a people on a journey who insist on living consistent with the conviction that God is the lord of history. They thus refuse to resort to violence in order to secure their survival."[52] For Hauerwas, convictions about the truthfullness of God's reign must be embodied in daily life. "Christians are people who remain convinced that the truthfullness of their beliefs must be demonstrated in their lives."[53] The church's political nature as well as their convictions about the person and work of Jesus must be visible in their practices, particularly their embodiment of the peaceful, nonviolent life of Jesus.[54] Hauerwas states, "What makes the church the church is its faithful manifestation of the peaceable kingdom in the world. As such, the church does not have a social ethic; it is a social ethic."[55] In so doing, the church bears witness to the reality of the kingdom and provides a foretaste of it.

Jesus, in his life and work, serves as an embodiment of the kingdom of God. In a similar way, as the Christian community follows in the way of Jesus, it too provides a foretaste of the kingdom. In other words, by living rightly in the world—that is, by living in such a way that reflects their seeing and accepting of the world as God's world and our own lives as God's creatures[56]—the church shows the world what it truly is: "the creation of a good God who is known through the people of Israel and the life, death, and resurrection of Jesus Christ."[57] This again returns to the concept of witness. As Ariaan Baan observes, "For Hauerwas, the goal of the vocation of the church is not just that it witnesses to God. The church has been called to teach mankind about what kind of world we live in and what kind of creatures we are."[58] The church engages in the task of witness through its lived existence, an existence that is necessarily communal since the practices of

---

50. Hauerwas and Willimon, *Resident Aliens*, 67.
51. Hauerwas, *Matthew*, 24.
52. Hauerwas, *Community of Character*, 10.
53. Hauerwas, *Christian Existence Today*, 10.
54. Gingerich, "Church as Kingdom," 130.
55. Hauerwas, *Peaceable Kingdom*, 99.
56. Hauerwas, *Matthew*, 84.
57. Hauerwas, *Peaceable Kingdom*, 15.
58. Baan, "Stanley Hauerwas and the Necessity of Witness," 39.

the Christian are only observable in community. The church's mission is to testify to the truthfullness of their claims about who God is and what he has done. In so doing, the church becomes a "faithful manifestation of the peaceable kingdom in the world."[59] For Hauerwas, this occurs primarily through the church's practical life in a violent world as they subsist in the time between the establishment of the kingdom and its consummation. The church exists as a peaceable people who inhabit a violent world, testifying to the goodness of God's creation and the lordship of Christ, the one whose life constitutes this people and proves the futility of violence as a way of life. But for Hauerwas this nonviolent, political life does not come naturally to the members of the Christian community. Christians must be trained and incorporated into the life of a community that makes possible the very practices that are indicative of the kingdom, "a body constituted by disciplines that create the capacity to resist the disciplines of the body associated with the modern nation-state."[60] The church is a community that trains its people in the way of the kingdom, the way of virtue and peace.

The Church as a School of Virtue and Peaceable Living

Hauerwas argues that the beliefs of the Christian life are embodied in the church's practical life, practices that form its parishioners to be people of virtue. "The truest politics, therefore, is concerned with the development of virtue."[61] Virtue describes the manner in which the Christian community lives as followers of Christ. Commenting on Jesus's rebuke of the hypocrisy of the pious, Hauerwas argues that such an admonition "suggests that it matters not only that we follow Jesus but that how we do so is crucial for what it means to be his visible people. One of the languages the church has found helpful to explore this 'how' has been the language of the virtues."[62] Adapting aspects of both Aristotle's and Thomas's thought, Hauerwas argues that just as an Aristotelian account of the virtues involved an apprentice following and learning from a master, so too the Christian must learn

---

59. Hauerwas, *Peaceable Kingdom*, 99.

60. Hauerwas, *In Good Company*, 26.

61. Hauerwas, *Community of Character*, 2. Larsen is also helpful here. He summarizes that for Hauerwas "a virtue is a *moral* habit ordered towards the reliable production of a good life. The complex of virtues that we acquire makes our character" (Larsen, "How I Think Hauerwas Thinks about Theology," 27, italics his). But it is important, as I have noted above, to remember Hauerwas's conception of virtue is intricately tied to the ecclesial community's task of exemplifying Christ (Hauerwas, *Matthew*, 68). Virtue is not just the task of the individual, but the task of the community as a whole.

62. Hauerwas, *Matthew*, 74.

to follow Jesus if they are to actually know him.[63] Incorporation into the Christian community is necessary in order to obtain the habits and characters required to know and live the Christian story faithfully. As Mark Ryan notes, "For him virtues are skills Christians learn in community that enable them to go on being who they are—which is to say, talking as they talk. Cultivating the right virtues allows Christians to pass down their story through generations and thus sustain the political community called church."[64] John B. Thomson believes that it is through remembering the narrative of those past saints who have lived as faithful witnesses that Christians will cultivate the virtues necessary to live faithfully in the present. "For Hauerwas, a church is a school of virtue rooted in an apprentice model of education, whose authorities, the saints, are those who have more fully appropriated and displayed the faith and, in particular are able to educate other disciples in living and dying in ways appropriate to the story."[65] The church trains its members to be a people who embody the way of their Lord and the life of the kingdom, forming them through the story of Jesus to be a people whose lives reflect the truthfullness of their story.

According to Hauerwas, the cultivation of virtue is essential to the Christian community's vocation. For Hauerwas, Christ sought to establish "a transformed people capable of living peaceably in a violent world."[66] The virtues, then, are a description of "the shared life made possible through Christ."[67] The church must possess the courage to tell its story truthfully and "form its citizens virtuously" in a violent world,[68] living hopefully and patiently as they cling to reality of Christ's reign in the face of worldly powers and embody the love of God in Christ. Yet it seems that each of these virtues is understood in relationship to peace and nonviolence.[69] For Hau-

---

63. Hauerwas and Willimon, *Resident Aliens*, 55.
64. Ryan, *Politics of Practical Reason*, 101–2.
65. Thomson, *Ecclesiology of Stanley Hauerwas*, 19.
66. Hauerwas, *Peaceable Kingdom*, 83.
67. Hauerwas, *Matthew*, 65.
68. Hauerwas, *Against the Nations*, 130; Hauerwas, *Peaceable Kingdom*, 104–5.

69. Jennifer Herdt observes that Hauerwas displays little interest in developing a revival of virtue ethics, but is more focused on describing the character of the church. She argues that Hauerwas views the virtues "teleologically and socially, as necessary for being the community of peace that is the Church" (Herdt, "Hauerwas among the Virtues," 211). The virtues, as we have noted above, describe the path toward the ideal life. For the Christian community, this "good life" is God's peaceable kingdom. And since the church is the community that is grounded on Christ's absolute refusal to resort to violence in the face of power and commitment to providing a foretaste of the peaceable kingdom's inbreaking, the church must fundamentally be characterized by its peaceable living. It seems, then, that all the other virtues are to be understood in relationship

erwas, "Nonviolence is not just one implication among others that can be drawn from our Christian beliefs; it is at the very heart of our understanding of God. . . . [It] is integral to the shape of Christian convictions."[70] As Sean Larsen argues, for Hauerwas, "pacifism is therefore not a commitment meant to make the world 'a better place' . . . but a response to the truth of God's non-violent rule from the cross."[71] He goes on to observe, "Pacifism then becomes the *sine qua non*, a hallmark of Christian life."[72] The church is a community of apprentices who are learning how to live peaceably as they follow after their Lord, the king who refused to use coercion and whose kingdom is an alternative to violence. Peace, then, is the telos of the Christian community. The church's liturgy trains its members to perform the story of the kingdom faithfully and thereby become a people of peace.

One of the principle tasks of the church is training its members to follow Jesus as faithful witnesses through remembrance of the Christian narrative. For Hauerwas, humans are formed by the stories they receive. Rommel argues that for Hauerwas, the larger Christian story must become determinative in our lives. "Overcoming of the limits of one's own [*story*] is only possible if a true *story* becomes the central, primary leitmotif (*determinative story*), and this in turn can only happen in a community of virtue formation."[73] Story and narrative, as I have already demonstrated, are important themes in Hauerwas's writing. He writes, "A narrative must not only provide an intelligible pattern that links contingent events of our lives; it must also provide us a way to go. A story of who we are must give us the power to make our actions consistent with our identity."[74] Thomson provides a helpful explanation of the relationship between story and identity. "Identity is therefore not rooted in rationality as an abstraction, but requires a 'narrative to give our life coherence,' a 'truth' reinforced by the

---

to peace and the realization of true peace within the Christian community. If virtues are descriptions of the life of the church and nonviolence a characteristic of a faithful community, peace no longer seems to be one of the virtues but essential to the very character of the church and the *telos* of God's people (Hauerwas, *Christian Existence Today*, 90, 95).

70. Hauerwas, *Peaceable Kingdom*, xvii–xvi.

71. Larsen, "How I Think Hauerwas Thinks about Theology," 34.

72. Larsen, "How I Think Hauerwas Thinks about Theology," 34. Hartmut von Sass explains that, for Hauerwas, pacifism is an "inevitable outcome" of his belief that Christians anticipate the eventual triumph of Christ and are called to resist the urge to counter violence with more violence (Sass, "Politik des Pazifismus," 43–44).

73. Rommel, *Ekklesiologie und Ethik bei Stanley Hauerwas*, 23, italics his, my translation.

74. Hauerwas, *Christian Existence Today*, 31.

intentional and teleological pattern of human living."⁷⁵ It is only within the church that we can hear the truthful story of God's reign in Christ, one that provides a meaningful account of our past and does not result in violence.⁷⁶ Additionally, it is within the church that a true and coherent sense of self is attainable, one where human creatures recognize and accept their place in God's created order. As Mark Ryan observes, Hauerwas believes that we must be trained to see the world rightly. "Our ability to see correctly what is before us depends on our proper formation in a community."⁷⁷ One of the church's central tasks, then, is remembrance. As it continually reminds its members of this story, it instills in them the habits required to live as faithful witnesses to the kingdom.⁷⁸ In so doing, they allow the story of Jesus to become the central story of their lives and formative of their identities. "Christians become able to see through these false claims and descriptions of reality, because they see in the death and resurrection of Jesus that, what seemed like powerlessness was in fact the victory of truth over falsehood and violence."⁷⁹

For Hauerwas, the Christian narrative must be embodied in the practices of the Christian community. "The sacraments enact the story of Jesus and, thus, form a community in his image. We could not be the church without them. For the story of Jesus is not simply one that is told; it must be enacted."⁸⁰ The liturgical practices and sacraments of the church, then, concretize the story of Jesus in visible form. Baptism marks entrance into the Christian community as through it we are "made a human being after the likeness of Christ. . . . Through baptism we are made the human beings we

75. Thomson, *Ecclesiology of Stanley Hauerwas*, 133.

76. Hauerwas, *Christian Existence Today*, 38.

77. Ryan, *Politics of Practical Reason*, 120.

78. For Hauerwas, remembering "implies not merely recalling something whose actuality has come and gone, but keeping the formative past alive by embodying God's past actions within her present ones" (Ryan, *Politics of Practical Reason*, 132). This understanding of memory differs slightly from Zizioulas's. For Zizioulas, *anamnesis* in the Eucharist returns us to the cross and the work of the Holy Spirit transports us from there into the *eschaton*. However, for Hauerwas, *anamnesis* is remembering the work of Christ and the alternative nature of his community. Memory is more oriented toward the past and present than it is to the eschatological future. Furthermore, it does not involve an ontological, punctiliar event in which personhood is experienced. Yet for both Hauerwas and Zizioulas the anamnetic task is formative and enables participation in the life of Christ. However, even this act of participation is fundamentally different. Zizioulas adopts a more ontological framework, while Hauerwas focuses predominantly on the manner in which participation in Jesus's story provides the Christian community with an empirical form.

79. Rasmusson, *Church as Polis*, 185.

80. Hauerwas, *Peaceable Kingdom*, 107–8.

were created to be."⁸¹ Baptism inaugurates the individual into the Christian story wherein they rightly see themselves as creatures created to follow in the way of Jesus.⁸² Through baptism our disparate stories are reconstituted and, since our identity is intrinsically tied to our stories and histories, we are given a new meaning and identity, becoming a part of the story embodied in Jesus's death and resurrection as well as the community that his work established. The celebration of the Eucharist points forward to the eschatological meal and "reminds Christians we are not of 'this world.'"⁸³ In this act of communal celebration, Christian discipleship is grounded in the eschatological promise of the kingdom.⁸⁴ Liturgical practice becomes the means through which the Christian story is reenacted. The liturgical life of the church trains church members to remember Christ's work of peace.⁸⁵ Christian practices such as forgiveness, hospitality, and truthful speech are all essential for correctly embodying the reign of God in Christ and for rightly forming the individual members of the Christian community. As Victoria Lorrimar observes, "For Hauerwas, baptism, the Eucharist, and other practices of the church do not represent 'efficacious signs of grace . . . by which divine life is dispensed to us.' Rather, enacting churchly practices forms character; these practices serve as gestures that point to the story of Christ."⁸⁶ The church's liturgical practices serve as marks of the eschatological kingdom and train Christians to rightly appropriate and embody the peaceable kingdom of God.⁸⁷

The kingdom of God as embodied in the life of Christ grounds Hauerwas's understanding of ecclesiology. The church is an alternative polis, providing a foretaste of the eschatological kingdom. As its members imitate the peaceable and political character of their Savior, they bear witness to his story and his revelation of the world as created by and for God. But the peaceable life is unnatural, even for those who have been initiated into the Christian community through baptism. Thus, the church must teach its members to embody the kingdom. Accordingly, the church is a school of virtue, training its members to live as faithful witnesses whose very lives make visible the truthfullness of the Christian narrative.

---

81. Hauerwas, *Cross-Shattered Church*, 121.
82. Hauerwas and Willimon, *Resident Aliens*, 52.
83. Hauerwas, *In Good Company*, 162.
84. Schlabach, "Continuity and Sacrament, or Not," 193.
85. Hauerwas, *Community of Character*, 108.
86. Lorrimar, "Church and Christ in the Work of Stanley Hauerwas," 318–19.
87. Hauerwas, *Christian Existence Today*, 107.

ECCLESIO-ANTHROPOLOGY OF STANLEY HAUERWAS

Having delineated Hauerwas's ecclesiology in the previous section, it is now time for me to articulate how these ecclesiological commitments robustly inform his understanding of humanity. For Hauerwas, the church is a community formed by the story of Jesus. As an alternative polis shaped by the rule of God in Christ, the ecclesial community's mission is to bear witness to the peaceable kingdom. The church's practices are the means through which the church bears witness to the story of Jesus. Furthermore, these practices train the members of the ecclesial community to be a people of virtue whose lives testify to the story of God's reign in Jesus Christ. The church's telos, peaceful existence together with God, is an inaugurated reality that gives shape to the Christian community in the present. Knowing that it is God who brings about this end, members of the church can live as "eschatological" people in the present. In light of the above discussion, the elements of Hauerwas's ecclesio-anthropology begin to emerge. Ecclesiology is pivotal in Hauerwas's account of humanity as it is only with the church that true humanity is revealed, and it is only in embodying the Christian narrative that human creatures can be rightly formed. Put simply, within the church we learn what it means to be human and are formed rightly as God's creatures in God's world. Hauerwas's ecclesio-anthropology is narrative in shape, political in nature, eschatological in orientation, and holds peaceful existence as its eschatological telos.[88]

The Narrative Shape of the Self

Hauerwas's emphasis on the church's role in forming the individual through the Christian narrative highlights a distinctive element of his ecclesio-anthropology: the narrative shape of the self. In the telling, hearing, and embodying of the Christian story, we are rightly formed as human creatures. "For it is my deepest conviction that Christianity is training in how to be human."[89] Within the church we are able to learn what it means to live as

---

88. Hauerwas would undoubtedly prefer the terminology *eschaton* over *telos*; this is the distinctive end to the Christian narrative. As Wells observes, for Hauerwas, "the cardinal virtues are those suited to the notion of *telos*, and the theological virtues—to which Hauerwas adds a few of his own, notably peacemaking—are those whose anticipate the *eschaton*" (Wells, *Transforming Fate into Destiny*, 35). The eschatological world is the end or conclusion to the Christian narrative. However, in this section I am focusing more on the *type* of person present in that eschatological existence. In other words, in the conclusion to the Christian story, faithful witnesses will possess a certain type of character, one suited for their eschatological participation in the peaceable kingdom.

89. Hauerwas, *Approaching the End*, xvii.

God's creatures in God's world.[90] This refashioning of self-understandings in light of the Christian story contains two elements that are worth noting. First, it involves the realization of the contingency of human creatures. Reoriented by the work of Christ, "we see ourselves and our lives as part of God's story."[91] A right view of the world, as told through the story of the church, understands that human creatures exist as contingent beings. "The very description, 'creature,' is itself a story that provides a truthful account of our lives."[92] The Christian narrative reveals that human beings possess a contingent existence, contingent on the gratuity of their Creator and this larger story must become determinative of our lives.[93] Second, this refashioning of self-understandings involves learning that the significance of our lives is found in the unique vocation we receive from God. He writes, "We are contingent beings whose meaning and significance is determined by something other than ourselves."[94] This meaning lies primarily in bearing witness to and embodying the peaceable kingdom. For Hauerwas, this relates directly to his understanding of the *imago Dei*. Not only does the story of the kingdom provide a proper orientation for one's life, it also reveals that "the only significant theological difference between humans and animals lies in God's giving humans a unique *purpose*. Herein lies what it means for God to create humans in God's image."[95] The Christian narrative is the only way that the disparate events of human life are unified and the only way that the individual's story gains coherence. As Herman Paul notes, "Narrative coherence occurs when human lives are lived in acknowledgement of such Biblical grammatical rules as that God is the creator of this world, that humans live in the world in order to praise their creator, and that the creator is also the redeemer, who shall restore all things so as to bring the world to its completion."[96]

But this story must be received from the Christian community. For Hauerwas, "The only way we can know the character of the world, the only way we know ourselves, the only way we know God is by one person telling another."[97] This implies that human beings possess not only a contingent existence with respect to their Creator, but also an intrinsically interdependent

---

90. Rommel, *Ekklesiologie und Ethik bei Stanley Hauerwas*, 16.
91. Hauerwas and Willimon, *Resident Aliens*, 67.
92. Hauerwas, *Work of Theology*, 29.
93. Rommel, *Ekklesiologie und Ethik bei Stanley Hauerwas*, 23.
94. Hauerwas and Willimon, *Resident Aliens*, 67.
95. Hauerwas and Berkman, "Chief End of All Flesh," 199, italics original.
96. Paul, "Stanley Hauerwas," 18.
97. Hauerwas, *Approaching the End*, 38.

existence in regard to other members of human community.[98] Hauerwas's depiction of the church as a witness and as epistemologically central to understanding the story of Jesus reveals that human beings are intrinsically interdependent.[99] Apart from this community, we cannot know the purposes for which we were created or the story that gives our life coherence. This interdependence is highlighted in Hauerwas's understanding of the shape of human self-understandings. Every human creature is formed by the stories of their communities. These stories provide different accounts of reality, the moral life, and the skills necessary to flourish. For Hauerwas, ecclesiology reveals that human creatures are contingent creatures, born "in the middle" of these narratives.[100] As a result, the self is subsequent to the community.[101] "Story is a more determinative category than self. Indeed, our very notion of 'self' only makes sense as part of a more determinative narrative. We can only make sense of our lives, to the extent that we can make sense of our lives at all, by telling stories about our lives."[102] Consequently, our lives and sense of self are dependent upon the communities in which we subsist and whose practices we embody. While Zizioulas views human persons as social due to his relational ontology and how that pertains to the *imago Trinitatis*, Hauerwas does not seem concerned with any notions of metaphysical or ontological union between persons. Yet he nevertheless maintains that human creatures are social in that they are formed and shaped by their communities, depending upon them for the development of their identities.

For Hauerwas, the interdependent nature of human beings also extends to humanity's achievement of the virtuous end to which it was created. In order for human beings to achieve their end and become creatures of virtue, we must be formed by a particular kind of community. Charles Pinches avers, "Hauerwas is deadly serious in his belief that we desperately need one another to be cured of our own self-deceptions."[103] It is only within the Christian community that we can both hear and become the human

---

98. Brock and Hauerwas, *Beginnings*, 42.

99. Hauerwas and Willimon, *Resident Aliens*, 94.

100. Gunton, "Church as a School of Virtue?," 211.

101. Hauerwas, *Christian Existence Today*, 28. Hauerwas even goes so far as to argue that the individual's "self" is subordinate to the community since selves are formed and discovered only within certain communities and their narratives and traditions. He writes, "Community joins us with others to further the growth of a tradition whose manifold storylines are meant to help individuals identify and navigate the path to the good. The self is subordinate to the community rather than vice versa, for we discover the self through a community's narrated tradition" (*Peaceable Kingdom*, 28).

102. Hauerwas, *Sanctify Them in the Truth*, 101.

103. Pinches, "Considering Stanley Hauerwas," 197.

creatures we were created to be. For Hauerwas, "Christians are not simply called to do the 'right thing,' but rather we are expected to be holy. Such holiness is not an individual achievement but comes from being made part of a community in which we discover the truth about our lives."[104] It is quite clear that Hauerwas believes that the individual must be formed in the Christian community in order to understand Christian truth. As Mark Ryan notes, "Hauerwas believes that (given that language is internally related to the world) one must be formed in Christian ways of speaking in order to understand Christian truth claims."[105] But perhaps this line of reasoning can be taken a step further: not only is Christian formation the epistemological foundation for understanding Christian truth, but since Hauerwas believes that truth is embodied in communal practices, subsisting in a Christian community is required in order to *be* the type of *beings* Christians claim to be. Therefore, if (1) narratives and embodied practices shape the self and (2) the only true narrative is embodied and told within the context of the church, it seems that (3) only those within the church are being shaped rightly by the true narrative—that is, the story of Jesus. Therefore, (4) it seems that either humanity is possessable in varying degrees or only members of the church can attain true humanity. While Hauerwas does not explicitly state that those outside of the Christian community are fully or truly human, the shape of his logic appears to entail either an exclusivist or dynamic account of humanity. For Hauerwas, "To be a Christian is the fullest expression of what it means to be a human being."[106] While Hauerwas is reluctant to provide robust metaphysical definitions for his understanding of humanity, he does seem to view the church as central to experiencing or obtaining the type of existence God desires for his creatures.

The Political Shape of Human Identity

Given the need for such formation within the Christian community and the political nature of the church, another key element of Hauerwas's ecclesio-anthropology emerges: the inherently political nature of human identity.[107]

104. Hauerwas, *In Good Company*, 155.
105. Ryan, *Politics of Practical Reason*, 112.
106. Hauerwas, *Approaching the End*, 184.
107. The term "political" is being used here to describe how communities function in relation to their ruling authorities and the stories that determine the necessary habits and skills required to flourish. This is somewhat similar conceptually to Zizioulas's understanding of an individual's identity being constituted in Christ or Adam. Hauerwas constructs a similar polarity: either we are being trained as disciples of Caesar or of Jesus. In fact, both understand a "non-Jesus" constitutedness as leading inherently to individualism, although for drastically different reasons.

For Hauerwas, the embodiment and worship of a particular kingdom is intrinsic to human existence. Accordingly, to be a member of the church is to participate in an alternative politics to the politics of the world, one that refuses to use power and coercion in order to solidify its existence.[108] Ecclesial existence is political. As Rasmusson observes, "To be a disciple therefore is to be part of the new polis that has the Gospels as constitution. As a life of discipleship, Christian life thus concerns the formation, or rather the transformation, of people through the tradition-formed community called the church."[109] But given that Jesus is the embodiment of the kingdom and possesses an intrinsically political nature as king, those who follow him must also be political beings as witnesses to this kingdom and king. The very nature of this alternative polis requires that the church be a community of people whose practices and behaviors are indicative of the type of people that they have become a part of. Consequently, their lives as witnesses are subversive to the politics of the world as they represent "an alternative to the violence of Rome as well as those who would overthrow Rome with violence."[110] The church embodies an alternative politics that is enacted in the lives of its members who, as faithful witnesses, testify to the true kingdom.

But if human action is intelligible in light of political commitments and our actions reveal and formulate these identities, Hauerwas appears to construct a largely functional account of the human creature. I use the term "functional" to describe how a human creature's identity is formulated through their actions and how their meaning arises from the roles they are called to perform. This is particularly evident in Hauerwas's discussion of the *imago Dei*, which he understands in terms of the purpose for which God has created humanity.[111] This unique vocation of serving as a manifestation of God's peaceable kingdom is revealed and realized in the church. While politics is the larger, supervening framework for understanding human action, our political orientation is revealed through the shape of our lives. "Any community and polity is known and should be judged by the kind of people it develops."[112] Caesar's kingdom is only recognizable due to the violent practices that its adherents exemplify. Similarly, the Christian story is recognized as true insofar as its practices are embodied in the lives

---

108. Hauerwas, *Matthew*, 29.
109. Rasmusson, *Church as Polis*, 179.
110. Hauerwas, *Matthew*, 67.
111. Hauerwas and Berkman, "Chief End of All Flesh," 199.
112. Hauerwas, *Community of Character*, 2.

of a particular community called church.[113] But on both accounts, human action reveals and forms human identity. Hauerwas repeatedly rejects the notion that human beliefs can be abstracted from action. He writes, "Our convictions embody our morality; our beliefs are our actions."[114] It seems, therefore, that for Hauerwas politics is a fundamental category for understanding human identity and behavior, particularly as derived from his reading of how the Christian story creates the church. Consequently, if the Christian narrative is true and the kingdom is really ruled by a king, then a community of human beings must exist whose very lives embody this conviction.[115] And, as I have argued above, the primary characteristic of this community is its eschatologically oriented commitment to peaceful living.

An Eschatological Orientation

Furthermore, Hauerwas's emphasis on the narrative shape of the human life also implies that temporal finitude is intrinsic to human existence. Samuel Wells notes that for Hauerwas the very concept of narrative implies a beginning and an end.[116] And since human creatures are historical, born in time and in communities, if narrative implies a beginning and end, for Hauerwas, temporal finitude is intrinsic to creatureliness. "The acknowledgement that we are timeful beings does not come easy given our proclivity to avoid the reality that we have a beginning and an end."[117] Hauerwas argues, "We should view time not as something to be lived through, nor life as an end in itself, but rather see life as the gift of time enough for love."[118] Once human temporal finitude has been accepted, the challenge is no longer to ensure one's survival, as that would be futile. Rather, the challenge is to live faithfully in present time—that is, acquiring the proper set of formative habits that ensure the development of character. In the previous chapter, I demonstrated that Balthasar views human finitude as something that the ecclesial person is able to transcend due to their reception of the kenotic mission of Christ.[119] In contrast, Hauerwas views finitude as essential to what it means to be a human creature. Additionally, while Balthasar argued that the only meaningful form of human action was accomplished through the reception

---

113. Kerr, *Christ, History and Apocalyptic*, 97.
114. Hauerwas, *Peaceable Kingdom*, 16.
115. Hauerwas, *Christian Existence Today*, 11.
116. Wells, *Transforming Fate into Destiny*, 35.
117. Hauerwas, *Work of Theology*, 102.
118. Hauerwas and Bondi, "Memory, Community and the Reasons for Living," 445.
119. Balthasar, *TD II*, 290–91.

of divine life and action upon the cosmic stage,[120] for Hauerwas human action rightly corresponds to the kingdom when it recognizes God's unique place as ruler and sustainer of his world.[121]

In light of this, another characteristic of his ecclesio-anthropology appears: humanity's eschatological orientation. As Samuel Wells observes, "Hauerwas is committed to a view of human existence as historical, bounded by creation and *eschaton*, embedded in particularities and contingencies, far removed from ideals and abstractions."[122] The church trains its members with this narrative and, in so doing, gives an eschatological shape to their existence. No longer obsessed with ensuring their survival, they can live as God created them to be: a timeful people living in apocalyptic time. Hauerwas argues that members of the church are a timeful people—that is, a people who exist in God's time.[123] While those outside the church attempt to perpetuate their existence through violence, the narrative of the church teaches its members that they are truly creatures of time. "Salvation is God's creation of a new society which invites each person to become part of a time that the nations cannot provide."[124] Closely connected with narrative,[125] this eschatological orientation enables Christians to live as the creatures God created them to be—namely, as peaceful witnesses. However, the *eschaton* is not a future point in linear time but "the time God enacted in the Son."[126] An eschatological orientation, then, involves a new type of seeing—that is, we are able to see the world as God's inaugurated new creation and live accordingly. "The world is not what it appears to be, because sin has scarred the world's appearance. The world has been redeemed—but to see the world's redemption, to see Jesus, requires that we be caught up in

---

120. Balthasar, *TD III*, 263.

121. Hauerwas, *Approaching the End*, 151.

122. Wells, *Transforming Fate into Destiny*, 33.

123. Hauerwas, *Without Apology*, 53. Hauerwas writes, "For God's time is eternity, and as God is Trinity, eternity does not mean timelessness, but rather eternity describes the reality of a time that is more than time itself" (*Without Apology*, 53). Hauerwas's account of the *eschaton* seems to appropriate aspects of Barth's view of divine time. Eternity, in this sense, is not the extension of historical time but rather a different type of time. Consequently, the *eschaton* is not a place in future time but rather eternal time's subsistence in the present, historical time (Hauerwas, *Matthew*, 24).

124. Hauerwas, *Christian Existence Today*, 48.

125. Hauerwas, *Matthew*, 23. Hauerwas, for his part, admits he is unable to delineate the relationship between narrative and time. "The relation between time and narrative is complex. That is my way to say that I am unsure how to even begin to understand whether time is metaphysically the condition for the possibility of narrative or whether time can never be known without a narrative" (Hauerwas, *Work of Theology*, 93n10).

126. Hauerwas, *Work of Theology*, 100.

the joy that comes from serving him."[127] But this is not wishful thinking. Rather, it is a matter of seeing the world rightly. As eschatologically oriented creatures, the community of the church looks forward to the full realization of the kingdom knowing that "God has already made history come out right."[128] But if, as I have argued above, a storied humanity implies that human identity is only rightly realized within the church or exists in a higher degree therein, for Hauerwas, to be most truly human is to be communally conformed through the Christian narrative and, therefore, eschatologically oriented to the peaceful kingdom.

Peaceful Existence as Humanity's Telos

Peace stands as foundational to Hauerwas's account of the person and work of Christ, the essence of the kingdom, and the nature of the church. In fact, Hauerwas acknowledges that it is essential to rightly understanding the Gospels and faithfully witnessing to the kingdom.[129] In other words, for Hauerwas nonviolence and pacifism are at the very heart of what it means to be a worshipper of Jesus. Therefore, an account of Hauerwas's ecclesio-anthropology would be incomplete without understanding that peaceful existence is the true eschatological telos of human existence. Peaceful living, as the chief characteristic of the eschatological kingdom, serves as humanity's telos. Consequently, peaceable living and peacemaking seem to serve as the ground upon which the other virtues are intelligible. In other words, the virtues describe the habits and skills required for members of the Christian community to live together peaceably. The church's liturgy practices and embodies the peaceful life. This is, after all, the goal of discipleship: following Jesus in the way of his kingdom. For Hauerwas, the church teaches us ultimately that humanity was created in the image of God to be a people of peace.

Peaceful Living as Humanity's Eschatological Telos

Christians "have been created for peace."[130] The central nature of peaceful living is intricately tied to Hauerwas's understanding of the person, work, and reign of Christ and, by extension, his understanding of the image of

---

127. Hauerwas, *Matthew*, 247.
128. Hauerwas and Willimon, *Resident Aliens*, 87.
129. Hauerwas, *Matthew*, 21.
130. Hauerwas, *Christian Existence Today*, 95.

God. He writes, "In Genesis 1, the image of God is part of the vision of a peaceable creation, both between human and animal and between animal and animal, a peace where it is not necessary to sacrifice one for another."[131] Depicted in the person and work of Christ, Hauerwas argues that the rule of God explicitly denounces violence and coercion. As Lorrimar notes, Hauerwas's "insistence on the peaceable nature of the church's witness derives from the nonviolence that pervades the nature of Jesus' life, death, and resurrection."[132] Since Christians serve as a foretaste of the kingdom, a kingdom ultimately understood by its peaceable nature, their lives must witness to this peaceful living. And if the kingdom is the telos for "truly" formed human beings, peaceful living appears to be the fulfillment of human identity: we are a people who were designed for peace. "For Christians to live as the image of Christ means to live according to the call of the Kingdom of God. In Gethsemane—in taking up the way of the Cross—Christ shows us clearly that the way of the kingdom of God is not the way of violence."[133] But, as we have discussed above, for Hauerwas the way of Christ must be learned and received in community. "Like any skill, the virtues must be learned and coordinated into an individual's life."[134] All human creatures subsist in communities, narratives, and embodied practices that reflect their theological commitments. Therefore, the peaceful telos and way of life is one that must be taught and practiced in community.

Peace and the Virtues

Hauerwas argues that humans are habitual creatures, necessitating certain skills if they are to faithfully embody their communal narratives. Virtues describe the set of habits indicative of the Christian's received narrative, enabling the Christian community to witness to the peaceable kingdom. For Hauerwas,

> The virtues of patience, courage, hope, and charity must reign if the community is to sustain its existence. For without patience the church may be tempted to apocalyptic fantasy; without courage the church would fail to hold fast to the traditions from which it draws its life; without hope the church risks losing sight

---

131. Hauerwas and Berkman, "Chief End of All Flesh," 206.
132. Lorrimar, "Church and Christ in the Work of Stanley Hauerwas," 323.
133. Hauerwas and Berkman, "Chief End of All Flesh," 206.
134. Hauerwas, *Community of Character*, 115.

of its tasks; and without charity the church would not manifest the kind of life made possible by God.[135]

The virtues are the skills and habits we must embody in order to live peacefully and, therefore, faithfully bear witness to God's kingdom. Mark Ryan sees virtue as indicative of the very narrative that Christians have received. "If the Christian story as the ultimate structure of one's personal story implies that the moral life requires transformation, the virtues are the qualities of character a Christian seeks to attain and embody. A virtue is a disposition of the agent—a 'readiness' in him or her—to perform particular kinds of action."[136] In other words, the virtues describe the way of life of a people who have been created and transformed for a life of resistance—that is, a life of peace. In fact, for Hauerwas, these virtues are only possible because of the type of people they have become and the narrative they have received. As virtues, habits, and skills are all communally dependent, the virtues reflect the type of interpersonal relations valued within the Christian community.[137] Consequently, Christians must be trained in the virtuous life if they are to faithfully bear witness to it.

Furthermore, the appropriation of virtuous habits is important if humans are to possess character—that is, if our lives are to be "befitting one who has heard God's call."[138] According to Hauerwas, character is "the qualification or determination of our self-agency, formed by our having certain intentions (and beliefs) rather than others."[139] A person who possesses character can be trusted to act with consistency—that is, in accordance with their narrative.[140] In other words, who they are and what they do cohere.[141] But it is only within the church that the necessary practices and habits are present to form consistent agents since it is the center of virtue, training them for peaceable existence. For Hauerwas, "Character depends on the development of those habits we call virtues."[142] For the Christian commu-

---

135. Hauerwas, *Community of Character*, 68.
136. Ryan, *Politics of Practical Reason*, 121.
137. Hauerwas, *Christian Existence Today*, 90.
138. Hauerwas, *Peaceable Kingdom*, 33.
139. Hauerwas, *Character and the Christian Life*, 115.
140. Hauerwas, *Work of Theology*, 73n10.

141. However, Hauerwas notes that the manner in which action and identity fail to cohere in human beings is one of the things that distinguishes us from God. Appropriating aspects of Aquinas's view of God as *actus puris*, Hauerwas argues that, unlike God, human persons are never able "to be wholly in our acts" and that this is one of the reasons why we need communal formation and truthful narratives (Hauerwas, *Work of Theology*, 88).

142. Hauerwas, *Work of Theology*, 71.

nity, the virtues describe the skills that its members must acquire in order to live with fidelity to the new creation inaugurated in Christ. And since Christianity reveals "the way things are," it seems that for Hauerwas human creatures were designed for virtuous existence practiced and embodied within a truthful community, the church.

Enacting and Practicing Peaceful Living through Liturgy

As human beings are habitual creatures and find their telos in peaceful living, the church's liturgy rightly forms human identity in accordance with the story of God's action in the world. By participation in liturgical action, one becomes a liturgical being.[143] But liturgy is not an end in itself. It serves as a means of discipleship: teaching us "to see and accept the world as God's world . . . [and] to learn to be a creature of God."[144] In other words, as Lorrimar observes, for Hauerwas "enacting churchly practices forms character."[145] Through incorporation into the body of Christ and participation in the life of the church, human beings are trained to be creatures in God's story. For, as Lawson observes, "the Church is an alternative polis of resident aliens where virtue and character are nurtured."[146] While Zizioulas views liturgy, specifically the Eucharist, as actualizing personhood, for Hauerwas the emphasis is more on progressive formation.[147] In many ways, this is similar to Balthasar's account of the church's sacramental action as formative of human personhood.[148] Hauerwas understands liturgical practices as forming the communities' vision of the eschatological kingdom.[149] Furthermore, the liturgy teaches human creatures how to respond rightly to their tradition and narrative. "Through liturgy we are shaped to live rightly the story of God, to become part of that story, and are thus able to recognize and respond

---

143. Hauerwas, *Work of Theology*, 45.

144. Hauerwas, *Matthew*, 84.

145. Lorrimar, "Church and Christ in the Work of Stanley Hauerwas," 318.

146. Lawson, "Theological Formation in the Church," 343.

147. Hauerwas, *In Good Company*, 155.

148. As I have noted above, Hauerwas has expressed reluctance to use the language of persons or personhood, especially as it pertains to Christian ethics (Hauerwas, "Must a Patient?," 598). For Hauerwas, this is an appeal to universal categories that denigrate the specificity of the Christian story vis-à-vis the formation of human identity. However, he does allow for the employment of the term "person" from an explicitly Christian framework (*Approaching the End*, 59). This is similar to how Balthasar construes personhood as a fundamentally *theological* category, defined predominantly through participation in the *missio Christi*.

149. Herdt, "Hauerwas among the Virtues," 217.

to the saints in our midst."[150] Again, this emphasis on the nature of liturgy indicates that human creatures are liturgically formed. The habits and skills they practice, particularly as it is reflective of their communally informed and received narratives, do not simply shape human desires but also shape human beings to be people of a particular type of character. Furthermore, if the Christian community is the only community of creatures rightly formed by a true narrative, then peace must be essential to what it means to be truly human. In other words, to be a rightly formed human creature is to be *homo pacem*. The church, as an alternative polis, reveals that humans qua humans are eschatologically oriented and liturgically formed to be creatures of peace that bear witness to the peaceable kingdom of God.

For Hauerwas, the pinnacle of human existence lies in participation in the peaceable kingdom of God and in the very life of Christ. Daniel Bell identifies that Hauerwas's primary concern with liberal Protestantism is its commitment to abstracting principles from the life of Christ that dissolve the very heart of discipleship. "Discipleship is not merely a matter of following rules or principles Jesus discloses but of ontological union, of participation in a new way of life, that Jesus effects as disciples are joined to Christ through the church."[151] But Bell's observation can be taken a step further. For Hauerwas, discipleship in the path of peace is not just a participation in a new way of life. More than that, as Christian communities participate in the path of Christ they are participating in the life and obedience of Christ.[152] "Through baptism we are made participants in the humanity of Christ, which means ours is a shared humanity because Christ took upon himself the whole of human existence."[153] Recall that for Hauerwas, the person and work of Christ are inseparable. Since Hauerwas maintains that Christology is the narrative that shapes ecclesiology, the church cannot be separated from the one who constitutes it.[154] As Herdt observes, "We receive from God in the church's daily practices (including but not limited to the sacraments) the virtues we require to participate in the divine life."[155] The practices and liturgical acts of the church train the Christian community to be a people of peace. In so doing, Hauerwas's ecclesiology reveals humanity's eschatological telos as revealed through their narrative. Humanity was designed for peaceful existence.

150. Hauerwas, *Christian Existence Today*, 107.
151. Bell, "Way of God with the World," 118.
152. Hauerwas, *Cross-Shattered Church*, 121.
153. Hauerwas, *Cross-Shattered Church*, 121.
154. Hauerwas, *Community of Character*, 37.
155. Herdt, "Hauerwas among the Virtues," 215.

CONCLUSION

In the previous two chapters, I demonstrated that for both Zizioulas and Balthasar ecclesiology provides vital insight into our understanding of humanity. The same is true for Hauerwas. Since from Hauerwas's framework the church is an intrinsically political institution, a community that bears witness in both word and deed to the peaceable kingdom of God, ecclesial persons are political, virtuous beings whose understanding of the world has been reshaped by the narrative of God, as the church forms and shapes them into authentic witnesses to the kingdom of God. For Hauerwas, the church serves as the center point of his theological inquiry as it is only within the church that reality is seen for what it truly is. Additionally, it is within the church that humanity experiences a foretaste of its eschatological telos: participation in the peaceable kingdom of God. The church exists as an alternative polis, providing a witness and foretaste of the peaceable kingdom of God.[156] Subverting the violent stories of the world, it provides a true account of the created world and forms its citizens to live as a people who rightly bear witness to the story of Jesus. As a historical people, it is a community that tells and retells the Christian narrative. The church embodies the image of God to the rest of creation as it mirrors God's peaceful rule and rejection of coercion. Through baptism the individual is gathered into the body of the church, "a community whose politics is rooted in another way than that which predominates the world" as they refuse to depend upon violence to ensure their survival.[157] The church's liturgical life forms its members as it cultivates virtue, training them through communal discipleship to be a people of character.

Hauerwas's ecclesio-anthropology is rooted in this vision of the church as a foretaste and witness of the kingdom. Four particular characteristics have emerged that are distinctive of Hauerwas's ecclesio-anthropology: the narrative shape of the self, the political nature and eschatological orientation of personhood, and humanity's peaceful telos. For Hauerwas, human creatures are shaped by communal narratives and the church provides the only true narrative account for the human person. This seems to imply either that only ecclesial persons possess true personhood or that ecclesial persons possess a higher degree of personhood than non-ecclesial persons. Incorporated into the life of the church through baptism, the individual becomes a part of a community and receives a new "political" constitution wherein they are reidentified as citizens of the alternative polis: the

---

156. Hauerwas, *Peaceable Kingdom*, 97.
157. Hauerwas, *Approaching the End*, 62.

kingdom of God. Hauerwas insists that the convictions of Christianity are not abstracted doctrinal principles but embodied practices. Through participation in its communal practices and liturgical actions, human creatures embody their identity and are trained toward their peaceful existence. It is only a virtuous person who, subsisting in community, can truly embody the peaceable kingdom and fulfill the purpose for which humans were created: to be faithful witnesses and tellers of God's story. The church then is not only the place where humanity is observed in its truest sense; it is also the place into which humans must enter in order to be formed into the people they were created to be. Ultimately, for Hauerwas, ecclesiology reveals that we are fundamentally *homo pacem*—that is, beings whose very life is to be grounded in peace.

5

Zizioulas, Balthasar, and Hauerwas in Dialogue

At this point, it is now time to move beyond description and toward synthesis. Here, I will place my three interlocutors in dialogue with one another in order to better learn from them how to go about the process of *doing* ecclesio-anthropology. The goal of this chapter is not to put forth a Free Church critique of these three figures, but to articulate principles that should guide ecclesio-anthropology in general. These principles will then direct my project as I move forward. Since, as I have argued in the introduction, ecclesio-anthropology seeks to discern how the church's nature, mission, practices, and *telos* inform our understanding of anthropology, this chapter will engage each of those four loci insofar as they pertain to our inquiry into the human subject. In each section, I will begin by first triangulating the three figures on one of the aforementioned loci. In so doing, differences, questions, and areas of concern will naturally arise. As I engage the differing positions of my interlocutors, I will move toward articulating key theses that will serve as a governing principle in this particular area of ecclesio-anthropology on a general level. All of this will be aimed toward my constructive work in the next chapter. There, I will seek to construct an explicitly Free Church ecclesio-anthropology, using these four theses and critiques as helpful guardrails.

GROUNDED IN AND FOR GOD

In the preceding chapters, I have demonstrated that Hauerwas, Zizioulas, and Balthasar present different approaches to grounding ecclesiology, the identity of ecclesial members, and humanity itself. Three options have emerged in their respective proposals: intra-Trinitarian life, christological mission, or christological narrative.[1] Zizioulas's approach takes the first of these three options as he states the church is grounded in intra-Trinitarian relationships.[2] Arguing that the persons of the Trinity exist in an "event of love" and a unity of relationships, Zizioulas posits that the church's true being involves a subsistence in intra-Trinitarian life—namely, in the Son-Father relationship.[3] The Spirit then enables the church to become an image of the Trinity as its members become open to and for one another.[4] In contrast, for both Balthasar and Hauerwas the ecclesial community is predominantly understood in terms of Christology.[5] Yet this emerges in two different ways. For Hauerwas, the story of Jesus constitutes the ecclesial community as he subverts worldly power and realizes a new, political life in the inauguration of the kingdom of God. The church then stands as an alternative polis, a community of witnesses to the inaugurated rule of Christ.[6] Balthasar, on the other hand, views the Christian community as grounded in the kenotic mission of Christ. The Son pours himself out in his redemptive work, and,

---

1. Here, I am not suggesting this list is exhaustive of all the possible ways of grounding ecclesiology or humanity. Rather, I am stating these are three important options that emerge in the work of my interlocutors.

2. Zizioulas, *One and the Many*, 15.

3. Zizioulas, *Being as Communion*, 110.

4. Zizioulas, *Communion and Otherness*, 6.

5. Hauerwas is frequently criticized for his failure to clearly articulate the Spirit's work in his theological project, particularly as it pertains to moral formation and ethics. We will return to this briefly below. However, it is important to note that, for Hauerwas, Christology grounds ecclesiology. The church is a "community that Jesus calls into existence" to exemplify his life and provide a foretaste of the kingdom (Hauerwas, *Matthew*, 68). Accordingly, Christology plays a governing role in Hauerwas's ecclesiology. While Balthasar, more than Hauerwas, readily emphasizes the Spirit's distinctive role in the Christian community's participation in the mission of Christ, he is still adamant that Christology is what constitutes ecclesial being. He writes, "The Church, however, is 'Christ living on'; she is, to use Paul's great analogy, *Christ's body*" (Balthasar, *Spouse of the Word*, 144, italics his). He goes on to note, "The simile of a body answers the question 'Who is the Church?' only in a negative sense; she is, and cannot be other than, an extension, a communication, a partaking of the personality of Christ" (Balthasar, *Spouse of the Word*, 145). It is then clear why Healy and Schindler conclude that for Balthasar "the Church is both the abiding presence of the incarnate Christ and the continuation of his mission" (Healy and Schindler, "For the Life of the World," 55).

6. Hauerwas, *Community of Character*, 49.

in so doing, fashions a community birthed for and from his mission. The church then perpetuates this mission as it completes his eucharistic action and offers a redeemed world back to the Father.

If all three of my interlocutors understand that the church is grounded in the action of God, how does this inform each of their approaches to anthropology? For Zizioulas, personhood itself is an event of communion.[7] The Spirit brings theotic communion with God into the present during the celebration of the Eucharist. In so doing, Zizioulas also appears to construe personhood as a punctiliar event.[8] In contrast, Balthasar presents the human creature as a 'being in becoming'—that is, the members of the ecclesial community are perpetually conforming to a specific divine idea through a kenotic *disponibilité* to the will and mission of God.[9] Personhood is something the individual rational subject becomes as they relinquish false self-identities and find themselves in their divinely elected vocation.[10] Human subjects are *in via* to the full realization of personhood they receive as a gift from God. Finally, Hauerwas emphasizes the Christian narrative as the fundamental ground for the church's identity. Human beings possess a narrated existence, necessarily existing in a community whose embodied and enacted beliefs form them into people of character.[11] He describes the church as "a people . . . formed by a story which places their history in the texture of the world."[12] And since the church possesses the only truthful narrative, it is only within the church that human subjects can be rightly formed.[13] In summary, for Zizioulas, the church is the place where personhood is realized in a punctiliar event; for Balthasar and Hauerwas, it is the place where human creatures are progressively formed.

The Creator-Creature Relationship in Zizioulas's Ontology

For Zizioulas, the ecclesial community subsists in the Son-Father relationship.[14] Apart from this subsistence, humanity is beleaguered with the problem of ontological necessity wherein they are unable to determine their

---

7. Zizioulas, *Being as Communion*, 213–14.
8. Zizioulas, *Communion and Otherness*, 85.
9. Balthasar, *TD III*, 263.
10. Balthasar, *TD III*, 271.
11. Hauerwas, *Christian Existence Today*, 106.
12. Hauerwas, *Community of Character*, 15.
13. Hauerwas, *Approaching the End*, xvii.
14. Zizioulas, *Communion and Otherness*, 109.

own mode of existence and are constrained by their nature.[15] In contrast, Zizioulas conceives of the Godhead as an event of loving community where each person exists for and in communion with the other. It is the persons of the Godhead and not an impersonal divine essence that determines God's mode of being. Zizioulas posits it is by subsisting in the Son-Father relationship that the human creature is transformed into an ecclesial person.[16] He writes, "In Christ, therefore, every man acquires *his* particularity, *his* hypostasis, *his* personhood, precisely because, by being constituted as a being in and through the same relationship which constitutes Christ's being, he is as unique and unrepeatable and worthy of eternal survival as Christ is."[17] For Zizioulas, the only way one is able to obtain true personhood and the only path to human fulfillment is through the appropriation of the Son's mode of being.

Zizioulas attempts to articulate a view of personhood that affirms the particularity of the creature and the Creator as well as the distinction between the two. However, Cumin and Volf are rightly worried that Zizioulas's project is unsuccessful as he ends up blurring the line separating the Creator from his creatures. As Cumin rightly observes, "For Zizioulas, to be created is to receive one's existence as a 'given datum' and that this 'givenness' is somehow existentially restrictive. . . . Thus it would seem that for Zizioulas, 'created' and 'person' are fundamentally incommensurable."[18] "Creation" is tragically limited by its inability to govern its own mode of existence. The created being simply exists on account of its nature and the actions of another. In contrast, God exists freely in the event of communion, a liberty that is essential to Zizioulas's understanding of personhood. Cumin goes on to note, "Both created being and given nature become antithetical to their counterparts personhood and relationality since the first two concepts are defined in terms of ontological limitation and the latter two are defined in terms of absolute freedom."[19] If freedom is located solely in the Father and necessity is the defining characteristic of creation, Zizioulas's depiction of

---

15. Zizioulas, *Being as Communion*, 51–52. Colin Gunton provides a helpful articulation of the problem of ontological necessity: "To establish the particularity of the human, ecclesiology is necessary because as part of nature, human beings are not free, but simply determined by (impersonal) nature" (Gunton, "Persons and Particularity," 102).

16. Zizioulas, *One and the Many*, 12.

17. Zizioulas, *Communion and Otherness*, 240, italics his. Elsewhere Zizioulas argues that in baptism the particular individual's hypostasis is identified with the hypostasis of Christ through baptism. He writes, "This adoption of man by God, the identification of his hypostasis with the hypostasis of the Son of God is the essence of baptism" (Zizioulas, *Being as Communion*, 56).

18. Cumin, "Looking for Personal Space," 362.

19. Cumin, "Looking for Personal Space," 362.

salvation as the freedom from necessity seems to entail equating salvation with the transcendence of creatureliness.[20] It seems, then, that for Zizioulas it is actually the creatureliness of the creature that must be transcended if humanity is to have fellowship with God.[21] In so doing, the very distinction between Creator and creature—namely, their respective modes of existence—must be dissolved. But if the manner in which creatures exist vis-à-vis their Creator must change, what then establishes the uniqueness of each? Zizioulas draws on the concept of *theosis* to describe the creature's eschatological state. But without the aid of "substance" as a theological category Zizioulas argues that the person's identity is constituted by their subsistence in a particular relationship. But every true human person's identity is grounded in their subsistence in the very same relationship that gives the Son his uniqueness. Furthermore, in the *eschaton* when *theosis* is realized on a permanent level, what maintains the creature's particularity as distinct from the Son?

Zizioulas could respond to such a critique by claiming that the particularity of the creature is maintained through their other relationships—namely, the relationship between two human creatures or the relationship between a human creature and a non-human creature. In so doing, it is the networks of relationships within the church and with other created realities that constitute the particularity of the various members, relationships that would also distinguish them from their Creator. But on second glance, this solution does not appear viable. As Edward Russell points out, for Zizioulas "*different* persons in their particularity are all being constituted by *the same* relation of the Son to the Father.*"*[22] How can different persons be ontologically constituted by other relationships when they are all constituted by the Son-Father relationship?[23] If the relationship between two human creatures is able to ensure their particularity, it then seems that their identity is no longer constituted *exclusively* by the Son-Father relationship. Yet that is precisely what Zizioulas claims. It seems then, as Volf notes, that the creature disappears within "'one vast ocean of being,' namely, in the divine person."[24]

---

20. Cumin, "Looking for Personal Space," 363.

21. Munteanu, "Homo eucharisticus," 197.

22. Russell, "Reconsidering Relational Anthropology," 182, italics his.

23. Russell, "Reconsidering Relational Anthropology," 183. Russell, for his part, thinks a robust pneumatology could alleviate this problem in Zizioulas's thought but that none is present.

24. Volf, *After Our Likeness*, 87.

The Christian Community, the Christian Narrative, and Christ

Hauerwas seems to have a similar problem, albeit on different terms. For Hauerwas, ecclesiology is grounded in the christological narrative. Jesus comes, proclaiming the kingdom of God, and constitutes a community whose central task is to exemplify the life of its Lord.[25] Discipleship within this community is described primarily in terms of learning to act consistently within its shared history as the community awaits the consummation of Christ's kingdom.[26] Hauerwas describes the church as an alternative polis that resists the allure of the violent practices indicative of earthly rule, thereby demonstrating the futility of earthly rulers. In so doing, the Christian seeks to make God's story their very own.[27] While certainly not disassociated from the Trinity, it is in the story of Jesus that God's rule is revealed.[28] The church is that community formed by the confession that "Jesus is Lord," living in peaceful expectation of their returning King and his inaugurated rule.

While it can appear at times that the narrative possesses equal agency to the one whose story it tells, at other times Hauerwas is clear on the distinction between Christ and the Christian community. He too seeks to maintain a distinction between Christ and the Christian community, as evidenced in his discussion of each's roles as it pertains to the kingdom of God and the end of history. Christ is the *autobaselia*, God's kingdom in person;[29] the church exists as a community of witnesses to that kingdom by acting and speaking truthfully.[30] But at other times, the church appears to just be the story of Jesus. This gives rise to Nathan Kerr's concern that Hauerwas's work increasingly moves toward coalescing Christology and ecclesiology. He writes, "Hauerwas seems to be moving progressively with *identifying* Jesus' 'story' with the ongoing lived narrative that is the church; that is, in its telling of it, the church *is* itself 'the story being told'—'the teller and the tale are one.'"[31] Kerr is concerned that in Hauerwas's schema ecclesiology and Christology become increasingly less distinct from one another. At times,

---

25. Hauerwas, *Matthew*, 68.
26. Hauerwas, *Community of Character*, 51, 60.
27. Hauerwas, *Christian Existence Today*, 107.
28. Hauerwas, *Peaceable Kingdom*, 83, 85.
29. Hauerwas, *Matthew*, 38.
30. Hauerwas, *Christian Existence Today*, 40; Hauerwas, *Peaceable Kingdom*, 26.
31. Kerr, *Christ, History and Apocalyptic*, 107, italics his. From Kerr's standpoint, the problem lies in Hauerwas's ecclesio-centric model. He is concerned Hauerwas has adopted "John Milbank's 'metanarrative' perspective upon the relationship of Jesus to the church," arguing this is a more recent development in Hauerwasian theology (Kerr, *Christ, History and Apocalyptic*, 107).

Jesus's story is the narrative that the Christian community tells through its embodied action. At other times, a distinction is maintained wherein particular parts of the story are reserved for Jesus alone. But which is it? Is the shape of the ecclesial community indicative of the story that forms it? Or are the ecclesial community's embodied practices the story itself?[32] For Kerr, "It seems as if Hauerwas's concern to integrate the history of the church into Jesus' story runs the risk of subordinating Jesus of Nazareth himself to a more 'metanarrative reality,' namely, the alternative *polis* of the church, according to whose historical existence alone Jesus is made 'present' and 'effective' in history."[33] In so doing, it seems that Jesus's *identity* becomes a function of the practices of the community. And if this is the case, what differentiates the tale from those who tell it? If the story of Jesus is embodied in ecclesial practices, what differentiates Jesus's identity as a particular being from the practices of the church? Hauerwas is notably reluctant to engage in metaphysical discussions, but it does seem that we need to be able to identify where the church ends and Jesus begins.

Maintaining the Universal and the Particular

Balthasar, for his part, would want to reject the notion that human creatures dissolve into the Son-Father relationship or a larger metanarrative. In fact, maintaining the particularity of the creature in light of God is one of the primary concerns of his project. He repeatedly critiques German idealism and Christian mysticism for failing to maintain particularity. It seems that he would level a similar critique against both Zizioulas and Hauerwas.[34] Balthasar fears that both German idealism and Christian mysticism continually dissolve the individual in the general categories of polis, *Geist*, or God. He attempts to circumvent this with an appeal to the missions of the Son and Spirit. In his mission, the Son completely surrenders himself to the Father's will in the incarnation, descending *ad infernem* and suffering a fate worse than that of any sinner.[35] In so doing, he reveals the form of divine love. The Spirit's mission is to appropriate this form to a particular community of love and return the world to God after molding it into the image of love itself.[36]

32. Hauerwas, *Approaching the End*, 186.
33. Kerr, *Christ, History and Apocalyptic*, 109.
34. Balthasar, TD I, 555–89.
35. Balthasar, TD IV, 346.
36. Balthasar, TD III, 186.

As I have outlined in chapter 3, for Balthasar the church is grounded in the kenotic mission of Christ. The members of the church are called not only to imitate their Lord, but to understand their very existence in light of self-surrender in service of God.[37] For Balthasar, personhood is defined as correspondence to God's idea of us and the process of becoming increasingly ready to serve the world in sacrificial love. It is a *disponsibilité* to receive and participate in the mission of Christ.[38] But since the earthly Jesus has completed his mission and returned to the Father, how does Balthasar distinguish between Christ's missional activity and the church's participation in it? For Balthasar, Jesus's earthly life is lived under the complete guidance of the Spirit.[39] In fact, Balthasar even goes so far as to say that the Spirit acts as the 'rule' of the Father for the incarnate Son. However, in his ascension, Jesus is no longer 'ruled' by the Spirit, but actively participates in the production of the Spirit. As the Spirit is poured out on the church, he not only still functions as the 'rule' of the Father and Son, but "is coextensive with [Christ's] fleshly and historical existence."[40] The same Spirit who served as the rule of the Father in the earthly life of the Son now rules over the church. The Son, having been stripped of everything in his kenotic descent, then returns to the Father with the church and all of creation in tow.

Yet again, we run into the problem of the relationship between the Creator and the creature. It seems that in Balthasar's larger framework of emanation and return, the ontological distinction between God and his creature is blurred. To a certain extent, this may be a result of Balthasar's insistence that the church is the perpetuation of the mission of Jesus. Given Balthasar's use of strong ontological language, this can appear to minimize the distinction between the theanthropic person and the members of his church.[41] Balthasar may well respond that the church perpetuates the hu-

---

37. Balthasar, *Spirit and Institution*, 134.

38. Balthasar, *TD IV*, 406. Balthasar writes that the recipient of divine grace "receives a mission that is 'cut from' Christ's and represents a portion of the Church's mission" (Balthasar, *TD III*, 527).

39. Balthasar, *TD III*, 188.

40. Healy, *Eschatology of Hans Urs von Balthasar*, 150.

41. This concern is heightened when one examines Balthasar's view of Mary as the type of the church in conjunction with Balthasar's insistence that identity is revealed in action. In many ways, Balthasar has Mary suffer in parallel to the incarnate Son, undergoing her own form of *kenosis ad infernum*, in addition to her role as mediator (Balthasar, *TD IV*, 356). But if this is indeed the case, the distinction between Christ and Mary begins to dissolve or, at the very least, they overlap considerably. If Mary is both *mediatrix* and *reconciliatrix*, does this not begin to impinge on Christ's uniqueness (cf. Balthasar, *TD III*, 311–12; Balthasar, *Spouse of the Word*, 183)? Lösel writes, "The impression that objective salvation is attributable not only to God, but also to Mary is

manity of Christ, but not his divinity. But then it must be remembered that from Balthasar's standpoint, the incarnation is the historicization of the mission of the Son. "The Church's entire eucharistic action . . . is nothing but an echo of the Lord's prior action of grace; it is the action, through the Son of the triune God."[42] It is not a "new" movement in God, but the perpetuation of the Father's self-emptying action that begets the Son who continues this outpouring in the incarnation. The church perpetuates *that* mission, completing the Son's kenotic action and returning to God. However, if the creature is to return this "poured-outness" back to God, it seems that this "poured-outness" must also be of like kind to God. But if this is the case, we seem to minimize the fact that God exists as a class unto himself. In other words, even if there were to be a void in God, the creature is not the *kind* of being that could fill it.[43]

For each of the three figures, their proposals offer a helpful starting point for ecclesio-anthropology: as human individuals are reconstituted, either ontologically (Zizioulas), vocationally (Balthasar), or narratively (Hauerwas), humanity finds its fulfillment in fellowship with God.[44] Hu-

---

further strengthened by Balthasar's statements about the solidarity of Mary with sinners, their humiliation and abandonment under the cross, their standing and suffering in the abyss of hell, or, finally, their suffering of their own hells" (Lösel, *Kreuzwege*, 260, my translation). For an extensive discussion of Balthasar's view of Mary as *co-redemptrix*, see Nichols, "Marian Co-Redemption."

42. Balthasar, *TD IV*, 405.

43. On the other side, Balthasar would argue the creature does not lose its particularity when it is gathered into divine life. Balthasar insists that in the Godhead there is room enough for the creature as a result of the infinite, absolute difference that exists there on account of the Son becoming Godforsakenness itself (Balthasar, *TD V*, 399). In fact, Balthasar argues this enables there to be eternal surprise in God, as surprise is the fruit of God and the creature coming to know one another in ever-abounding ways (Balthasar, *TD V*, 400). However, I am cautious about adopting such a stance as I believe it presumes to know more about the inner workings of divine life than is warranted. As Karen Kilby comments, "It seems that we find ourselves in rather difficult waters if we try to imagine what is in fact envisaged here; it is not particularly easy to offer a positive account of what 'distance' or 'difference,' much less infinite, absolute distance or difference, might look like in the Trinity" (Kilby, *Balthasar*, 111). Kilby is rightly worried that in order for Balthasar to substantiate such a claim, he would have to claim a great deal of insight into the inner life of God (Kilby, *Balthasar*, 112).

44. I have intentionally used the term "fellowship" in order to cover a range of views for each of the three figures, as we will see below. For Zizioulas, this communion takes the form of a theotic union with God in the filial relationship between Father and Son. Balthasar holds a similar view but attempts to robustly identify the creature's particularity. Communion with God, for Balthasar, will involve the creating of space within the Godhead for the individual to exist and retain elements of mystery and surprise. Hauerwas prefers not to speculate on how the individual relates to God metaphysically in the full inauguration of the kingdom but seeks to maintain a strict divide between

man fulfillment is a gift from God. Initiation into the ecclesial community involves the reception of a new mode of being or narrative. This new mode of existence is understood as the fulfillment of what it means to be human. My critiques of Zizioulas, Balthasar, and Hauerwas are indicative of a larger conceptual problem: the church is portrayed as grounded in divine action, yet it is too strongly identified with that which grounds it. Yet this is especially problematic since each recognizes the importance of maintaining the particularity of the creature and the distinctness of God. While I have already demonstrated how this is a goal in Balthasar's project, it is also present in Zizioulas's view of the person. He argues that persons recognize and accept the particularity of the other. Similarly, Hauerwas the distinction between the church and God is important, especially when considering who is responsible for determining the "end" of history. While the church is described as an entity created by and for God, all three figures fail to preserve the distinction between the creature and its Creator. Although the church is the body of Christ in a modest sense of participation, it must remain clear that the church is *not* Christ in a substantial sense. In other words, ecclesio-anthropology must be grounded in divine action because the church exists as a contingent community constituted through the work of God. Yet, it cannot remove or coalesce the distinction that exists between Creator and creature, between Christ and his church. As Kevin Vanhoozer writes, "The church is not constitutive of the Son's identity as are the Father and the Spirit; its relation to the Son is not substantival but covenantal, a matter of fellowship, not ontology."[45]

All three figures agree that the church is a contingent community, affirming the difference between the Creator and his creatures. However, on second glance their respective proposals seem to risk blurring the distinction between the church and the God it worships. This then results in an obfuscation of the difference between God and the individual members of the church. Our first thesis helps address this tension: *The church must be understood as a contingent community, constituted by God's acts in history. Yet the church's divine grounding cannot blur the distinction between the members who comprise it and the God who constitutes it.* This necessarily involves a theological approach to the church, as each of my interlocutors has argued it can only be rightly understood in light of divine action. But the focus of this thesis also addresses the necessary boundaries that maintain the relationship between the church and God. This is important because, while the church's

---

creature and Creator, one that would make both Zizioulas's and Balthasar's proposals untenable (Hauerwas, *Hannah's Child*, 283). Similarly, I have avoided the term "person" due to Hauerwas's reluctance to adopt such terminology.

45. Vanhoozer, *Biblical Authority after Babel*, 152.

identity is necessarily bound up in the God it serves, an appropriate distinction must be preserved since the church is a community of creatures.

A MISSIONED EXISTENCE

While the church's nature is rightly understood as grounded in and by God, the language of mission provides the overall trajectory for the church's existence. For each of my interlocutors, the mission of the church serves as an interpretive key for understanding the church's present earthly existence. For Zizioulas and Balthasar, the church's mission is to bring the world into the life of communal love that is the Trinity. Zizioulas argues that this is one of the church's primary purposes, as creation is alienated from God and its finitude must be transcended in communion with God. Biological hypostases are incapable of love because they do not possess the freedom to determine their own mode of existence.[46] However, when the individual joins the ecclesial community, they are incorporated into the unique filial relationship between Father and Son, a relationship grounded in love.[47] "The Church, in her very way of being, is the truly erotic mode of existence. She is the place where God's love as the love of a particular and ontologically unique being (the love of the Father for his only-begotten, i.e., uniquely loved, Son) is freely offered to his creation in the person of Christ."[48] The church's mission is to serve as a community of priests who seek to bring all of creation into eucharistic communion with God. For Balthasar, the church is constituted by the kenotic love of Christ. The "kenosis of Christ, consummated in the death on the cross, is the very point of origin of the Church and Christian as such."[49] As Peter Lüning points out, for Balthasar, humanity really and truly participates in the mission of Christ as we become co-actors with Christ.[50] The church's task, as *sacramentum mundi*, is to pour itself out as the perpetuation of Christ's mission in order to bring the world into communion with God.[51]

Alternatively, for Hauerwas, the church is a community whose existence is governed by the story of God's rule. This differs from Zizioulas's and Balthasar's portrayal of the church. In Hauerwas's approach, the church's vocation is clearly distinguished from that of its Lord. The church's mission

---

46. Zizioulas, *Being as Communion*, 57.
47. Zizioulas, *Lectures in Christian Dogmatics*, 31.
48. Zizioulas, *Communion and Otherness*, 79.
49. Balthasar, *Spouse of the Word*, 27.
50. Lüning, *Der Mensch im Angesicht des Gekreuzigten*, 345.
51. Balthasar, *New Elucidations*, 99.

is to live as a faithful community of witnesses, providing a foretaste of the eschatological, peaceable kingdom.[52] God alone is the one who will bring the kingdom to its consummation. As Robert Dean avers, "The world, though fallen, has been reconciled to God through the cross of Jesus Christ. The church, as the new creation community, lives in the power of the Spirit who raised Christ from the dead as a witness to the resurrection for the sake of the world which has not acknowledged, as of yet, its Reconciler and Lord."[53]

Each of these understandings of the church's mission then relates directly to their understanding of humanity's acquisition of true freedom. For Zizioulas, freedom is understood as freedom *from* ontological necessity and freedom *for* the other.[54] Uniquely possible in and through the church,[55] it involves a recognition that the other is constitutive of our own being and identity. The mission of the ecclesial person is then to extend this fellowship of love and communion to the rest of the created world.[56] Balthasar also views freedom as essential to the mission of the church and our understanding of humanity.[57] While every human creatures possesses finite freedom in virtue of God's gift in creation, it is only in the surrendering of this freedom that the human creature is able to participate in divine action.[58] It is in self-surrender and abnegation, typified by the *disponibilité* and receptivity of Mary, that humanity embraces its feminine nature and is freed to act.[59] Similarly, for Hauerwas, participation in the Christian community bestows a unique relationship on human creatures as they recognize their role as a witness to the redemption accomplished in Christ. In participating in the life of this community and being formed through its true story, the Christian becomes truly free.[60] Freedom for Hauerwas, like Balthasar, is freedom to act. But while Balthasar focuses on perpetuating the mission of Christ, for Hauerwas freedom is the ability to act consistently with a particular story and claim our particular actions as uniquely our own.[61]

---

52. Hauerwas, *With the Grain of the Universe*, 16.
53. Dean, *For the Life of the World*, 223.
54. Zizioulas, *One and the Many*, 12; Zizioulas, *Communion and Otherness*, 9.
55. Farrow, "Person and Nature," 112.
56. Zizioulas, *Eucharistic Communion and the World*, 137.
57. Balthasar, *Theological Anthropology*, 88.
58. Balthasar, *Christian State of Life*, 38–39.
59. Balthasar, *TD III*, 270.
60. Hauerwas, *Community of Character*, 2–3; Hauerwas, *Christian Existence Today*, 29.
61. Ryan, *Politics of Practical Reason*, 123.

Mission, Femininity, and Self-Abnegation

Yet again, however, we must address some questions that emerge in each of their respective projects. First, Balthasar's insistence on the feminine nature of the church is essential to his understanding of the human creature's vocation as one of self-abnegation. However, I am worried that such a reliance on nuptial imagery turns femininity into the means of divine personalization. As I have articulated above, Balthasar's ecclesio-anthropology seems to depict human creatureliness as fundamentally feminine in orientation. He writes, "The Church is not, purely and simply, Christ. She is not hypostatically united to God who dwells in her. In this opposition, therefore, she is receptive to her Head and so has a feminine role."[62] He goes on to state, "With God there can be no union of the same sex but only a feminine dependence on God, as taught by Paul and Augustine: no taking but only a being taken. As the individual believer lets himself be taken by God, becoming the handmaid of the Lord, so the Church awakens in him and, in feminine fashion, reflects the Spirit of the Lord."[63] The language here seems overtly sexualized and built upon the physical functions of the human body.[64] Ecclesial persons, like the rest of creation, hand themselves over to the Lord in a disposition of receptivity, receiving the mission and life he deposits within them. Here, it is hard to assuage the feeling that Balthasar is relying too heavily on the analogy of sexual procreation to explore the relationship between Christ and his church.

Indeed some have viewed Balthasar's account of femininity and sexual polarity as a cause for grave concern.[65] Beattie is critical of Balthasar on this account, arguing that his reliance on polarities denies women their own subjectivity and negates the inherent goodness of their bodies.[66] She observes that while Balthasar views all of creation as involving a series of poles (e.g., man and woman, individual and community, and Spirit and body), the polarity between man and woman "pervades the entire living creation."[67]

---

62. Balthasar, *Spouse of the Word*, 187.

63. Balthasar, *Spouse of the Word*, 188.

64. Kerr, *Twentieth-Century Catholic Theologians*, 143; Sain, "Through a Different Lens," 74.

65. Here, I will focus particularly on the critique of Tina Beattie, as she presents one of the most robust engagements with Balthasar's work. Agnetta Sutton, Barbara Sain, and Connie Crammer also present strong critiques of Balthasar's account of sexual differentiation. See also Crammer, "One Sex or Two?"; Sutton, "Complementarity and Symbolism of the Two Sexes," 418–33; Sain, "Through a Different Lens."

66. Beattie, *New Catholic Feminism*, 141.

67. Balthasar, *TD III*, 292.

Balthasar maintains a strong distinction between men and women based on his reading of Gen 2:21–23.[68] Yet, in so doing, he depicts true femininity as inherently passive and a means of masculine fulfillment.[69] Beattie finds this particularly problematic. She writes, "To exist as the answer to another's question is to be denied one's own sense of questioning subjectivity, and thus Balthasar perpetuates the Catholic idea of sexual complementarity in such a way that the woman complements—and completes—the man's existence, but at the cost of her own personal identity in the drama of salvation."[70] In other words, the woman's identity and distinctiveness is absorbed into her male counterpart, serving as a means of his fulfillment. This is typified in Mary whose subjectivity is lost as she witnesses the crucifixion and becomes the mother of the church. "Mary's unique and individual sense of personhood, identified with her maternity of Christ, is taken away from her and she becomes a collective entity, a 'woman' represented not by a woman's body but by the 'body' of the Church, which is in fact Christ's body."[71] In the end, "Balthasar does not attribute a single quality to the woman that is not derivative of or responsive to the man. She comes into being only to serve his ends and to fulfil his existence."[72] If Beattie's analysis is correct, it seems that Balthasar's account of sexual difference has actually devalued human embodiedness, not elevated it.

Beattie's critique could be extended to Balthasar's portrayal of humanity as a whole. Remember that for Balthasar humanity possesses an intrinsically "feminine" form. Edward Oakes notes that in Balthasar's project both men and women possess an intrinsically feminine disposition vis-à-vis their relationship with God.[73] Therefore if, as Beattie argues, Balthasar's portrayal of "femaleness" lacks a robust existence and subjectivity in and of itself, it also seems that men must abdicate their subjectivity if they are to achieve their telos. Neither men nor women possess any way of relating to God as subjects. Agneta Sutton observes, "If the proper response to God is like that of Mary,

---

68. For a detailed discussion of the role that this particular pericope plays in Balthasar's sexual polarity, see Zwank, *Geschlechteranthropologie in theologischer Perspektive?*, 217–31.

69. Zwank, *Geschlechteranthropologie in theologischer Perspektive?*, 218. Crammer writes, "Ultimately Balthasar reproduces the one-sex model in which the normative human being is implicitly male and Woman's definition is based around Man, particularly around what Man is seen to need Woman to be. The result of this methodology is that Woman in Balthasar's theology lacks substance, subjectivity, and a voice of her own" (Crammer, "One Sex or Two?," 102; cf. Kilby, *Balthasar*, 128–30).

70. Beattie, *New Catholic Feminism*, 102.

71. Beattie, *New Catholic Feminism*, 107.

72. Beattie, *New Catholic Feminism*, 108.

73. Oakes, *Pattern of Redemption*, 255.

then both man and woman must display characteristics of that response, such as receptiveness and submission."[74] Femininity, for Balthasar, becomes *the* mode of being that all of humanity, men and women alike, must appropriate in response to God. And, if the identity of the actors in his Theo-Drama is revealed through their action, we can say that in a very real sense men must "become" women.[75] Thus, as Sain notes, "Balthasar's vision contains no positive way for men to relate to God as men and that femininity is fundamentally inseparable from creatureliness."[76] In the end, divine action (masculinity) seems to absorb human action (feminine receptivity), as human (theological) persons exist only as a response. Furthermore, it seems that Karl Rahner's accusation of Gnosticism gains a little more credibility. While Rahner was worried that Balthasar's Christology is adoptionistic,[77] it seems that such a concern can be extended to Balthasar's view of all human creatures. But what then is the value of male and female bodies in such a framework, especially in comparison to the interior feminine form that lingers beneath the surface of all of humanity? At the very least, we can say that there is a legitimate worry that Balthasar has understood femaleness and maleness in mostly instrumental terms and in so doing the importance of physicality and corporeality has been diminished. Furthermore, it seems that the mission of the creature ends up consisting of the divesture of its creatureliness.

74. Sutton, "Complementarity and Symbolism of the Two Sexes," 423.

75. This also raises the concern that creatures (as feminine) become essential to God (as masculine). In other words, if women are the means through which men find their fulfillment and all creatures must adopt this feminine disposition in relationship to God, to what extent does the creature become an essential means of God's own self-fulfillment?

76. Sain, "Through a Different Lens," 91.

77. Rahner et al., *Karl Rahner in Dialogue*, 124–26. Rahner accuses Balthasar of a form of Gnosticism in which the humanity of Christ is superfluous compared to the spiritual or ideal *missio* and eternal *kenosis*. For Rahner, Balthasar's strongly kenotic orientation, historicized in the *missio* of the Son, betrays gnostic leanings that prioritize the spiritual over the material, denigrating the importance of the Son's embodiedness in the incarnation. Balthasar responds to Rahner's critique with a rather robust discussion of the fact that the Son has indeed taken on flesh in the incarnation to form the theandric person (Balthasar, *TL II*, 223–80). Additionally, it seems the full humanity of Christ is necessary in one sense if he is to serve as the concrete *analogia entis* and thus mediate between God and humanity. Yet, this does not help mitigate our present concern that the corporeality of other human beings has been minimized in Balthasar's project.

Ethics Outside of the Eucharist

While Zizioulas does not embrace Balthasar's account of Christian mission, his punctiliar account of human personhood presents a different problem vis-à-vis humanity's missioned existence. Recall that for Zizioulas, it is during the celebration of the Eucharist that the Spirit brings humanity's eschatological telos into the present. Therein, they experience a foretaste of *theosis*. This eschatological experience grounds Christian ethics as the Christian community seeks to embrace the rest of the world in eucharistic fellowship with God. The members of the church serve as priests, extending the gift and blessing of communion with God to the rest of the created order.[78] As demonstrated in Zizioulas's discussion of a eucharistic approach to ecology, Zizioulas argues that the church offers the world back to God so that it might receive true being.[79] The members of the ecclesial community do not serve as stewards or preservers of creation but strive to cultivate it so that creation can transcend the limitations of its own nature.[80]

But if this is the case, how can the human being live "eucharistically" after the celebration of the Eucharist has been completed? If, after the celebration is completed, the individual is no longer subsisting in the Son-Father relationship, they are no longer existing as an ecclesial person nor are they experiencing the *theosis* of the Eucharist. How then is it possible to welcome the rest of the created order into this celebration? For Zizioulas, this transition is not existential, but ontological. Furthermore, as I have argued above, personhood appears to be a punctiliar event. Yet if this ontological transformation is punctiliar, it seems to preclude a human creature from exhibiting an eschatological or theotic ethic in the present since we are no longer the kinds of beings capable of living this way. If biological hypostases are capable of living *for* the other in the same way that ecclesial hypostases are, then the merits of such an ontological distinction seem limited. Yet, if such a bifurcation is maintained, how can Christians live as persons and priests outside of the Eucharist? Outside of the Eucharist human beings are no longer the *kind* of beings that can live in a manner consistent with the free love of God. We revert from ecclesial persons to our prior state as individual, biological hypostases with all of the ethical limitations that this transition entails. Zizioulas is notably reluctant to examine Christian theology through the lens of Christian ethics, yet such a reply seems unsatisfactory.

---

78. Zizioulas, *Lectures in Christian Dogmatics*, 131.
79. Zizioulas, *Eucharistic Communion and the World*, 138.
80. Zizioulas, *Eucharistic Communion and the World*, 140.

To a certain extent, we have to bring ethical concerns to bear on our theological inquiry.

Zizioulas attempts to navigate this problem with the concept of a eucharistic or sacramental hypostasis. Zizioulas argues that the eucharistic hypostasis is that third ontological category.[81] Cortez notes that this alternative mode of being is characterized by ascetic practices that attempt to free the human subject from the laws of nature.[82] Informed by the Eucharist, this way of existing seeks to sacrifice on behalf of the other and prioritize the other over ourselves.[83] In so doing, the ecclesial community mediates the gift of fellowship with the rest of the world. However, as Zizioulas does not develop this category in great detail, it is hard to feel satisfied with his implementation of it. Consequently, the question remains unresolved: How can those not actively participating in the Eucharist live as persons and offer this personhood to the world?

Of our three interlocutors, it seems that only in Hauerwas's account is the gift of freedom truly viewed as freedom to act. Surely, Balthasar would affirm freedom to act in principle. After all, to be a person is to receive one's mission from God and act in the world under the guidance of the Spirit. As the individual relinquishes their autonomy, the Spirit elevates their freedom so that they can meaningfully act within the divine drama as a participant in the mission of Christ.[84] Hauerwas, in contrast, seeks to articulate an account of human agency and moral formation that is grounded in the Christian community's embodiment of the Christian narrative. The Christian, as one who sees and bears witness to the reality of God's reign in the world, can act faithfully within it. Yet this does not necessitate human withdrawal from society, but rather ecclesial persons are called to live truthfully within the world as faithful witnesses to the story of God's reign. In other words, this commitment is an insistence that the action of the Christian is different in kind from that of the non-Christian. This difference is indicative of certain political commitments. If we were to bolster Hauerwas's view of human action with Balthasar's view of the Spirit's work in the life of the laity, it seems that we could arrive at a satisfactory account of human action that maintains the tension of God's work within the Christian's life and the Christian's work within the world. For both Balthasar and Zizioulas, it is the Spirit's work in the life of the church that changes the kind of action its members engage in. Furthermore, for Balthasar it is the Spirit who enables

---

81. Zizioulas, *Communion and Otherness*, 69.
82. Cortez, *Christological Anthropology in Historical Perspective*, 186.
83. Cortez, *Christological Anthropology in Historical Perspective*, 187.
84. Balthasar, *TD III*, 534.

humanity to act coherently: "Grace gives man a center of gravity that, like a magnet, draws all the forces of his nature into a clear and definite pattern that is neither foreign nor cumbersome to the patterns already formed in his nature, but engages them, like idle laborers, in a task that is both pleasant and rewarding."[85]

Our second thesis seeks to articulate the manner in which the overall mission of the church informs our understanding of its members. As I will demonstrate below, each writer has a particular telos in mind that informs the church's mission. But while the church's telos describes where the ecclesial community is heading, the church's mission describes our task in the present and how we understand human action. Here we arrive at our second thesis: *Mission provides the supervening interpretive key for understanding the trajectory of the church and its life, involving the task of bearing witness to God's revelation in Christ and rightly relating to the world as God's redeemed creatures through the work of the Spirit*. Humanity is called to a specific task as it looks forward with hopeful expectation to the future God has promised for his people. And this mission is only accomplished insofar as the Spirit works to enable the church to be the people God has called it to be.

LITURGY AND HUMAN FORMATION

While mission provides a larger framework for understanding how the church exists in the present, this mission is realized within the church's liturgical life. For each of our interlocutors, the church is a liturgical community. Yet they differ in their understanding of how liturgical action affects the life of the church's members.[86] For Zizioulas, the Eucharist is the center of the church's life. As I have already noted above, during the celebration of the Eucharist the Spirit historicizes the *eschaton*, bringing it into the present and enabling human participation in divine life.[87] Consequently, the liturgical action of the church is constitutive of human personhood, a personhood that is experienced in the Eucharist celebration and received from the Spirit as a gift.[88]

---

85. Balthasar, *Christian State of Life*, 74.

86. Here, I am choosing to describe the action of the church primarily as liturgical. This is not over against a sacramental account of such action, as surely all three figures would affirm that the church's liturgy *is* sacramental, albeit emphasizing this point to varying degrees.

87. Zizioulas, *Eucharistic Communion and the World*, 34.

88. Zizioulas, *Eucharistic Communion and the World*, 28.

In contrast, both Balthasar and Hauerwas view the liturgical life of the church as formative of human beings. Instead of viewing the liturgical action of the church as changing the individual's ontological or metaphysical makeup, a formative view of liturgy focuses on how it trains human creatures to live, perform, and relate rightly and thereby flourish as a human creature. While Balthasar agrees with Zizioulas that the Eucharist is the center of ecclesial identity,[89] this is understood principally in terms of a progressive participation in the mission of Christ. "We are to assimilate our own 'I' more and more completely to our God-given mission and to discover in this mission our own identity."[90] The sacraments, particularly the Eucharist, become the primary means through which this assimilation takes place as the individual receives their true identity from God.[91] Furthermore, Christ "distributes his death, spilling it as life into the womb of the Church," which enables its members to attain fullness of personhood.[92] In Hauerwas's account, the church's liturgy enables the ecclesial community to embody the Christian story, a narrative that forms its members. However, this does not make the liturgical acts superfluous, but instead they are necessary for the embodiment of Christlikeness and the development of true character.[93] "In the enactment, in Baptism and Eucharist, we are made part of a common history that requires continuous celebration to be rightly remembered. It is through Baptism and Eucharist that our lives are engrafted onto the life of the one that makes our unity possible."[94] This act of remembering the church's story is formative and teaches the Christian community to live rightly. "Through liturgy we are shaped to live rightly the story of God."[95] Liturgical action tells the church's story and in so doing forms members into their telos: *homo pacem*. Whereas in Zizioulas's account personhood is experienced in a punctiliar fashion, for both Hauerwas and Balthasar ecclesial beings are being "built up" into their telos through the liturgical life of the ecclesial community.

In all three accounts, *the church's liturgical action is essential to human fulfillment and proper formation.* As we have discussed above, for all three figures, the church's liturgical life properly forms human beings so that they

89. Balthasar, *Spirit and Institution*, 240.
90. Balthasar, *TD III*, 271.
91. It is beyond the scope of this current section to provide a full critique of Balthasar's kenotic and receptive account of human personhood. However, I will return to it briefly below in our discussion of the church's *telos*.
92. Balthasar, *TD IV*, 359.
93. Hauerwas, *Approaching the End*, 196–97.
94. Hauerwas, *Christian Existence Today*, 53.
95. Hauerwas, *Christian Existence Today*, 107.

might find their fulfillment in fellowship with God. This appears to be the case for Zizioulas as well since it is only within the ecclesial community that the individual's existential despair can find resolution. However, this emphasis on the liturgical action of the church reveals that all three figures understand the church's liturgical life as enabling human beings to experience what it means to be a human creature in the fullest sense. The church's liturgy becomes the means through which humans are able to rightly exist as creatures-in-fellowship with God. The church is then essential to the fulfilment of human existence in any strong or meaningful sense. While they differ quite strongly on what occurs in the particular sacraments, they stand in agreement on the liturgical disposition of human persons. To be human is to worship and to be formed through our worship.

Personhood, Communion, and the Non-Christian

Yet if the life of the church is essential to rightly forming or experiencing existence, how are we to understand the distinction that this demands between those who participate in the church's liturgical life and those who do not? Zizioulas's ecclesio-anthropology presents a strong ontological distinction between the Christian and non-Christian. Subsisting in the Son-Father relationship, members of the ecclesial community acquire the Son's mode of being and are reconstituted as ecclesial persons. For Zizioulas, it is in this moment that the members of the ecclesial community become the *imago Dei*, possessing divine freedom.[96] In contrast, those outside of the church remain biological hypostases and seem to be neither persons nor in the image of God. While Zizioulas has left open the possibility that non-Christians could in fact be persons,[97] such an assertion is difficult to reconcile with the logic of his larger framework. If "man cannot realize his personhood outside the Church, or else the Church is ultimately irrelevant and should be made redundant,"[98] it seems that the church is the exclusive location where the event of communion is realized. As Ciraulo notes, this appears to be the logical conclusion of his theology if personhood is received through the Eucharist.[99] Ciraulo posits that, while for Zizioulas baptism is the only

96. Zizioulas, *Communion and Otherness*, 292.

97. Zizioulas claims to be agnostic regarding both the personhood and salvation of persons outside of the church. He states, "The agnosticism and uncertainty concern only those who do not believe in Christ and are not members of his Church. . . . As far as we know, the Church as the Body of Christ is the only sure and safe way to God" (Zizioulas, *One and the Many*, 397).

98. Zizioulas, *One and the Many*, 15.

99. Ciraulo, "Sacraments and Personhood," 995.

revealed means for obtaining personhood for the Christian community, perhaps personhood can exist in degrees outside of the Christian community as a journey toward full personhood.[100] But this again seems incompatible with Zizioulas's view of personhood. As Cortez avers, "Such a quantitative approach to personhood, though, suggests that personhood is at least partly an intrinsic capacity of the biological *hypostasis*, something Zizioulas explicitly rejects."[101] For Zizioulas, personhood is only experienced as a Christian participates in the celebration of the Eucharist. It seems that, for Zizioulas, personhood must either exist in varying degrees and is intrinsic to all biological hypostases, an idea Zizioulas outright rejects, or it is received in the Eucharist and only experienced by Christians.

Zizioulas is not unique in emphasizing an ontological gap between Christians and non-Christians, yet that does not make his proposal any less problematic. Since in Zizioulas's schema to be in the image of God means to exist as God himself exists, that is, as a person-in-communion, it seems that only Christians are in the image of God. Yet given the vital role the *imago* plays in discussions of Christian ethics,[102] Zizioulas's framework is particularly troubling. If Zizioulas is correct vis-à-vis the image, what resources does the Christian tradition have for describing how Christians should relate to non-Christians? And what governs this relationship? Zizioulas may respond that ecclesial persons function as priests and are tasked with bringing the non-Christian into eucharistic fellowship with the Triune God. But this in turn appears to create a "Great Chain of Being" wherein non-Christian humans and animals are functionally treated as if they are on the same tier since both are constrained by nature. Zizioulas does differentiate between human creatures and non-human creatures on the basis of God's call to the former. But this does not change the fact that the church appears to treat both groups as if they are essentially the same. Furthermore, what dissuades a bishop from forcibly baptizing people and initiating them into the ecclesial community? Such behavior would appear to give them the gift of freedom and communion with God.

Hauerwas, Balthasar, and Degreed Humanity

In contrast to Zizioulas, Balthasar argues that all of humanity is in the image of God, while personhood is something the individual becomes.

100. Ciraulo, "Sacraments and Personhood," 997.
101. Cortez, *Christological Anthropology in Historical Perspective*, 185.
102. Cf. Puffer, "Human Dignity after Augustine's *imago Dei*," 65–82; Schuele, "Uniquely Human," 5–16; Weiss, "Direct Divine Sanction," 23–38.

Balthasar's understanding of the *imago* involves the latent human potential for self-transcendence and the innate desire for a relationship with God.[103] Personhood, on the other hand, is understood predominantly in terms of action—namely, acceptance of one's mission in the divine drama. "Participation in the mission of Christ (or that which in the building up of the church Paul calls 'charisma' and which is given to each as his eternal idea with God and his social task)—that would be the actual core of the reality of the person."[104] The act of baptism reveals this intrinsic mission while the church's other liturgical rites enable the individual to be "built up into it" as they aspire to become a person. "The human conscious subject becomes a person in the theological sense through the unique way in which he is addressed by God and taken into his service, which always takes place within the Christological framework."[105] While Balthasar does not talk about humanity in quantitative terms, he certainly views personhood as a degreed reality. And since personhood is viewed as correspondence to God's idea of the individual, it seems that we can say that becoming a person is the fullest expression of humanity.

Hauerwas, as I have already noted, is reticent to appeal to the concept of "person."[106] Yet, similar to Balthasar, Hauerwas seems to argue that every human creature is in the image of God. He appears to describe the image in functional terms—that is, as a vocation assigned by God "to live according to the call of the kingdom."[107] Christians and non-Christians both have the same role in God's story and are in the image of God insofar as God has assigned both a particular purpose: "to act as an image of God's *rule* in the world."[108] On the one hand, the difference between Christians and non-Christians is epistemological. The Christian acknowledges their contingency—that is, the fact that they are a creature.[109] On the other hand, Christians are humans who exist in communities that form them so that they learn to live in accordance with the Christian story. Hauerwas writes, "I believe that to be a Christian is the fullest expression of what it means to

---

103. Balthasar, *Man is Created*, 30; cf. Robinson, *Understanding the* "imago Dei," 116.

104. Balthasar, "On the Concept of Person," 25.

105. Balthasar, *TD III*, 427.

106. Hauerwas, "Must a Patient?," 600. I do not think Hauerwas would disagree with Balthasar's or Zizioulas's appeal to the category of person as it is understood from a theological standpoint. In other words, Hauerwas seems to reject personhood as a conceptual category that can be universally appealed to in ethical discussions.

107. Hauerwas and Berkman, "Chief End of All Flesh," 206.

108. Hauerwas and Berkman, "Chief End of All Flesh," 205, italics original.

109. Brock and Hauerwas, *Beginnings*, 42.

be a human being."[110] This seems to indicate that both Christians and non-Christians share the same "ontological plane" of human being as creatures in the story of God.[111] While both Christians and non-Christians are understood as image bearers of God,[112] the difference between the two groups is that members of the church are being rightly formed as creatures in God's story and are able to act in light of it. Only the members of the ecclesial community are enabled to act in accordance with the Christian narrative, see the world rightly, and live as witnesses to the kingdom.[113] In so doing, he seems to allow room for a progressive experience of human fulfillment for those who are being drawn into the kingdom of peace.[114] Consequently, it appears that Hauerwas understands humanity as something that is experienced in degrees.[115] Human creatures become more or less human insofar as they are formed or deformed by communal narratives and practices.

However, a formative and degreed understanding of humanity could potentially be problematic as it suggests that those within the church are becoming increasingly more human than those outside of the church. Additionally, humanity or human nature has traditionally been understood as an issue of *kind*—that is, to be a certain kind of metaphysical or ontological being. Hauerwas could avoid this problem due to his reticence to engage in metaphysical speculation. Yet this raises another concern. As Joseph Rivera avers, an overemphasis on narrative's formative abilities and the malleability of human nature can end up resulting in the loss of agency. He writes, "If I have no nature, I am endlessly released from myself, which means I do not possess myself as a particular self. I am no longer, in this 'nature-less' framework, able to wield my agency as a subjective seat of noetic and affective powers poised for embodied action."[116] It seems then that any formative or degreed account of humanity will have to be nuanced in order to avoid some of these concerns.

---

110. Hauerwas, *Approaching the End*, 184.

111. Hauerwas, *Approaching the End*, 157. Hauerwas would undoubtedly bristle at my attempts to translate his thought into metaphysical categories. But to the extent that he argues for viewing liturgical practice as formative, it does seem he is advocating for a degree account of humanity, even if humanity is not a metaphysical category.

112. Hauerwas, *Approaching the End*, 44.

113. Hauerwas, *Work of Theology*, 88.

114. Hauerwas and Berkman, "Chief End of All Flesh," 205.

115. Hauerwas, *Approaching the End*, xvii.

116. Rivera, "Human Nature and the Limits of Plasticity," 42.

The Absence of the Spirit in Hauerwas's Project

Yet, while Hauerwas potentially avoids the ethical problems that may result from Zizioulas's project, his account of liturgy needs help from our other two interlocutors. For Hauerwas, the church is a community formed by the story of Jesus. Its central task is to form the lives of its members in this same story. This formation involves training in how to live as a human participant in God's story and properly worship him.[117] Arne Rasmusson provides a helpful summary: "As a life of discipleship, Christian life thus concerns the formation, or rather the transformation, of people through the tradition-formed community called the church."[118] This is an important point. The telos of humanity is the embodiment of the reign of God and it is through the church's liturgical life that humanity is properly formed toward this telos.[119]

Contra both Zizioulas and Balthasar, Hauerwas's account of the liturgical life of the church is rather silent in regards to the role and place of the Spirit. While Hauerwas emphasizes the manner in which the church's liturgical action forms human beings into people of character as they embody the Christian narrative, it is difficult to discern why the Holy Spirit's presence and work are essential to such action and, by extension, to human formation. As Nico Koopman observes, Trinitarian and pneumatological thinking do not play a strong role in Hauerwas's ethics or ecclesiology.[120] For the most part, it appears that the practices themselves are formative of human communities. The Holy Spirit appears, at best, to be an addendum to Hauerwas's project. In so doing, Hauerwas seems to construct a view of liturgical action that minimizes divine presence and action. Kelly Johnson writes, "The real problem is that this embodied and intelligible account of liturgical formation leaves talk about the Holy Spirit in at best a parenthetical role. Hauerwas does not deny or ignore the role of the Holy Spirit. But his pneumatological references read like caveats, reminders that he has not forgotten he should mention the Holy Spirit."[121] Hauerwas's approach does not provide a clear articulation of *why* the believing community is dependent on the continued work of the Spirit. Healy makes a similar observation regarding Hauerwas's perspective of the virtues. He criticizes Hauerwas for constructing a view of virtue that denigrates our dependence on "the

---

117. Hauerwas, *In Good Company*, 67–68, 216.
118. Rasmusson, *Church as Polis*, 194.
119. Hauerwas, *In Good Company*, 155.
120. Koopman, "Role of Pneumatology," 34–35.
121. Johnson, "Worshipping in Spirit and in Truth," 306.

ongoing, ever-renewed gift of life in Christ through the Holy Spirit that makes us more completely and authentically who we are."[122]

Furthermore, Healy is concerned that Hauerwas's conception of the Christian liturgical practices has been abstracted to the point that he coalesces disparate practices in a way that diminishes their distinctiveness. He argues that there are three ways a Christian practice can be enacted unsatisfactorily, which could lead to forming Christians against Christian teaching itself: (1) disingenuous performance, (2) poor performance, (3) incorrect performance.[123] For example, consider a self-centered children's minister. Every week, he attends church, teaches a lesson, recites the creeds, and teaches the children Bible stories. From outward appearances, it may seem that the church member is participating in the communal practices of the church, but inwardly he seeks praise from pastoral figures and influence over the future direction of the church. Hauerwas may claim that such disingenuous performances are not actually performing the Christian story. But then the question becomes, who is so free from the influence of sin that their performance is untainted from self-aggrandizement? Are such performances the exception or the rule of church life?

Hauerwas has since responded to these critiques and argued that the Spirit "is the agent that comes to rest on the body we call church."[124] Appropriating the work of Rowan Williams, Hauerwas argues that "the Holy Spirit is rightly understood to be the animating principle of the central practices that make the church the church; that is, it is the Spirit that makes preaching, baptism, and Eucharist more than just another way of communication, initiation, or sharing a meal."[125] The Spirit makes Christian practice qualitatively unique. Furthermore, he views the Holy Spirit as sanctifying our work

---

122. Healy, *Hauerwas*, 128.

123. Healy, *Hauerwas*, 110–16.

124. Hauerwas, *Work of Theology*, 50. See also Hauerwas and Wells, "Gift of the Church," 13–27. Lorrimar notes, "While Hauerwas does not offer a developed sacramentology, he comes much closer to a sacramental understanding of church practices than most Protestants" (Lorrimar, "Church and Christ in the Work of Stanley Hauerwas," 319). However, this does not assuage the concern that the Holy Spirit is unessential to his project, even if such an accusation can be leveled against Protestant and Free Church thinkers as well. In Hauerwas, the Christian narrative seems to be doing all of the sacramental work but it is unclear how the Spirit is essential to the process of growing in Christlikeness. As Tiina Allik writes, "It could be said that Hauerwas does not fully incorporate into his thinking the notion that both justification and sanctification, when they occur, are never just the result of our own efforts" ("Narrative Approaches to Human Personhood," 312).

125. Hauerwas, *Work of Theology*, 39.

and guiding the Christian community.¹²⁶ If Hauerwas were to clarify *how* the Spirit qualitatively transforms Christian work, I believe that it would help assuage some of my earlier concerns, particularly as it relates to different practices. Yet it is still unclear if the Spirit is essential or accidental to Hauerwas's account of moral formation within the church and the church's liturgical life. Particularly, given Hauerwas's emphasis on the church's role in training its members in virtuous living, one would hope for a stronger articulation of the pedagogical task of the Holy Spirit. While practices in general may be formative, it seems that the church's relationship to the Holy Spirit as well as his presence within the liturgy needs greater articulation in Hauerwas's thought.

Zizioulas's and Balthasar's Spirit-ed Account of Liturgy

Both Zizioulas and Balthasar have a more robust account of the Spirit's function in the liturgical life of the church. It is the presence and work of the Spirit within the church's liturgy that makes it effective. Balthasar, in addressing the concepts of the witness and proclamation of the Word, argues that the Spirit is essential. "It follows that the word of God cannot be uttered by the mouth of man unless the latter is empowered by the Holy Spirit."[127] According to Balthasar, the Spirit's presence and work enables the Christian community to speak truthfully, witness faithfully, tell the Christian story, be built up into their respective missions, and act meaningfully upon the world stage. The Spirit brings Christ's form to the church and there is no telling of the Christian story apart from his work as he appropriates the revelation of God to the people of God. While Hauerwas may agree with Balthasar's sentiment, it seems that Hauerwas's commitment to a certain understanding of habitus undermines the Spirit's role in the church's action. In other words, the church's action as mere "churchly" action is formative of the Christian community. In contrast, for Zizioulas, the Spirit's work is essential to understanding liturgical action as it is only in and through the Spirit that the church is able to participate in eschatological realities.[128] For Zizioulas, the Spirit brings eschatological communion into the present.[129] Without his presence, the sacrament is meaningless. Consequently, for both Balthasar and Zizioulas, liturgical action is Spirit-ed—that is, the Spirit's

---

126. Hauerwas, *Work of Theology*, 50.
127. Balthasar, *TL III*, 329.
128. Zizioulas, *One and the Many*, 85.
129. Zizioulas, *Lectures in Christian Dogmatics*, 157.

work and presence is an essential aspect of what it means for the Eucharist or baptism to be formative liturgical rites.

Here we have discovered two proclivities that may need to be avoided vis-à-vis how the liturgy relates to our understanding of humanity. On the one side, there has been a tendency to construe human identity in ways that preclude the category from being meaningfully applied to non-Christians. On the other hand, Hauerwas has articulated an account of ecclesial action that is so robust that it seems to verge on excluding the Spirit's place in the life of the church. How can these two proclivities be circumvented? For the moment, we can at least identify the two poles that we must avoid. First, the *imago* cannot be denied of non-Christians. Genesis 9 seems to reinforce that after the fall humanity still remains in God's image and that this is the source of a particular kind of ethic.[130] While the image itself could be understood in functional or non-metaphysical terms, Zizioulas's approach to personhood and to the *imago Dei* appears to overemphasize the discontinuity between Christians and non-Christians. Even in a relational ontology, we would not want to say that any creature exists outside of a relationship with the triune God. Second, if the church's liturgy is formative, then it must be understood as more than just mere human action. It is Spirit-ed action. It is the Spirit's work that "catches up" the action of the ecclesial community, turning it in a God-ward manner.[131] The Spirit's work is essential to understanding the liturgical life of the church.

Zizioulas, Balthasar, and Hauerwas all view the church as a community whose liturgical life robustly informs our understanding of the "whatness" of humanity. From here, our third thesis emerges: *human creatures are rightly and progressively formed through their covenantal participation in the Spirit-ed liturgical action of the church so as to become the type of people ready for eternal fellowship with God.* For all three figures, the church's liturgy plays a vital role in our understanding of human identity and formation. It is precisely through the church's liturgical action that humanity is rightly formed and achieves its telos. The church's liturgy teaches us how to properly worship God, forms us into people who love and hope rightly, and reminds us of our task of service to the world. Consequently, participation in the church's liturgical action becomes essential to human fulfillment.

---

130. Westermann, *Genesis 1–11*, 1:468; Hamilton, *Book of Genesis*, 1:315.
131. Balthasar, *TD I*, 646.

HUMAN IDENTITY AND THE ESCHATON

If the church's liturgical action and mission are both teleological, then it stands to reason that the church's telos is important to understanding its members. The church is a community that is destined for eternal fellowship with God. It is the community of the new creation. Therefore, the *eschaton* serves a pivotal role in understanding the church's true identity. Earlier, we saw that forr Zizioulas the church is a community of the *eschaton* "where man can get a taste of his eternal eschatological destiny, which is communion in God's very life."[132] The church proleptically experiences *theosis* in the present and the *eschaton* establishes its identity.[133] "The reality of the Church comes to it from the eschaton, so the identity of the Church is not limited to its created history. The Church receives its identity from that which is to come."[134] In Zizioulas's framework, time in the *eschaton* is depicted less as a series of successive moments and is understood as subsisting in the Son-Father relationship. To exist eschatologically in "God's time" is to permanently subsist in a relationship that was once experienced intermittently.

In contrast, for Balthasar there are three temporal planes: divine time, created time, and Christ's time—that is, the union of the two in the incarnation.[135] "Christ's time mediates between God's 'time' and world-time. Christ's time recapitulates and comprehends world-time while it also reveals God's super-time."[136] Balthasar rejects an *a*-temporal, Thomistic account of God's experience of time, arguing that God has his own kind

---

132. Zizioulas, *One and the Many*, 15.

133. In this section, I will use the term *eschaton* to refer to that future point in time where God's redemptive purposes are consummated. As such, it will include concepts such as the beatific vision, *theosis*, the resurrection of the body, or divinization. The term "eschatological" will be used primarily in a Hauerwasian sense since his use of the term is unique. For Hauerwas, the term "eschatological" has more to do with a way of seeing one's life retrospectively (Brock and Hauerwas, *Beginnings*, 59). In other words, eschatology or an eschatological vision is a way of seeing the world in light of the new reality inaugurated in Christ. For Hauerwas, a new eschatological vision enables the church to live in the new way of life made possible by Christ.

134. Zizioulas, *Lectures in Christian Dogmatics*, 129.

135. Balthasar, *TL III*, 186–90. For Balthasar, there is a difference between the *eschaton* and divine time. Divine time is simply the time in which God exists. God then creates space for "created time" in the act of creation *ex-nihilo*. In the incarnation, the divine and human natures of Christ also unite divine and human "times" in one person. The church and, consequently, ecclesial persons subsists in "Christ's time" until the day when creaturely time is once again taken up into divine time. This final movement of God is the *eschaton*.

136. Balthasar, *TD V*, 30.

of time that is unique to him.¹³⁷ The church subsists in "Christ's-time" in virtue of its union with Christ and participation in his temporal existence.¹³⁸ While Zizioulas's focus on the *eschaton* is oriented toward relationships, for Balthasar the church does not experience the in-breaking of the *eschaton* in a punctiliar fashion during the liturgy of the Eucharist. Instead, the church exists in a unique kind of time. On the one hand, it possesses an eternal kind of existence as an idea in the mind of God.¹³⁹ Yet, on the other hand, in virtue of the incarnation the church is also historicized in the present just as Jesus once was.

Hauerwas, while reluctant to exposit the depths of divine time, agrees with Balthasar that God possesses his own kind of time.¹⁴⁰ Jesus has inaugurated a new "time" and a people of this "new time."¹⁴¹ For Hauerwas, this new time is predominantly understood in terms of seeing the world in a different way.¹⁴² Since the church knows that the story of Jesus ends with his peaceable reign over the earth, the members of the Christian community strive to act in accord with this vision.¹⁴³ Furthermore, an eschatological vision is vital for understanding Christian action. For Hauerwas, humanity's eschatological orientation is another way of saying that it is grounded in the story of God's redemptive work.¹⁴⁴

This leads to two distinct implications. First, human identity is dynamic and must be able to cohere across the "times" if it is to intelligibly

---

137. Balthasar, *TD V*, 30. For Balthasar, God is not *a*-temporal, but supra-temporal. Yet, Balthasar also quickly acknowledges the limits of human reason regarding the things of the divine. For Balthasar, acknowledging human rational capacities is apropos in the case of the concept of divine time.

138. Balthasar, *TD V*, 31.

139. Balthasar, *Man is Created*, 60–61. Here Balthasar is willingly appropriating Thomas's account of divine ideas. A similar move is made in Balthasar's discussion of Mary, where she exists in immaculate form before her birth as a divine idea. Moser is helpful here. He writes, "For Balthasar, the church is *supra*-, but not *a*-temporal. Just as Christ was a human being who grew from an embryo to a mature man, so too the church is caught up in the course of history" (Moser, *Love Itself is Understanding*, 27, italics his).

140. Hauerwas, *Matthew*, 24; Hauerwas, *Work of Theology*, 92–94.

141. Hauerwas, *Matthew*, 120; Wells, *Transforming Fate into Destiny*, 145.

142. For example, Hauerwas argues Christians have the time for forgiveness, confession of sin, the raising of children, and the cultivation of virtue (cf. Hauerwas, *Matthew*, 167). But this is not wishful thinking. As Rasmusson puts it, the thrust of Hauerwas's project is an "attempt to redescribe reality . . . in Christian terms" (Rasmusson, *Church as Polis*, 189). A new creation has been inaugurated in Jesus, a creation in which the Christian community exists.

143. Brock and Hauerwas, *Beginnings*, 114.

144. Hauerwas, *Matthew*, 247.

describe human creatures. In other words, there must be continuity between the "I" am today and who "I" will be in the *eschaton*. This is an emphasis of Hauerwas's and Balthasar's projects. Second, the human being is ultimately an eschatological creature. Not only do each of the three figures view human identity as cohering between two times, but they also argue that human beings only find fulfillment in the *eschaton*. The church is an inherently eschatological community; the people who comprise this community must also possess an eschatological character as well.

Over-Realizing Theosis

Despite their helpful starting points in elucidating how the eschatological nature of the church informs our understanding of human identity, a proclivity to over-realize the *eschaton* emerges in the work of Zizioulas and Hauerwas.[145] For Zizioulas, *theosis* is experienced in the Eucharist and the entire kingdom of God is present in that moment. And, while the realization of the kingdom remains a future reality, it appears to also become a present reality *in toto* albeit in a punctiliar fashion. Volf argues that Zizioulas over-realizes the *eschaton* because of his failure to properly understand the nature of grace as dealing with sin and not created existence as such, viewing salvation solely in terms of liberation from one's biological hypostasis. He writes, "Hence this process of becoming a person can come about only from the direction of God and as a total eschatological transcending (not annihilation!) of biological existence. Furthermore, according to Zizioulas salvation is an *ontological constituting* of the human being into a person."[146] As a result, Volf avers that Zizioulas portrays human persons and the ecclesial community entirely as an eschatological reality.[147] This indeed seems

---

145. The accusation of an "over-realized" eschatology is notoriously nebulous and difficult to articulate. However, it seeks to address the question: How much of the *eschaton* may we say is present before we have simply turned the present into the *eschaton*? While on the one hand such a question can seem arbitrary, its purpose is to articulate the extent to which the resurrection of the flesh and consummation of the kingdom play a role in our understanding of moral formation as well as human perfection and fulfillment. In other words, if we are indeed beings who are continuously becoming, what is the anthropological significance of the resurrected state?

146. Volf, *After Our Likeness*, 101, italics his.

147. Volf, *After Our Likeness*, 102. Russell agrees with Volf's assessment of Zizioulas's account of personhood and the church. He writes, "There is a tension here in Zizioulas's thought, but in his writing the emphasis is on (over-)realized eschatology as his rejection of the person as *simul iustus et peccator* shows" (Russell, "Reconsidering Relational Anthropology," 180). Because Zizioulas's account of salvation consists in the ontological event of transcending the biological hypostasis and becoming a new,

to be the case. If the person cannot exist outside of *theosis*, and *theosis* is only present within the celebration of the Eucharist, it appears that humans revert back to a non-personal mode of existence once the liturgical rite is completed.

Yet perhaps an even larger issue lurks in Zizioulas's scheme. Zizioulas argues, as we have outlined above, that the Spirit historicizes *theosis* during the celebration of the Eucharist, bringing the experience of the kingdom and theotic union into the present. However, it is unclear what Zizioulas intends to communicate with this description. At times, Zizioulas appears to describe the Eucharist as a moment in which we merely *experience a foretaste of theosis*. At other times he tends to describe the Eucharist as a historicization of *theosis*—that is, the bringing of the *eschaton* into the present. Yet, I wonder if this latter description can really be the case. One of the essential aspects of the eschatological kingdom of God seems to be its permanence. It is inaugurated in Christ and is a kingdom that will know no end (cf. Dan 7:14).[148] But if one of the essential components of the kingdom is its permanence and this historicizing of the kingdom only occurs during the liturgy, how can such a kingdom and its relationships exist temporarily? Does this then mean that the church experiences something different in kind or something analogous to the kingdom, but not the kingdom itself? At best, it appears to be a facsimile or symbol of the kingdom, but it does not seem that we can classify it as a foretaste of *theosis* qua *theosis*.

Living as the New Creation

A similar accusation of an over-realized eschatology can be applied to Hauerwas's project. Repeatedly advocating that the new creation has come in Jesus, Hauerwas calls Christians to see the world as it truly is and live in accordance with the new reality inaugurated through Jesus.[149] Eschatology

---

ecclesial hypostasis, a tension between the future and the present aspects of personhood cannot be maintained. Russell concludes that Zizioulas's approach ignores the "spatio-temporal" nature of human beings.

148. Describing the eschatological kingdom as permanent is not the same thing as describing it as static. Many accounts of *theosis* would describe it as an eternal process—that is, an eternal trajectory of becoming increasingly united to God. Yet this is very different from describing it as a process that is fundamentally punctiliar, repeatedly starting and stopping, beginning and ending.

149. In discussing how the Sermon on the Mount informs Christian ethics, Hauerwas argues it begins with a call to see the world rightly before instructing the Christian community on how to live. He writes, "The whole Sermon is not about how to be better individual Christians, it is a picture of the way the church is to look. The Sermon is *eschatological*. It is concerned with the end of things—the final direction toward which

involves understanding the present in light of God's promised end. Presently, the church is an alternative polis that is wholly capable of living as an alternative to the politics of the world.[150] However, politics is understood predominantly in terms of actions undertaken. As the community instills a certain set of habits in its members, they become a people of character. According to Hauerwas, character is the ability to consistently act in light of a particular story.[151] It is that moment when our habits have rightly formed us.[152]

But an important question emerges when reading Hauerwas's theology: to what extent do we need to "become" before we can rightly "be"? Hauerwas rightly centers Christian virtue within the Christian community but in so doing seems to describe Christians as the type of creatures who have the requisite constitution for a completely holy life in the present. But this leads one to wonder: what if the bodily resurrection is an essential aspect of Christian sanctification and moral formation? If this is the case, eschatological accounts of human identity may need to offer an explanation for the discontinuity between life *in via* and the future life we aspire to obtain in fellowship with God. However, at times, Hauerwas seems to try to preserve the distinction between "already" and "not yet" with the category of the apocalyptic—that is, the time between Christ's first and second advent.[153] But this tension seems to only play a minor role in explaining the formation of habits and the limits of achieving a moral life in the present. If this is indeed true, a larger issue looms in Hauerwas's understanding of how the *eschaton* informs our account of human identity. In fact, he seems to minimize the importance of Christ's return. Nathan Kerr writes, "Even though Hauerwas will readily admit that there is still a *future* to be had for this ecclesial society, his failure to articulate any real disjunction between this future and the *parousia* of the singular human being Jesus Christ means that this future must really be conceived teleologically as *always-already*

God is moving the world." He then continues to explain that, for the Christian community, seeing the world rightly is of primary importance. "The eschatological context helps explain why the Sermon begins, not by telling us what to do, but by helping us to *see*. We can only act within that world which we see" (Hauerwas and Willimon, *Resident Aliens*, 88, italics his).

150. Hauerwas, *Matthew*, 157.
151. Hauerwas, *Community of Character*, 10.
152. Hauerwas, *Sanctify Them in the Truth*, 90.
153. Hauerwas readily recognizes the church's existence between the advents of Christ. He writes, "Although the delay of the *parousia*, the return of Christ, is fully admitted in Matthew (24:48; 25:5, 19), this delay serves to underscore Matthew's interest in the formation of community rather than to diffuse it. The church is in on the long haul, living in that difficult time between one advent and the next" (Hauerwas and Willimon, *Resident Aliens*, 86).

present in the church's political life here and now."[154] Kerr's point is an important one. While Hauerwas's description of the kingdom is appealing, we must admit that many of the characteristics of the Christian life are uniquely appropriate in the present. In many ways, the here and now is not the then and there of the *eschaton*. Practices such as seeking reconciliation when wronged (Matt 18:15–16), praying for evangelistic opportunities (Col 4:3–4), bearing one another's burdens (Gal 6:2), and maintaining peaceful living (Rom 12:18) do not appear to be characteristic of our life together once our Lord has returned. But if that is the case, it seems to communicate that the "time" for such actions will eventually come to a close. Yet, occasionally, Hauerwas's writing appears to dissolve this tension. Furthermore, in 1 Cor 15:40, Paul describes the Christian hope. It is not merely that Christ will come and resolve the tensions of this present existence or remove the forces of evil, but it is also that in his coming he will consummate a transformation of humanity itself, a transformation that is required for his presence with his people.[155] The already/not-yet aspect of the kingdom applies not only to the shape of Christ's rule, but also to those citizens of the kingdom.

Balthasar's Rebuttal

Balthasar's view of the church's relationship to the *eschaton* is markedly different from the other two figures. Like Zizioulas, he argues that it is the church's task to offer the world eucharistically to God. Like Hauerwas, he argues that the church exists in the unique time of Christ. However, there is a distinct difference on each point. Vis-à-vis Zizioulas, while Balthasar does affirm the church's eucharistic mission, this entails a still future deification for the entire cosmos that is progressively experienced now through the church's sacramental life.[156] For Balthasar, it is the Son's descent, beginning in the incarnation and continuing *ad infernem*, that inaugurates this new time. Consequently, the present "Christ time" in which the church exists is readily identified as a time of suffering and refinement that will eventually be completed through the soul's journey in purgatory. Upon death or the completion of purgatory, the person is united with their divine idea and

154. Kerr, *Christ, History and Apocalyptic*, 124, italics his.

155. On this verse, David Garland writes, "The body that is raised will be transformed into something entirely different from what is known on earth and appropriate for heavenly existence. . . . Paul's point is that the resurrection body is not a reanimated corpse but something of a completely different order that is appropriate to celestial existence" (Garland, *1 Corinthians*, 731–32).

156. Healy, *Eschatology of Hans Urs von Balthasar*, 214; Deane-Drummond, "Breadth of Glory," 55.

participates in the inner life of God.[157] However, in the present, the individual person has been called to a task even while the task's fulfillment is only realized in the *eschaton*.[158] While we do not need to adopt Balthasar's larger schema vis-à-vis the world's relationship to God or his belief in purgatory, his approach does reveal a certain temperance we must maintain when we approach the topic of humanity's existence in time. Balthasar's framework emphasizes notable future "checkpoints" that remind us why resurrection and deification are vital moments in the Christian life. If indeed the telos of human existence is fellowship with God, it is only transfigured human creatures that can experience this life. The life of obedience, the process of increasingly identifying with the mission of Christ, and, finally, purgatory, all involve the relinquishing of false images of self so that we can become the kind of people capable of enjoying God.[159]

Hauerwas, Zizioulas, and Balthasar each provide stimulus to acknowledge the manner in which the *eschaton* informs our present understanding of the church. The church is a community *in via*—that is, a community on the road to fellowship with God. While the church is an eschatological institution, it also exists presently within historical time. The church is simultaneously the "Bride-to-Be" and the "Bride-Made-Ready" (cf. Eph 5:25–27; Rev 21:2). Minimizing the eschatological nature of the church fails to understand the extent to which the hope of the Lord's return should inform the ethos of this community. As Hauerwas makes clear, the church is a community who knows that it is not responsible for changing the course of world history and who knows how its narrative ends.[160] Yet over-realizing the *eschaton*, as some of our interlocutors can be prone to do, ends up minimizing the extent to which the resurrection of the body informs our understanding of human fulfillment and formation. Balthasar's thinking provides a helpful addition. The church is not merely an eschatological community; it is also a proleptic one. I am not suggesting that we adopt Balthasar's view of purgatory or God's super-time. I am merely noting that he effectively guards against over-realizing the *eschaton* in that the church remains a community *in via*. Its identity, and the identity of its members, must therefore be understood from within the tension of these two poles. The resurrection of the body is not a mere accidental addendum to the story of the people of God but fundamentally shapes our understanding of the transformation of creaturely life in the world to come.

---

157. Balthasar, *TD V*, 391.
158. Balthasar, *Christian State of Life*, 82.
159. Balthasar, *Christian State of Life*, 128.
160. Hauerwas, *Sanctify Them in the Truth*, 103.

In light of this, my final thesis involves the eschatological telos of the church and the manner in which it informs our account of human identity: *the church's proleptic nature, subsisting in the time between the kingdom's inauguration and consummation, must inform our understanding of humanity while maintaining the importance of the future resurrection as fundamental to human fulfillment.* On the one hand, the church exists as an eschatological community, a community that will one day enjoy immediate fellowship with God in the eternal state. It is in the presence of God that we are rightly formed and fulfilled. Yet it is also a present reality, a community that exists in the "time between times" as its members await Christ's return. And if that is indeed the case, those who are given the promise of resurrection must be those same individuals who are resurrected. To put the matter rather crudely, the "I's" present within the ecclesial community who have been given the promise of eternal life must correspond to the "I's" who eventually inherit this promise. How then does this eschatological nature of the church inform the identity of its members? For each of our three interlocutors, their disparate accounts of what it means for the church to be an eschatological community leads to different approaches to how the *eschaton* informs our understanding of anthropology and human identity.

CONCLUSION

The previous three chapters of this project have been primarily descriptive. There, I identified John Zizioulas's, Hans Urs von Balthasar's, and Stanley Hauerwas's distinct approaches to ecclesio-anthropology. In this chapter, I have positioned my three interlocutors around the four key loci of ecclesio-anthropology: the church's nature, mission, practices, and telos. Each of these three figures presents a robust understanding of anthropology that is informed by their accounts of the church and its function. Yet, certain questions and concerns have arisen from my engagement with them, which I have attempted to synthesize in the form of four key theses.

First, I inquired into what grounds ecclesiology and the identity of its members. Two options emerged: intra-Trinitarian relationships (Zizioulas) and Christology (Balthasar and Hauerwas). However, I found that linking the ontology or identity of the church too closely with that of the Trinity or the Son can blur the distinction between the Creator and his creature. I articulated the first of four theses: *The church must be understood as a contingent community, constituted by God's acts in history. Yet the church's divine grounding cannot blur the distinction between the members who comprise it and the God who constitutes it.* In other words, we cannot blur the distinction between individual human persons and God. The particularity of each must be maintained.

Second, I sought to elucidate the relationship between the church's mission and human identity. Specifically, I looked at how ecclesial persons are called to act in the world. Although they articulate different understandings of the mission of the church, both Balthasar and Zizioulas seem to portray human creatures as fundamentally passive. For Zizioulas, the church's mission is to offer the world communion with God in the Eucharist. Yet it seems difficult to determine how humans can live "eucharistic lives" outside of the liturgical event since they are no longer of the right ontological constitution. In Balthasar's case, a reliance on nuptial imagery leads to concerns about a lack of subjectivity in human creatures as they serve as the means to God's fulfillment. In contrast, Hauerwas argues that the Christian narrative enables human beings to become agents and act in accordance with a given story. Despite lingering concerns about the place of the Spirit in Hauerwas's framework, I noted that he helpfully portrays human freedom as the freedom to act. There I determined our second thesis: *mission provides the supervening interpretive key for understanding the trajectory of the church and its life, involving the task of bearing witness to God's revelation in Christ and rightly relating to the world as God's redeemed creatures through the work of the Spirit.*

Next, I discussed the relationship between the liturgical life of the church and human formation. There I discussed how all three figures agree that the church's liturgy is essential to our understanding of what it means to be a rightly formed human. Indeed, it is through the life of the church that humans properly become human in the truest sense. Yet Zizioulas's project seems to preclude non-Christians from being in the image of God or experiencing personhood. I argued that this is problematic given the ethical questions that emerge. Additionally, Hauerwas's project does not seem to adequately articulate a role for the Holy Spirit in human moral formation. But if the Holy Spirit is essential to our understanding of the *kind* of community we call church, as Balthasar and Zizioulas aver, it seems that we need to account for how the Spirit works in the life of the church to rightly form its members. Thus, we arrived at our third thesis: *human creatures are rightly and progressively formed through their covenantal participation in the Spirit-ed liturgical action of the church so as to become the type of people ready for eternal fellowship with God.*

Our final thesis involved the relationship between the *eschaton* and ecclesial identity. All three figures understand the church as informed by the *eschaton* and this eschatological nature significantly contributes to our understanding of the identity of the church's members. Yet I observed a strong proclivity to over-realize the *eschaton* in Zizioulas's and Hauerwas's projects. For Zizioulas, the kingdom of God arrives *in toto* during the celebration of the Eucharist. Similarly, Hauerwas's argument that the new creation has arrived in Christ and his conceptualization of the eschatological orientation of the church seems to minimize the need for the kingdom's consummation and the body's resurrection. Here Balthasar's appropriation of divine ideas was helpful in that it enabled us to maintain the necessary tension between what humans are (presently) and who they will become (eschatologically). The resurrection and glorification contribute meaningfully to our understanding of humanity. Thus, I articulated a fourth thesis: *the church's proleptic nature, subsisting in the time between the kingdom's inauguration and consummation, must inform our understanding of human while maintaining the importance of the future resurrection as fundamental to human fulfillment.*

Indeed, engaging the ecclesio-anthropologies of my three interlocutors has been a helpful and necessary first step. Yet, over the course of this chapter we have raised the tensions that must be maintained as I move forward in my project. I now turn to the construction of a Free Church ecclesio-anthropology.

6

Gathered Under the Rule of Christ

A Free Church Ecclesio-Anthropology[1]

As I discussed in the introduction, many have acknowledged that the Free Church tradition is not idiosyncratic in its Christology or eschatology. Yet the Free Church *is* unique in its approach to ecclesiology. Free Church ecclesiology argues the church is a community of "pilgrim people"—that is, believers who have freely gathered together under the lordship of Christ to mutually discern his will for ordering their worship and life.[2] It is important to recall one cannot speak on behalf of the Free Church but only as a member of this community. With that important caveat aside, in this chapter I will begin by further articulating an ecclesiology that is rooted

---

1. Elements of this chapter were previously published in Hill, "'Breathe on Us, O Breath of God,'" 79–98.

2. Within this definition, as I noted in chapter 1, I include the marks of freedom of conscience and worship, voluntary membership, congregationalist forms of governance, and an emphasis on the active participation of every member in the threefold office. Additionally, the independence of the local church from provincial or governmental control is intrinsic to this definition insofar as believers gather freely and recognize Christ as their Lord (Zimmerman, "Church and Empire," 474–77; Harmon, "Free Church Theology," 425–26). Understandably, such a definition necessarily delimits those traditions that will be included in the subsequent discussion. However, I believe such delimitation is necessary if the label is to be used in a meaningful way.

in the immediate lordship of Christ. While Catholics, Presbyterians, Anglicans, and Lutherans all agree Christ is Lord, there are implications particular to Free Church ecclesiology that emerge from such a commitment. I will begin this chapter by demonstrating the legitimacy of basing Free Church ecclesiology in the immediate lordship of Christ due to the significant historical voices within the Free Church tradition who make this move. Next, I will engage Ephesians 4–5 in order to elucidate the biblical logic that lies behind some of the key aspects of a lordship-based ecclesiology. From there I will show that the church is formed by Christ's direct rule, participates in a derivative form of his threefold office, and is the means through which God mediates his word, presence, and rule on the earth. This then leads us to the final section of this chapter and the climax of my project: the articulation of a Free Church ecclesio-anthropology. I will demonstrate four important anthropological implications that arise from Free Church ecclesial emphases: human creatures are Spirit-ed, communal, Christotelic beings that serve as God's embodied means of manifesting his word, presence, and reign on the earth.

HISTORICAL VOICES WITHIN THE FREE CHURCH TRADITION

Free Church thinkers have frequently made a connection between the immediate lordship of Christ and the shape of their ecclesiology. Malcolm Yarnell writes, "Like their continental forerunners, the English Baptists were driven to their unique positions by an overarching desire to fully obey Jesus Christ. Characteristic of their common ecclesiology, Continental Anabaptist and English Baptist alike, is the concern to follow the 'rule of Christ.'"[3] Similarly, Stephen Holmes writes,

> The primary doctrine of church among Baptists is a stress on the Lordship of Christ. Of course, all Christian denominations will claim this; the Baptist distinctive is applying this resolutely to the local congregation. . . . All the members of the local church are corporately responsible for discerning the mind of Christ for that people. Church meeting, however practiced, is the organizational expression of this belief.[4]

---

3. Yarnell, *Formation of Christian Doctrine*, 8. See Grenz, *Theology for the Community of God*, 464–71; McClendon, *Doctrine*, 2:364–67; Erickson, *Christian Theology*, 963–64; Jones, *Grammar of Christian Faith*, 2:603.

4. Holmes, *Baptist Theology*, 101.

While Holmes gives this insight regarding the role of the lordship of Christ to Baptist ecclesiology, I would argue it is a point of emphasis that is applicable to Free Churches as a whole.[5]

Early thinkers within the Baptist tradition emphasized Christ's unique right to rule his congregation. John Smyth, the founder of the first Baptist congregation of historical record,[6] wrote, "Let this therefor be set downe for an invincible truth that the true visible Church is the Kingdome of Christ, wher Christ the King only ruleth & raigneth in his owne lawes & officers & over his owne subjects."[7] For Smyth, the church is that community that is gathered under the rule of Christ. Consequently, the church is "free" in the sense that its liturgical life is not subject to the laws of the state or the censure of provincial authorities.[8] Similarly, for both Thomas Helwys and Isaac Backus, earthly rulers, as mere mortals, lack the power and authority to govern the spirituality and worship of the people of God. This power belongs to Christ alone.[9] The 1644 London Confession argues the church on earth is a sign of Christ's spiritual kingdom.[10] Therefore, the church submits to him and none other vis-à-vis its ecclesial life.[11] "Baptists believe Jesus

---

5. Pilgram Marpeck writes, "The Saints of God have been charged by the Lord to exercise judgment through the Holy Spirit.... No one is commanded to judge without the Holy Spirit, without whom no certain judgment is possible. That is why the Lord Jesus Christ first gave the Holy Spirit to those whom he empowered to judge so that they should certainly and truly judge" (*Writings of Pilgram Marpeck*, 334). See also Newson, "Ethics as Improvisation," 194–95; Yoder, *Body Politics*, 61–70; Jones, *Grammar of Christian Faith*, 2:641–44.

6. Harmon, "Free Church Theology," 430.

7. Smyth, *Works of John Smyth*, 352.

8. For Smyth, this includes the nature of the church's worship and the content of its prayers. Since Anglicanism practiced the baptism of infants, Smyth perceived that the Anglican church was not a true church. Consequently, any liturgical or doctrinal imposition from the Anglican church on local churches was antithetical to the direct rule of Christ. He writes, "The true constitution of the Chu. is of a new creature baptized into the Father, the Sonne, & the holy Ghost: the false constitution is of infants baptized: we professe therefor that al those Churches that baptise infants are of the same false constitution: & al those Chu. that baptize the new creature, those that are made Disciples by teaching, men confessing their faith & their sinnes, are of one constitution" (Smyth, *Works of John Smyth*, 565).

9. Helwys, *Short Declaration of the Mistery of Iniquity*, 1; Backus, *Isaac Backus on Church, State, and Calvinism*, 314–15.

10. "London Confession, 1644," in Lumpkin, *Baptist Confessions of Faith*, 169.

11. "London Confession, 1644," in Lumpkin, *Baptist Confessions of Faith*, 170. Joseph Kinghorn writes, "*Public worship is a central point where the professors of the religion of Christ visibly unite as his subjects for the purposes of obeying the various parts of his will.... It is in the Church of Christ, that Christians as a body obey their Lord*" (*Life and Works of Joseph Kinghorn*, 2:72, italics his).

exercises his sovereign, gracious, kingly rule over every individual believer and every local congregation. To be a Christian is to bow the knee to Christ's rule over your life through repentance and faith. To be a church is to strive to conform every aspect of congregational life to the will of Christ."[12] Chute et al., note that such an emphasis is not unique to Baptists, but is indicative of Free Church commitments to the manner in which the local church relates to Christ.[13]

The relationship between the immediate lordship of Christ and ecclesiology is also a prominent theme within Anabaptism. For Balthasar Hubmaier, the church is comprised of those who have surrendered their lives "to live henceforth according to the Word, will, and rule of Christ, to arrange and direct [their] doing and leaving undone according to him and also to strive under his banner until death."[14] Bernard Rothmann argued that the church is founded on the confession of Christ as its Lord and is a community that "adheres solely to the words of Christ" and strives "to do his will."[15] Pilgram Marpeck emphasized that the true church was characterized by the voluntary submission of each member to the will of Christ.[16] Even church discipline is viewed through the lens of training church members to walk in obedience to Christ and better embody his rule.[17] In the Waterland Confession (1580), Christ's kingly office is directly linked to the constitution of a new spiritual people who are learned of Christ and live in fellowship with him.[18] The saints possess a different manner of life as they are ruled and taught of the Holy Spirit and the Word.[19] The people of God gather because, in so doing, God is present in the local congregation and guides them to understand and discern his will through the Holy Spirit.[20]

While the above survey is far from exhaustive, it seems that there is in fact ample historical precedent for grounding Free Church ecclesiology in the immediate lordship of Christ.[21] Regenerate believers gather together

---

12. Chute et al., *Baptist Story*, 330.

13. Chute et al., *Baptist Story*, 330.

14. Hubmaier, *Balthasar Hubmaier*, 85.

15. Rothmann, "Restitution," 106.

16. Marpeck, *Writings of Pilgram Marpeck*, 550–53.

17. Hubmaier, *Balthasar Hubmaier*, 85–86. See Simons, *Complete Writings of Menno Simons*, 396–405.

18. x Lumpkin, *Baptist Confessions of Faith*, 53.

19. "The Waterland Confession," in Lumpkin, *Baptist Confessions of Faith*, 53.

20. "The Waterland Confession," in Lumpkin, *Baptist Confessions of Faith*, 59.

21. The lordship of Christ will be used as a shorthand to include the rule and ministry of Christ over a local congregation as well as the church's desire to continually reform its practices, liturgy, and lifestyle to better correspond to the kingdom and serve as a witness to the world.

to discern Christ's will so that they might order their lives, worship, and ministry accordingly. In many ways, this is indicative of the Free Church's appeal to Matthew 18:20 as a *locus classicus* when discussing the integrity of their ecclesiology.[22] For Free Church thinkers, Christ's rule is directly mediated to his local church that is then tasked with discerning his will for their lives and worship. If this is the case, then it is also true that his rule is not extrinsically mediated to the local church by provincial nor governmental authorities.

A LORDSHIP ECCLESIOLOGY

In Genesis 1, Yahweh's declaration of "Let there be" brings into existence a world that responds to his command. Similarly, Christ's declaration to his disciples that they "will receive power" from the Holy Spirit and thereby "will be [his] witnesses" calls the people of the new creation into being.[23] In this section, I will highlight some of the key themes of a lordship ecclesiology through explicit engagement with a particular biblical text. Given the Free Church's emphasis on returning to the grammar of the New Testament church, it is important to engage a key passage of Scripture in order to articulate a Free Church ecclesiology.[24] In Ephesians 4–5, Paul encourages the church to structure its worship and life in accordance with the victory of God in Christ so that they might best embody his kingdom as they communally grow in Christlikeness.[25] Therefore, it is appropriate to begin here

---

22. See Colwell, "Church as Sacrament," 55–58; Marpeck, *Writings of Pilgram Marpeck*, 331; Allison, *Sojourners and Strangers*, 278; Chute et al., *Baptist Story*, 337; "The Waterland Confession," in Lumpkin, *Baptist Confessions of Faith*, 59.

23. Ian McFarland provides a helpful articulation of the relationship between the created world and the Creator God. He argues it is primarily one of obedience. Creation is under the command of the Word and its very existence is an act of submission to the one who has called it into being (McFarland, *From Nothing*, 62). And insofar as that is true, we may also say the creatures of the new creation exist in a relationship of obedience under the command of the Word.

24. Here, I am not attempting to put forth a definitive biblical foundation for Free Church ecclesiology, but instead wish to provide an example of how a key biblical text may be seen to support the kind of lordship ecclesiology I articulate below. Undoubtedly, there are other ways of reading this passage and other points of emphasis present within it. My goal is to show that the church gathers to meet its Lord and be formed in wisdom, a point I believe Ephesians 5 highlights in a unique way.

25. It is beyond the scope of this chapter to argue convincingly for Pauline authorship of Ephesians. However, for my present purposes, this is not a vital part of my argument. Suffice it to say, there is enough scholarly consensus vis-à-vis the Pauline nature of the letter, whether that be from Paul's mature thinking or from someone whose thinking was informed by the apostle. For an overview of the various arguments, see Johnson, *Writings of the New Testament*, 407–12; Brown, *Introduction to the New Testament*, 627–30.

as I seek to demonstrate how Christ's direct rule provides the local church with its shape and form.

Christ's Rule and the Shape of the Local Church

Paul begins his letter to the Ephesian church with an articulation of the victory God has accomplished through Jesus's death, resurrection, and ascension. Timothy Gombis argues that Paul understands God's action in the world as that which sets the agenda for how the church participates in God's work in the world.[26] For Gombis, Eph 1:20—2:22 serves as a depiction of divine warfare where God defeats evil powers, exalts Christ as cosmic Lord and King, and sets apart the church as the gathered temple that manifests and celebrates his victory.[27] "The basic thrust of Paul's story is that God has defeated the fallen powers and authorities in Christ Jesus and has installed Christ Jesus as cosmic ruler over all of reality. God is manifesting his victory by creating the church, in which he is overcoming the effects of evil powers on his world."[28] For Paul, Christ is Lord over creation and is the one to whom all things will be subjugated. In Eph 1:10, Paul states that all of creation has been "brought under the headship of" (ἀνακεφαλαιόω) Christ. Arnold suggests that this term signifies that Christ stands as the agent of bringing all of creation under God's sovereignty.[29] If creation was thrown into a state of disharmony because of the fall, Hoehner rightly recognizes that ἀνακεφαλαιόω also communicates the re-integration of creation through the rule of Christ.[30] The church, as the body of Christ, relates to Christ's rule in a unique way: it is the community that is shaped by his rule and to

---

26. Gombis, *Drama of Ephesians*, 85.

27. Gombis, *Drama of Ephesians*, 90.

28. Gombis, *Drama of Ephesians*, 86. Frank Thielman also sees this narrative arc of God's triumph in Christ over the enemies of God's people, particularly in Paul's quotation of Ps 68:18 in Eph 4:7–8. He writes, "Paul's interest in Ps. 68:18, therefore, lay not only in the 'gifts' that the psalm mentions and that ... were given to people, but also in the psalm's expression of God's triumph over his enemies" (Thielman, "Ephesians," 823–25).

29. Arnold, *Ephesians*, 89.

30. Hoehner, *Ephesians*, 221. Thielman argues this reading overlaps with how the verb ἀνακεφαλαιόω and noun ἀνακεφαλαίωσις were used in antiquity, citing the Roman rhetorical theorist Quintilian. He writes "If Paul used the term in Eph. 1:10 with this common oratorical and literary meaning, then he is metaphorically describing God's plan to sum up the disparate creation in Christ. Just as an orator or writer draws together the elements of an argument and shows how they demonstrate the chief point of the speech or composition, so Christ will bring order to the universe" (Thielman, *Ephesians*, 67).

whom he communicates the blessings of redemption.[31] The church's status as a monument of Christ's victory differentiates it from the surrounding world and its communities.[32] Christine Gerber notes that Christology and soteriology play a prominent role in Ephesians. She argues that these two loci then set the foundation for the letter's ecclesiology in that the disparate individuals of the church are gathered together into one body of reconciled members united under their one Head.[33] Christ is identified as Lord of all creation and the church is that community that rightly recognizes the world as belonging to God.[34]

Yet how does Christ's rule materialize within the life of his church? In order to better answer this question, it is necessary to take a step back and look at Christ's ministry in Ephesians as a whole. Paul describes Jesus Christ as the means through which the knowledge, blessings, and kingdom of God are communicated. Regarding the knowledge of God, Paul describes Jesus as the one who makes plain the "wisdom and insight of God" (1:9). He is the one who enables believers to hear the revelation of God (1:13) and proclaims the benefits of salvation (2:17). As prophet par excellence, it is only insofar as Christ indwells his people that the immeasurable depth of God's love is revealed to them (3:17). Furthermore, Christ serves the church as priest, communicating the blessings of redemption and granting believers access to God the Father. Paul describes Christ as the one who makes atonement for sin (2:13; 5:2), grants peace with God as the very embodiment of *shalom* (2:13–17), and cleanses his church of all impurity (5:27). While the church is predestined for holiness (1:4), Christ's priestly work realizes this holiness (5:26).[35] Perhaps most importantly, Christ is the means through which humanity is granted access to God the Father (3:12). Finally, Christ is

---

31. The language of the church as the body of Christ appears frequently in Ephesians (1:23; 2:16; 3:6; 4:4, 12, 16; 5:29–30). Gerber argues the "head-body metaphor" is used by Paul to communicate the unique, hierarchical relationship between Christ and his church (Gerber, "Die alte Braut und Christi Leib," 207–8).

32. Darko, *No Longer Living as the Gentiles*, 32.

33. Gerber, "Die alte Braut und Christi Leib," 218.

34. Hauerwas, *Peaceable Kingdom*, 100.

35. As Greg Lyons observes, "Ephesians has sixteen occurrences of the Greek word-family (ἁγι-/ἁγν-) translated, holy, holiness, sanctify, sanctification in holiness. The church is defined in terms of holiness" (Lyons, "Church and Holiness in Ephesians," 242). Markus Barth argues the language of ἁγίους καὶ ἀμώμους κατενώπιον αὐτοῦ in Eph 1:4 conveys strong thematic parallels to the old covenant sacrificial systems. "The adjective 'holy' has a strong priestly element. . . . The attributed 'blameless' alludes to the indispensable quality of sacrificial animals (Exod 29:1, 38; Lev 22:19–26); perhaps also to the exclusion of cripples from priestly office (Lev 21:17–23; cf. II Sam 5:8)" (Barth, *Ephesians*, 1:113; cf. Thielman, *Ephesians*, 49).

the one who rules and leads his people into eschatological rest. I have already noted the arc of cosmic victory throughout the letter. But this is particularly important for how the cosmic reign of Christ governs the life of the church. For example, the church's ethos is informed by its recognition of the king and kingdom to whom it belongs (5:5), while masters are to treat their slaves in a manner indicative of their knowledge that they too are ruled (6:9). Additionally, the reintegration of creation under Christ's rule begins in a church that rightly identifies him as the exalted ruler of all (1:10, 20–23). Christ rules over his church as the priest who grants access to God and communicates the blessings of redemption, the prophet who reveals the living God, and the king who leads his people triumphantly to eschatological rest.

Calvin provides a helpful resource for understanding Christ's ministry over his body with his articulation of the *munus triplex*. For Calvin, Jesus Christ rules over his church as prophet, priest, and king.[36] As prophet, he makes known the grace of God, training his people in the wisdom of God.[37] As priest, Christ stands as mediator between God and humanity, securing the favor of God on their behalf. In virtue of his priestly ministry, the Christian community has access to God the Father as they are sanctified and cleansed, receiving the benefits of Christ himself.[38] Finally, as king, Christ is the defender and preserver of his church, leading his people to a place of spiritual blessedness and rest.[39] Michael Horton expands Calvin's three categories, viewing them through the lens of mediation.[40] For Horton, both the prophet and priest served as mediators between God and his people. In Israel, the prophet spoke God's word, bringing announcements from God of covenantal blessing, impending judgment, and future restoration.[41]

---

36. Calvin, *Institutes*, 2.15.1. It is worth noting that this articulation is not unique to Calvin or the Reformed tradition. Augustine, John Chrysostom, and Cyril speak of Christ as the priest whose work accomplishes redemption and forgiveness. Predating Calvin, Thomas Aquinas also speaks of Jesus's ministry in this threefold way (Aquinas, *ST* 3.31.2 and 1–3). For an overview of the history of these titles in the patristic era as well as their application to the baptized, see Congar, "Sur la trilogie," 97–115.

37. Calvin, *Institutes*, 2.15.2.

38. Calvin, *Institutes*, 2.15.6. As Macaskill rightly notes, for Calvin the benefits of Christ cannot be separated from his person. Highlighting some similarities between the Reformed and Lutheran traditions, he writes, "The most striking point of commonality that emerges is that the participatory dimension of salvation is a matter of the personal presence of Christ. . . . Salvation is not a matter of receiving benefits secured by Christ, but receiving Christ himself, and with him those benefits" (Macaskill, *Union with Christ in the New Testament*, 97–98).

39. Calvin, *Institutes*, 2.15.3.

40. Horton, *Lord and Servant*, 211.

41. Horton, *Lord and Servant*, 218.

Prophets also clarified God's intentions in particular instances.[42] The priest interceded in the event of a covenantal violation, securing the favor of God and eschatological entrance into his presence.[43] Meanwhile, the king was the means through which God secured Sabbath rest for his people and mediated his universal reign.[44] These three roles are fulfilled in Jesus Christ as he secures God's favor and access into God's presence, speaks God's word to God's people, establishes Sabbath rest, and realizes the reign of God in the present.

But how does the rule of God in Christ provide the church with its form and shape? Jonathan Leeman argues that political communities are united under a common governing authority.[45] "Membership in Christ's assembly, whatever that assembly is, implies some rule, some criteria, some expectation that binds or characterizes every member in contradistinction to nonmembers."[46] Christ's community is united around a particular authority figure in virtue of the Spirit's work in writing the law of God on human hearts and opening human eyes to the reign of God in Christ (cf. 2 Cor 3:3; 4:5). It is his presence and unifying work that distinguishes members of this community from non-members. In the new covenant, the Spirit internalizes the law of God within the people of God (cf. Jer 31:33a). In so doing, the Spirit conforms the people of God to the rule of God in Christ and enlightens them to his authority.[47] In many ways, then, the Spirit of Christ is the Spirit of discipleship, enabling the Christian community to learn what it means to confess Christ as Lord.[48] Additionally, the Spirit grants a new way of relating to God in the new covenant (cf. Jer 31:33b–34). As the revealer of the love of God, the Holy Spirit unites the lost in relationship with the one who rules over all. As Balthasar rightly observes, the Spirit of God "is that

---

42. Horton, *Lord and Servant*, 212.

43. Horton, *Lord and Servant*, 210–11.

44. Horton, *Lord and Servant*, 243–47.

45. Leeman, *Political Church*, 114.

46. Leeman, *Political Church*, 110.

47. Sherman, *Covenant, Community, and the Spirit*, 198.

48. Discipleship is essential to Free Church ecclesiology. McClendon writes, "From the rule of God—a consent-seeking, creative, salvific rule—comes *membership* that consents to that rule. In baptist parlance, that has meant receiving the Spirit, obeying the gospel, receiving Christ, taking up discipleship. It implies a disciple church" (McClendon, *Doctrine*, 2:367, italics his). The church is that community which gathers to submit to the direct rule of Christ. Anabaptist and Baptist churches have heavily emphasized the task of church discipline wherein the community takes responsibility for training its individual members to follow in the ways of Christ (cf. Finger, *Contemporary Anabaptist Theology*, 113–31; Leer, "Which Future Church (Form)?," 44; Freeman, *Contesting Catholicity*, 241).

by which God discloses himself as God, to what is not God."[49] Both God and his rule in Christ are made known to his people through the Spirit who then unites the Christian community under Christ.

Therefore, the lordship of Christ involves a new way of relating, both to the God who rules and the law he has given, that grants the Christian community its shape. But how does this distinctly mark the shape of the church? Barth is helpful here. He argues that the church is the earthly, historical form of Christ's body.[50] For Barth, God has revealed himself in the incarnation and the church exists as that community to whom the Spirit has appropriated this revelation.[51] It is well recognized that the image of *corpus Christi* plays a dominant role in Barth's ecclesiology.[52] For Barth this language, at minimum, communicates the church's existence as one of obedience to its Lord.[53] The church is a response to the incarnation and its central task is to hear and respond to Christ.[54] As Kimlyn Bender notes, for Barth, "Christ remains Lord, as the church must remain servant.... There is thus an irreversible order between Christ and his people, the community of the church, and Christ then provides the basis for the church's own organization and law."[55] In hearing and responding to Christ, the church emerges with a unique shape. His authority is the criterion to which its members respond and around which they unite. Christ's rule serves as the church's organizing principle, and its life is properly understood in light of its submission to the dominion of its Head, Jesus Christ.

Returning to Ephesians 4 and 5, Paul instructs the church to press into this new form of life made possible by God's victory in Christ. Having already learned (μανθάνω) Christ (4:19), they now gather in order to discern (δοκιμάζω in 5:10) and understand (συνίημι in 5:17) his will. Yet given the emphasis on maturation in Ephesians 4, Paul seems to suggest that the tasks of discerning, understanding, and obeying the will of Christ are intended to give the local community a particular shape: loving continuity with its Lord (4:15–16). Communal maturation, then, is understood in terms of rightly embodying the rule of Christ and is tied to Christian practice, particularly the use of spiritual gifts in service of the body. In calling the church to live as

---

49. Balthasar, *TL III*, 63.

50. Barth, *Church Dogmatics*, IV/2, 614–15. Henceforth, it will be cited merely as *CD*. See also Sonderegger, "Life of Christ, the Life of the Church," 195.

51. Barth, *CD* IV/1, 647; Barth, *CD* IV/3.2, 761.

52. Brom, "Church on its Way to Community," 30.

53. Barth, *Church and the Churches*, 10.

54. Barth, *Church and the Churches*, 49.

55. Bender, *Karl Barth's Christological Ecclesiology*, 104–5.

a visible manifestation of Christ's rule, Paul establishes a hierarchy in which the church orders its life according to the will of its Lord. Christians are called to discern what is "pleasing" to God (εὐάρεστος in 5:10) and to understand his will (θέλημα in 5:17). The church does not seek its own interests or will, but the will of him who has called it into being and given it life. Best argues that, while the injunction to discern the will of God is biblical, it is inherently vague, providing "little help in making practical decisions."[56] But perhaps this description is unnecessarily pejorative. After all, Paul has just given them a list of particular behaviors to avoid, including covetousness (5:3), foolish talk (5:4), and sexual immorality (5:5). As Markus Barth recognizes, Paul's exhortation to discern the will of the Lord is more than a mere intellectual exercise, but involves recognition and holistic conformation to God's desire for his people.[57] As the church seeks its Lord's will, the community becomes the type of people God has called them to be.[58]

However, the *primary context* in which Christians discern the will of Christ is the local gathering of believers. It is primarily within this local worship gathering that Jews and Gentiles are to perceive the implications of the victory of God in Christ, conforming their lives in Christlikeness. There are several clues that signify this section's presumed liturgical context. First, Paul either directly cites or alludes to Old Testament language throughout Eph 4:17—5:20. While some of these connections may be indebted to Paul's familiarity with a Jewish tradition of ethical instruction, according to Thielman a few seem to recall specific biblical contexts.[59] For our present purposes, one is of particular import. Thielman notes that the language of speaking "the truth with his neighbor" in Eph 4:25 seems to allude to the broader context of Zech 8:16.[60] In Zechariah 8, God details his promise to restore his people in the eschatological future. Zechariah highlights truthful speech as one aspect of how God's people will conduct themselves in the future when they are gathered to worship Israel's God with the nations (Zech 8:20–23). Similarly, "truthful speech" must characterize God's people now, in the gathered new covenant community of Jews and Gentiles as a proleptic realization of this eschatological future. If

---

56. Best, *Critical and Exegetical Commentary on Ephesians*, 491.

57. Barth, *Ephesians*, 2:605.

58. Kammler argues that within the Pauline corpus and the writings of John, Jesus Christ is declared as the exclusive Lord of his church, the one who both creates and preserves his people. For Kammler, it is this confession that emerges as both the truth of the gospel and the tie that binds the people of God together in Christian unity ("Die Wahrheit des Evangeliums," 150).

59. Thielman, "Ephesians," 825–26.

60. Thielman, "Ephesians," 826.

the allusion to Zechariah describes the life of God's people who have been *gathered to worship* Israel's God along with the nations, Paul's invocation of this passage seems to presuppose a focus on the gathered life of this new in Ephesians 4–5—that is, how they behave when they have gathered together to worship God. Second, Gourges observes that it might be the case that the three lines of Eph 5:14 served together as a baptismal hymn.[61] Gourges notes not only that there are more references to baptism in Ephesians than any other Pauline letter,[62] but also that "the hymn of Eph 5:14 is concerned with identifying the light that shines with Christ whose presence will henceforth illuminate the existence of the baptized."[63] Additionally, it seems that this baptismal hymn serves as a hinge within the pericope, heightening the focus on the worship of the community. Third, the end of the section, verses 19–21, seems to further clarify that this injunction presupposes a worship context.[64] After all, it is within the local worship meeting that Christians gather to sing, praise their Lord, and interact with other Christians.[65] It may be most natural, then, to read the entire passage, verses 5–21, as addressing the liturgical context. If this is the case, as Schnackenburg argues, then Paul is contrasting the distinct nature of Christian worship, one that is empowered and produced by the Spirit, with the sexually immoral practices that characterized pagan worship.[66] Consequently, even the positive commands (e.g., thanksgiving, walking as children of the light, and seeking to discern the will of the Lord) can be viewed primarily as communal behaviors carried out within the context of the local worship gathering under the guidance of the Spirit. Best argues that the reason for such an abrupt transition from "discerning Christ's will" in verse 17 to corporate worship in verses 18–21 might be because it is within the gathering of Christians that individuals are able to learn from one another. In sharing their personal experiences and mistakes, the wisdom of the entire community is cultivated.[67] But again,

---

61. Gourges identifies five clues that this particular line was borrowed from another source: (1) it shifts significantly from the surrounding context; (2) it is preceded by a formula of introduction; (3) it differs in style, containing assonance, rhythm, and elements of parallelism; (4) it differs vis-à-vis its vocabulary; and (5) there are multiple attestations within the Pauline corpus. He concludes, "The union of these clues as well as the poetic and lyrical style of Eph. 5:14 prompts us to see a form of the hymnal genre without a doubt borrowed from the liturgy of communities and reproduced only in part" Gourges, "'Réveille-toi...' (Ep 5,14)," 229.

62. Gourges, "'Réveille-toi...' (Ep 5,14)," 377.

63. Gourges, "'Réveille-toi...' (Ep 5,14)," 380.

64. Talbert, *Ephesians and Colossians*, 129.

65. Muddiman, *Epistle to the Ephesians*, 248.

66. Schnackenburg, *Ephesians*, 237.

67. Best, *Critical and Exegetical Commentary on Ephesians*, 506.

this mutual edification takes place when Christians gather together. Fourth, as Christine Gerber argues, this coheres well with the letter's emphasis on the local church and the communal life that Jews and Gentiles now share together.[68] She rightly points out that the "one-ness" language of Ephesians 4 is focused primarily on "the unity of Jewish and non-Jewish people and in the unity of believers in everyday life."[69] While it matters that Jewish and non-Jewish Christians in disparate parts of the globe are members of the same body, what is more important for Paul's purposes is how this unity informs the manner in which Jewish and non-Jewish Christians interact and worship when they exist in the same local. It is primarily in the worship gathering that the unity between Jews and Gentiles must be demonstrated.

However, it is not just that the church seeks to discern Christ's will and rule, a point on which all Christian traditions would agree to an extent. Rather, this behavior is primarily designated as the task of the *local* church as an instantiation of the universal church. We can take this a step further. Not only does the local church engage in discerning Christ's rule for that congregation, but Christians gather together corporately *for the purpose of* pursuing the Lord's will, obtaining wisdom for godly witness, and offering praise to God as they await the consummation of the kingdom.[70] One of the primary reasons Christians gather together is to discern the nature of Christ's rule and to allow it to shape the nature of their life together.

---

68. Gerber, "Die alte Braut und Christi Leib," 218.

69. Gerber, "Die alte Braut und Christi Leib," 218. However, in my view, Gerber goes too far in disconnecting the local from the universal, particularly given the cosmic language that is prevalent throughout the letter. As I identified above, Gerber rightly recognizes that ecclesiology in Ephesians is intimately tied to Christology and soteriology. However, Paul's letter includes references to the universal scope of the Fatherhood of God (3:14–15), the election of the Christian community (1:4), the universal lordship of Christ (1:10; 20–23), and God's triumph over all demonic powers (1:20–22; 6:10–18). If the headship of Christ is cosmic and salvation is depicted as pre-temporal and cosmic in scope, it seems any ecclesiological implications must contain a universal element as well. Furthermore, Paul repeatedly uses the first-person plural pronoun to refer to realities that the church has experienced (cf. 2:4–10), even though it does not appear he is a part of the Ephesian church. While the emphasis is placed on the local church and its daily life, it seems best to view this as an instantiation or sign of the universal church.

70. Throughout this chapter, "witness" will be used to describe the manner in which the ecclesial community's life or acts of proclamation are not revelatory in and of themselves. Instead, the church's life and proclamation refer back to God's act of revelation in Jesus Christ. "Witness" describes how Christian identity and action is predicated on divine action, which then leads to a consistent series of actions, characterizing one's life as a citizen of kingdom. This may include evangelism, preaching, truth-telling, or other proclamatory ventures, but these would then be ways in which one's identity as a witness to the resurrection is embodied in particular actions.

The Church's Participation in Christ's Threefold Office

The church is shaped by the rule of Christ. The connection between Christ's rule and the church helps maintain my first thesis from the previous chapter as it situates the church's relationship to God in a way that maintains the distinctiveness and particularity of each. Now it is time to turn to examine how Christ's rule over the ecclesial community informs our understanding of the church's mission. Simply put, the church shares in the ministry of its Lord. Participating in his priesthood and prophethood, the church mediates access to God and communicates the word of God and the blessings of redemption to the world through the agency of the Spirit. Participating in Christ's kingship, the church discerns Christ's rule and embodies it, providing a visible manifestation of his kingdom in the present.

As the church responds obediently to the rule of its Lord, it recognizes that its mission and ministry come from him. In 2 Cor 5:15–20, Paul defends his ministry to the Corinthian church by noting that his vocation is rooted in what God has done in Christ.[71] After describing how the new reality inaugurated in Christ and Paul's own conversion have changed his perspective of humanity (2:16), Paul proceeds to explain how God's act of reconciliation in Christ informs his present ministry.[72] While God has reconciled the world in Christ, Paul shares in the ministry of reconciliation (5:18) and the proclamation of the message of reconciliation (5:19). The language of reconciliation indicates "a change in the social relationships of people previously at enmity with each other."[73] However, Paul nuances his use of the term in that reconciliation always moves from God to humanity.[74] Harris points out that there are four aspects of reconciliation in Pauline thought: (1) God is the initiator of reconciliation, (2) Christ was God's agent in achieving reconciliation, (3) human beings are the objects and principal beneficiaries of reconciliation, (4) reconciliation is an accomplished act from God's side but must be appropriated to particular members of humanity.[75] Paul's task is to communicate the reality of a reconciliation that has already taken place in Christ. His ministry and preaching "reconcile" only insofar as God promises to appropriate reconciliation to particular individuals through Paul by the agency of the Spirit.[76]

---

71. Matera, *II Corinthians*, 126.
72. Harris, *Second Epistle to the Corinthians*, 427.
73. Matera, *II Corinthians*, 138.
74. Guthrie, *2 Corinthians*, 309.
75. Harris, *Second Epistle to the Corinthians*, 436–38.
76. Webster rightly cautions us to maintain an asymmetry in our presentation of divine and human action when we describe the church's task of mediation; see Webster, *Word and Church*, 195–96, 226–27.

But is the ministry of reconciliation unique to the apostles or is it the mission of the entire church? Many commentators argue that the ministry of reconciliation is exclusively given to Paul and the apostles, casting them in the mold of Old Testament prophets.[77] But while this may be Paul's point in this particular pericope, it seems that from a larger standpoint the church *does* in fact share in the ministry of reconciliation. Paul frequently describes other non-apostolic Christians as his "co-laborers" who assist him in his ministry (cf. Rom 16:3, 9; Phil 2:25; 4:3; Phlm 1). If Epaphroditus is Paul's co-laborer, then he is working alongside Paul in Paul's ministry. And if Paul's ministry is the ministry of reconciliation and Epaphroditus is laboring *with* him, then Epaphroditus is also participating in the ministry of reconciliation. Additionally, insofar as the ministry of the prophets and apostles shapes Christian ministry at large (cf. Eph 2:20–21), it seems that the ministry and mission of the church is a continuation of this apostolic mission. There is a level of continuity between the ministry of the apostles and the ministry of the rest of the body of Christ. Therefore, it seems that we can say that the church as a whole shares in the ministry of reconciliation as ministers of the new covenant and in so doing they share in the ministry of Christ.

Earlier, I argued that Christ rules over his church as prophet, priest, and king. He mediates the blessings and word of God to the people of God. He also governs their life together as he leads them to a place of eschatological rest. Now I am arguing that the church shares in a derivative form of Christ's ministry. The line of reasoning goes as follows:

1. Christ rules over his church as prophet, priest, and king, mediating the word and blessings of God and leading them to a place of eschatological rest.

2. The rule of Christ shapes and forms the church as it responds to him in obedience.

3. Christ gives the church a share in his ministry, commissioning them as ministers of the new covenant.

4. Therefore, if Christ's ministry over his church takes the form of his threefold office and if the church shares in Christ's ministry, the church's obedient response to the rule of Christ takes the shape of a derivative sharing in Christ's threefold office.

---

77. Cf. Barnett, *Second Epistle to the Corinthians*, 301; Harris, *Second Epistle to the Corinthians*, 438.

Yet does this resolve our problem in a satisfactory manner? Surely, as I have already argued in chapter 5, there are aspects of Christ's ministry that are unique to him. Christ alone makes atonement for sin, is the agent of reconciliation, serves as the ultimate revelation of God, and inaugurates and consummates his kingdom. He alone is the *Urkönig*, *Urpriester*, and *Urprophet*. However, Scripture does seem to depict the church as participating in some aspects of his threefold ministry.

The Priesthood of the Church

Priesthood is primarily concerned with the responsibilities of mediating access to God and interceding before God on behalf of other human creatures. While Christ is the unique mediator between God and humanity, the New Testament predicates both of these priestly tasks of the church albeit through the agency of the Spirit.[78] Intercession involves beseeching the Lord of the covenant to act favorably and mercifully with his people. Throughout his epistles, Paul reminds his church of his intercession on their behalf as he asks the Lord to give them insight and wisdom (cf. 1 Cor 1:4–7) and the ability to live in a manner that pleases the Lord (cf. Col 1:9–11). Furthermore, Paul instructs the church to follow in his example by praying and making intercession for others (cf. Eph 6:19; 1 Tim 2:1–2). Additionally, the New Testament consistently depicts the church as the new temple—that is, the place where God dwells by his Spirit.[79] In Israel, the temple served as the place where Yahweh uniquely manifested his presence.[80] Insofar as worship was conducted in the temple, the priests were "dealing with the person, character, will, purpose, and presence of Yahweh."[81] In describing the church as the new temple where God dwells by his Spirit, the writers of the New Testament are depicting the church as the place where believers have access to God.[82] This seems to intimate that when human beings are initiated into the church, they are welcomed into the very place where God dwells by his Spirit and are granted access to him. As Thomas Torrance concludes, the

---

78. Franklin, *Being Human, Being Church*, 198.
79. Cf. 1 Cor 3:16–17; 2 Cor 6:16; Eph 2:20–22; 1 Tim 3:15; Heb 3:6; 10:21–22.
80. Block, *For the Glory of God*, 205.
81. Brueggemann, *Theology of the Old Testament*, 650.
82. Greene, "Spirit in the Temple," 737–39. Karen Jobes comments on 1 Pet 2:5, "The Christian community is portrayed as a temple, implying that now it—not a literal stone building—is the place of God's earthly dwelling by the Spirit, a place of true worship and of acceptable sacrifice" (Jobes, *1 Peter*, 148).

application of priestly language to the church is a constant theme throughout the New Testament and the church participates in Christ's priesthood.[83]

The church shares in the priesthood of Christ and is the means through which God communicates his presence and the blessings of the new covenant by the agency of the Spirit. In *Concerning the Ministry*, Martin Luther identifies seven priestly functions: the teaching and preaching of the Word, the performance of baptism, the administration of the Lord's Supper, the binding and loosing of sins, the act of praying for one another, sacrifice, and exercising discernment vis-à-vis doctrine and spirits.[84] As Timothy George points out, for Martin Luther and John Calvin the priesthood of all believers involved the vocation of every member to serve, intercede on behalf of, and proclaim the promises of God to one another. It was also a call to engage the world in service and witness.[85] On the one hand, this priestly vocation involves intercession. The church is tasked with "bringing the concerns of the world to God in faithful prayerfullness, and bringing the concerns of God to the world in proclamation."[86] On the other hand, the church is the place where the blessings of the new covenant are mediated to the rest of creation through the agency of the Spirit. Maintaining the Spirit's agency is important to our understanding of the church's mediation. Webster notes, "The mediating reality . . . does not replace or embody or even 'represent' that which is mediated, but is as it were an empty space in which that which is mediated is left free to be and act."[87] Here, I find Zizioulas's concept of the priestly task of the church to be a helpful supplement. Recall that for Zizioulas the church's very identity is eucharistic in that it seeks to bring

---

83. Torrance writes, "[The New Testament] also applies priestly language to the Church, showing that the Church is given to participate in His ministry, in word, deed, and life; in word, by proclaiming the Gospel to the nations by prayer and worship and praise and thanksgiving, in life and deed, by self-sacrifice, by ministering humbly to the needs of others, and by presenting our bodies in worship to God" (Torrance, *Royal Priesthood*, 21–22).

84. Luther, *LW*, 40:21–32. Anizor and Voss rightly point out that for Luther the priesthood of all believers concerns the obligation and vocation of every Christian, even if Luther recognized that some members of the community take on distinct roles in an official capacity (Anizor and Voss, *Representing Christ*, 77).

85. George, "Priesthood of All Believers," 292–93. Nagel argues the communal nature of the priesthood is essential to our understanding of it. This is because a priest is always in relationship to something else (God) mediating on behalf of someone else (the community) (Nagel, "Luther and the Priesthood of All Believers," 278). As I will demonstrate below, the same sentiment can also be applied to the prophethood of the church.

86. Greggs, "Priesthood of No Believer," 391. Jenson and Wilhite describe intercession as the cataphatic side of ecclesial mediation (*Church*, 151–52).

87. Webster, *Word and Church*, 226.

the world into union with God.⁸⁸ In so doing, the church gives the world its true being in the life of God.⁸⁹ As discussed in the previous chapter, I have found Zizioulas's view of creation to be deficient. Yet, the church *does* fill the earth with the presence of God insofar as God promises to manifest himself through his people and condescends to meet with them.⁹⁰ Furthermore, without accepting Zizioulas's conception of theosis, we can still affirm that as priests to creation the church seeks to bring creation into fellowship with God and seeks to mediate the blessings of forgiveness and peace to creation.⁹¹ As the church gathers, it is the means through which God moves creation to its intended goal.

The Prophethood of the Church

The New Testament also portrays the church as participating in Christ's prophethood. The fathers and prophets of Israel longed for a day when the prophetic gift would be ubiquitously dispersed among God's people (cf. Num 11:30; Joel 2:28).⁹² The future expectation of the expansion of the prophetic office is particularly important since Peter explicitly connects Pentecost to the hope of Joel (cf. Acts 2:15–21). The coming of the Spirit at Pentecost marks the inauguration of this new age wherein the former hope of a universal prophethood is realized. Keener, highlighting Peter's sermon in Acts 2, notes that the outpouring of the Spirit and the expansion of the gift of prophecy were viewed as signs of the inauguration of the *eschaton*.⁹³ The prophetic ministry involved the task of pointing the people of God backward to the covenant and forward to God's promised redemption.⁹⁴ While Christ alone is the unparalleled revelation of God (Heb 1:1–3), the Christian community bears witness to the revelation of God's mercy in Christ (cf. 1 Pet 2:9). In speaking the truth to one another (Eph 4:25), singing hymns and spiritual songs to one another (Eph 5:19), and admonishing one another (Col 3:16), the Christian community is tasked with bearing witness to the covenant inaugurated in Christ in order to call its members back to fidelity. These tasks involve both aspects of the prophetic task, as

---

88. Zizioulas, *Eucharistic Communion and the World*, 137.
89. Zizioulas, *Communion and Otherness*, 60.
90. Colwell, *Promise and Presence*, 86–87.
91. Greggs, "Priesthood of No Believer," 395.
92. Freeman, "Mediating Ministry and the Renewal of the Church," 397.
93. Keener, *Acts*, 1:874–79.
94. Rad, *Message of the Prophets*, 93–94, 100–1.

members of the ecclesial community look back to the covenant while looking forward with the expectation of the Lord's return.

Sharing in Christ's prophetic ministry, the church as a whole is the means through which God mediates his revelatory word to his people and to his world. As a prophetic community, the church bears witness to God's proclamation of reconciliation, judgment, and eschatological hope. In virtue of the Spirit's work, the church is the means through which God communicates his word to his creatures. The Spirit is sent to remind the disciples of the revelation of Christ (cf. John 14:26) and to empower them to be a community who proclaims it (cf. Acts 1:8). John Colwell writes, "While the Holy Spirit may mediate God's presence and action through the means of any aspect of the material creation, God has not promised to do so.... God has promised to speak and act through the Church."[95] In many ways, this prophetic ministry is an embodied word. The Christian community is shaped by the presence and work of the Spirit to be a visible display of Christ's presence. While in the Old Testament particular prophets were raised to call the people of God to covenantal obedience, warn of approaching judgment, or point forward to eschatological hope, in the new covenant this task is universalized to the entire body. In virtue of their anointing in the Spirit, every member of the church body is authorized to participate in the prophetic ministry of Christ.

The church's prophetic ministry is both extrinsically and intrinsically oriented. On the one hand, this prophetic task is extrinsically oriented toward the watching world. The church proclaims the message of reconciliation, calling all of humanity to recognize their place as creatures in God's world.[96] For example, James McClendon notes that even in the event of martyrdom, martyrhood involves the opponents of the faith and the surrounding culture just as much as it involves the martyr. The followers of Christ engage those who are antagonistic to the gospel in their refusal to abandon the faith in the face of death, trusting that God is a faithful king and that our lives belong to him.[97] Yet on the other hand, the church's prophetic ministry is intrinsically oriented. Members of the church must remind one another of the revelation that they have received from God in Christ and call one another back to covenantal faithfullness. The task of admonition is given to each member insofar as they are indwelt with the Spirit. Additionally, in the Old Testament prophets pointed forward eschatologically to the

---

95. Colwell, *Promise and Presence*, 111.
96. Barth, *Church and the Churches*, 10.
97. McClendon, *Witness*, 3:347.

consummation of God's kingdom. In the same way, the church reminds its members of God's promised redemption.

The Kingship of the Church

The New Testament also describes the church as participating in Christ's kingly office. In Rev 5:6–10, John's vision of the heavenly throne room culminates in the recognition that Christ alone is worthy to open the scrolls of judgment. Yet the elders' song includes one illocution that is important for my present purposes: "You have made them a kingdom (βασιλείαν) and priests to our God, and they shall reign (βασιλεύσουσιν) on the earth" (Rev 5:9–10). In describing the unparalleled authority of the church's crucified and resurrected Lord, the elders seem to intimate that the supremacy of Christ results in the installation of the church as a community of ruled rulers. The resurrection of Christ results in his exaltation and the exaltation of his followers. Not only does the Christian community cling to the promise of reigning with Christ in the new heavens and new earth (cf. 2 Tim 2:12), but this eschatologically future reign is inaugurated in the present.[98] Additionally, while the apostles are primary witnesses and possess a unique authority in orienting the church's life and practice (cf. Eph 2:20; 1 John 1:5), the church has the responsibility of discerning and applying this teaching in their own lives (cf. 2 Thess 2:15; Heb 13:7).

Believers participate in the kingship of Christ by embodying his reign and discerning his will together.[99] In so doing, their lives possess a derivative authority as authoritative witnesses to the revelation of God in Christ. As Steve Harmon rightly recognizes, the church confesses that ultimate authority solely belongs to the Triune God.[100] Yet as the Spirit internalizes the Law of God within the ecclesial community, its members possess a derivative authority as they strive to respond to God in obedience and worship.[101]

---

98. See Beale, *John's Use of the Old Testament in Revelation*, 157–60; Schnackenburg, *God's Rule and Kingdom*, 330–31; Osborne, *Revelation*, 261.

99. Bebbington goes so far as to state that the kingship of all believers is one of the key contributions of Baptist ecclesiology and serves as one of the movement's three core convictions along with regenerate church membership and believer's baptism (Bebbington, *Baptists through the Centuries*, 285). I will return to this below when I discuss the topic of discernment as an ecclesial practice.

100. Harmon, *Towards Baptist Catholicity*, 27.

101. Harmon, *Towards Baptist Catholicity*, 37. This serves as a key illustration in the fundamental difference between God's authority and the church's derivative participation. Yahweh is king of his creation because he stands as its Author and Creator. His authority is intrinsic to his identity. While the promise of the new covenant internalizes the Law of God, it does so only because of the indwelling of the Spirit. The new

Their lives become authoritative displays of the gospel. Members of the church also recognize that the Spirit works *through* the other members of the community to conform them to Christlikeness. Recalling our discussion of Ephesians 5, members of the church are called to mutual formation in order to attain communal maturation and wisdom. Discipleship is essential to Free Church ecclesiology.[102] The Spirit conforms the people of God so that they live in accordance with the rule of God in Christ. He teaches the people of God how to follow their King.

The Uniqueness of a Free Church Lordship Ecclesiology

Yet is this articulation of the church's participation in the *munus triplex* unique to the Free Church? According to the Catholic doctrine, "The whole People of God participates in these three offices of Christ and bears the responsibilities for mission and service that flow out from them."[103] As priests, the baptized are set aside as "a spiritual house and a holy priesthood."[104] Sharing in Christ's prophetic office, the people of God serve as Christ's witnesses in the world.[105] Participating in Christ's royal office, the church recognizes that Christ's kingship is typified in service and commits to serving its Head as well as the poor and suffering.[106] Catholic thinkers such as Benedict Ashley and Donald Goergen have argued that laity and priesthood alike participate in the threefold office of Christ.[107] Ashley affirms that all of the baptized are priests insofar as the church shares in the sacrifice of its Head.[108] Yet he maintains that there is a distinction between the priesthood of the laity and the priesthood of the ordained as only the latter provide

---

covenant community possesses this authority not in virtue of its essence, but in virtue of God's gift. Yahweh possesses authority in virtue of his status as Creator, while the members of the Christian community possess authority in virtue of their standing of authorized citizens.

102. See Finger, *Contemporary Anabaptist Theology*, 113–31; Leer, "Which Future Church (Form)?," 44; Freeman, *Contesting Catholicity*, 241.

103. Catholic Church, *Catechism of the Catholic Church*, 783.

104. Catholic Church, *Catechism of the Catholic Church*, 784.

105. Catholic Church, *Catechism of the Catholic Church*, 785.

106. Catholic Church, *Catechism of the Catholic Church*, 786.

107. Küng, *Church*, 80.

108. Ashley, "Priesthood of Christ," 151–52. Hans Küng, while by no means indicative of the Catholic tradition, helpfully clarifies in arguing that every member of the church participates in the priesthood of Christ, giving them the authority to teach, forgive sins, and distribute the elements of the Lord's Supper. However, for Küng there is a difference between possessing this authority and exercising it. Only the priest is *authorized* to actualize their latent authority (Küng, *Church*, 80).

GATHERED UNDER THE RULE OF CHRIST 169

order to the ecclesial community and serve as the basis for its unity.[109] Similarly, Goergen notes that the term "priest" cannot be used univocally between the baptized and the ordained even though both are understood properly through the lens of Christology.[110] In each case there seems to be an objective distinction between the priesthood of the laity and the priesthood of the clergy.

For Richard Belcher, a Presbyterian, the church continues the ministry of Christ and carries out his mission as the body of Christ.[111] According to Belcher, the entire church is empowered by Christ to carry out their mission as prophets, priests, and kings. Elders, as priests, are responsible for governing the life of the church and ensuring that the church's worship honors God.[112] The members of the laity carry out their priestly vocation by participating in the worship service and their commitment to offering their lives in service of God.[113] A similar framework is present in Belcher's presentation of the kingship and prophethood of the church. Belcher's proposal seems to present two different *modes* of participating in Christ's threefold office. The elders' participation in the *munus triplex* is characterized by active oversight and care for the spiritual life of the laity through "the activities of leading, guiding, and ruling."[114] In contrast, the laity's participation in the *munus triplex* is characterized more by their application of the rule of Christ in their daily lives and a commitment to walking before him with fidelity. To be sure, Belcher is clear that there is only one priest and one ministry that grounds the church's mission. The church participates in Christ's ministry.[115] However, the manner in which a member is authorized to act in light of their participation differs depending on their status.

Yet it is here that the Free Church is unique, especially when we focus on the kingship of all believers. In Catholic, Orthodox, and Anglican ecclesiologies, a distinction of kind is drawn between the laity's and priesthood's participation in Christ's ministry. As Curtis Freeman observes, "In both the Protestant and Catholic accounts, the participation of the laity in the ministry of Christ is decidedly asymmetrical compared to the participation of the clergy."[116] In so far as the priest's and laity's participation in the kingship

109. Ashley, "Priesthood of Christ," 154.
110. Goergen, "Priest, Prophet, King," 187–88.
111. Belcher, *Prophet, Priest, and King*, 178.
112. Belcher, *Prophet, Priest, and King*, 170.
113. Belcher, *Prophet, Priest, and King*, 172.
114. Belcher, *Prophet, Priest, and King*, 175.
115. Belcher, *Prophet, Priest, and King*, 171.
116. Freeman, *Contesting Catholicity*, 221.

of Christ is different in kind, their ability to act in light of it will be as well. Presbyterian ecclesiologies tend to focus on how Christ endows the church with power, power that is exercised by specific representatives.[117] In many ways, this eschews the concern by creating two different modes of participating in the *munus triplex*. Members still exercise authority; however the task of governing, instructing, and caring for the body rests primarily in the ruling and teaching elders. In contrast, for the Free Church every member of the church *directly* and *actively* shares in Christ's threefold ministry. Furthermore, every member is thereby authorized to act in light of it. In the Free Church every member is anointed by the Spirit to share directly in Christ's ministry, a vocation that is indicative of the Free Church's emphasis on regenerate church membership. As a community of regenerate, Spirit-indwelt believers, every member of the community is tasked with discerning the mind of Christ *in the Spirit* and is authorized to do so by that selfsame Spirit. The authorization of individual members is a result of the Spirit's ability to discern the mind of Christ and his pedagogical work in shaping them as true disciples. The difference, then, between a Free Church ecclesiology built on the immediate lordship of Christ and other lordship ecclesiologies is on the level of who actively participates in the ministry of Christ.

For the Free Church, the church's participation in the *munus triplex* is inherent and both the community and the individual are equiprimal.[118] On the one hand, this participation is collective. The entire church shares in the priestly and prophetic ministry of Christ, mediating God's word, presence, and covenantal blessings to the world. In discussing the priesthood of all believers, Elizabeth Newman notes that the "royal priesthood is not an individual right, but a gift given to the whole."[119] Insofar as this is a result of the believer's incorporation into the new covenant, it must be viewed as a task of the covenanted community. As Paul Fiddes observes, the individual Christian's identity as priest is derived from their inclusion into a community of priests (the church).[120] The corporate nature of the priesthood is logically prior to the individual's identity as priest.[121] The prophethood

---

117. See Horton, *Christian Faith*, 855–58; Clowney, *Church*, 202–12.
118. Bebbington, *Baptists through the Centuries*, 61–62.
119. Newman, "Priesthood of All Believers," 61.
120. Fiddes, *Tracks and Traces*, 69.
121. Newman, "Priesthood of All Believers," 60. George Hunsinger's articulation of the *koinonia*-relationship between the church and Christ is helpful for articulating the relationship of the individual's participation in the church's priesthood. Hunsinger describes this relationship as follows: "Term *a* dwells in term *b* even as *b* dwells in *a*, with the result that they coexist in a unity-in-distinction. In such a relation neither *a* nor *b* loses its identity, but rather the distinctive identity of each is sustained, fulfilled

of all believers must also be understood along communal lines. The nature of the prophetic vocation requires a revealer, a message, and, of course, the audience to whom the message is addressed. God reveals his message to and through his servants as they serve as the means of his self-revelation. Moreover, the kingship of all believers must also be understood communally. The task of embodying the rule of the kingdom is dependent upon the communal life of the church. The impetus is placed on the entire community to reflect the rule of Christ. In virtue of their sharing in Christ's kingly ministry, each member of the community exercises care for and over other members, sometimes resulting in church discipline. It is the task of the local community to guard the health of these baptized disciples and to ensure that they continue to live a life of cruciformity and corporate discipleship.[122] The practice of communal discernment also does not happen in isolation, but is the task of the community in its gathered life together. For the Free Church, every member of the gathered community actively participates in Christ's threefold office. It is the kingship, priesthood, and prophethood of all believers.

However, on the other hand, Free Churches have historically emphasized the importance of the individual. Grenz writes, "The congregationalists viewed the church as the product of the coming together of individual Christians rather than the individual Christian being the product of the church."[123] There is a collective and communal nature to the individual's participation in the *munus triplex*. However, the individual cannot be lost in the larger whole. While at times there may be a need to emphasize the collective or corporate nature of the church, the church is a fellowship of believers-in-community. Therefore, there is also an essential individuality.[124] It is individuals who freely join the church, are united to this community in baptism, and voice concerns about the church's liturgical or doctrinal life. Therefore, it seems that we must say that the individual and the corporate dimensions of Free Church ecclesiology are mutually dependent.[125]

---

and enhanced." In other words, Christ (*a*) dwells in the believer (*b*) and is logically prior to the believer. Yet we cannot talk about the believer or the church without reference to Christ as Christ grounds it ontologically (Hunsinger, "Baptism and the Soteriology of Forgiveness," 348–49). Similarly, the individual believer is indeed a priest insofar as his priesthood is grounded in the larger priesthood of the church.

122. Fiddes, *Tracks and Traces*, 136.
123. Grenz, *Theology for the Community of God*, 469.
124. Fiddes et al., *Baptists and the Communion of Saints*, 17.
125. Geldbach, *Freikirchen*, 35–36.

Ecclesial Practices and the *Munus Triplex*

Above I have argued that the church's identity and mission are best understood in light of its participation in Christ's threefold office. It is now time to turn and examine how this informs our understanding of a few of the church's liturgical practices: baptism, the Lord's Supper, and communal discernment.[126]

Baptism

Like most Christian communities, baptism in the Free Church marks one's entrance into the ecclesial community. However, in Free Churches the practice of baptism is uniquely related to discipleship given its placement after conversion. It is believers who are baptized as they continue in the journey of discipleship. Baptism is also the moment when the individual is initiated into the priesthood, prophethood, and kingship of all believers and anointed for ministry.[127] Recalling our thesis from the previous chapter, it is important to view baptism as a "Spirit-ed" practice where God acts to further form his people to become the kind of community ready for life with him. Anthony Siegrist observes that while baptism simultaneously bears witness to the redemption wrought in Christ and proclaims the initiate's inclusion in God's salvific plan, it is primarily a performative sign wherein the initiate is acted upon by God.[128] "Through the power of the Holy Spirit baptism enables people to live as followers of Jesus—to desire, intend, and perform this way of life."[129] Baptism in the New Testament is closely associated with

---

126. It is important here to recall my definition of a liturgical practice from the introduction. There I argued a liturgical practice describes specific practices that are performed regularly and correctly by the covenanted members of the ecclesial community when they gather together for worship in response to divine revelation that shapes and rightly forms its members for the purpose of attaining the community's *telos*. Undoubtedly, there are more practices that could be included in this brief survey. Perhaps most notably, the proclamation of the word, the exercise of church discipline, and the practice of evangelism are not included here despite the fact all three are strong points of emphasis in Free Churches. However, these practices are not unique to the Free Church. Reformed and Lutheran churches emphasize the preaching of the word, Catholic churches exercise communal church discipline, and the majority of Christian traditions engage in evangelism. Additionally, while baptism, the Lord's Supper, and communal discernment may be practiced in other traditions, Free Churches practice them in distinctive ways.

127. Newman, "Priesthood of All Believers," 65; Fiddes, *Tracks and Traces*, 119.

128. Siegrist, *Participating Witness*, 95, 157. Siegrist draws this language of "co-witness" specifically from Marpeck, Writings *of Pilgram Marpeck*, 197.

129. Siegrist, *Participating Witness*, 161.

living the new way of life made possible through the resurrection of Christ (cf. Rom 6; Eph 5:14). As Anthony Cross writes, "In the New Testament baptism frequently occurs within exhortations to Christians to live out their profession of faith in Christ which was made in their baptism."[130] Baptism prepares the individual to embody the reign of God and welcomes them into a community wherein they are called to discern Christ's rule together.

The Lord's Supper

Not only is baptism a formative event wherein the initiate is anointed and empowered for participation in the church's ministry, but it also provides access to the Lord's Table. While there has been a proclivity among American Baptists to view the celebration of the Eucharist as an ordinance solely involving remembrance of the new covenant's inauguration, for some early Baptists and Anabaptists Christ was present in the ceremony.[131] "The breaking of bread and drinking from the cup become a true participation in the body and blood of Christ."[132] As a prophetic act of proclamation, the church looks back to the inauguration of the new covenant, remembering its identity as new covenant people while simultaneously looking forward

---

130. Cross, *Recovering the Evangelical Sacrament*, 94.

131. For Baptists, articulations of divine presence in the Lord's Supper normally involved an appeal to Reformed accounts of Christ's "spiritual presence" (see Haykin, "'His Soul-Refreshing Presence,'"177–93; Bebbington, *Baptists through the Centuries*, 185). There also seems to be some precedent for this type of thinking within Anabaptism. The Schleitheim Confession of 1527 clearly describes the rite as an act of remembrance. However, as C. Arnold Snyder argues from the early Anabaptist hymns of Peter Riedemann and Hans Hut, some believed Christ was still present in the celebration. "There was no presence of Christ *in the elements* of the Anabaptist Lord's Supper. The bread and the wine were not seen as instruments to *convey* grace. This does not mean, however, that the Anabaptists denied the living presence of Christ in and with their celebration of the Supper" (Snyder, *Following in the Footsteps of Christ*, 105, italics his). Consequently, some contemporary Anabaptists argue the Lord is present in the "love of the community" during the ceremony (see Boyd, "Community as Sacrament," 56–57). While the differences are important, for my present purposes it is enough to articulate that there is precedent within both groups to view the Lord as present within the celebration of the Lord's Supper.

132. Marpeck, *Writings of Pilgram Marpeck*, 270. Similarly, while Menno Simons extols the anamnetic function of the Lord's Supper, he also writes, "We have to observe that the Holy Supper is the communion of the body and blood of Christ. . . . For wherever this Holy Supper is celebrated with such faith, love, attentiveness, peace, unity of heart and mind, there Jesus Christ is present with His grace, Spirit, and promise" (Simons, *Complete Writings of Menno Simons*, 146–48). For an analysis of various Anabaptist views of divine presence in the Lord's Supper, see Rempel, *Lord's Supper in Anabaptism*.

to Christ's return.[133] Yet the celebration of the Eucharist is also a priestly act. Members of the church gather around the Lord's Table in order to come and meet with the Lord who presents himself to his people. Fiddes argues that the Lord's Supper is a means through which "Christ takes hold more firmly" of believers' bodies and then "uses them as a means of his presence in the world."[134] And as outsiders are welcomed into the church, they are brought to the place where God has promised to meet with his people and order their lives. Finally, the celebration of the Lord's Supper is a kingly act. Nicholas Perrin argues that the command to "do this in remembrance of me" (cf. Luke 22:20; 1 Cor 11:25) is more than cognitive recall. Anamnesis involves "a communal praxis which embodies and re-enacts Jesus's self-giving in the life of the community."[135] It is a practice that calls its participants to a life of cruciformity, that is, the practice calls the church to embody the life and the rule of its king.

Communal Discernment

For Smyth and many other Free Church thinkers, Christ meets the Christian community in the gathering of two or three believers and is directly present as their king. Every member is responsible for discerning Christ's will for the local congregation, communicating his rule to the other members of the body, and embodying his will for their lives. When the church gathers together, one of their primary tasks is to discern the will of Christ and every member is needed in the process. While the goal of the practice is to better embody Christ's reign, it requires members who are committed to speaking truth and living out their prophetic vocation. James McClendon argues that the task of discernment differs from strictly democratic forms of polity in that members do not seek the consensus or will of the community. Instead, members strive to discern the will of God. "Discernment is rather a communal *practice*, deliberately undertaken, in which issues of moment for the ongoing life of God's people are addressed in meeting, brought under mutual study in the light of all Scripture and all experience, committed to ultimate authority in earnest prayer, and at last brought to the judgment of

---

133. Freeman writes, "The *anamnesis* in which the church remembers Jesus in the Supper stands in continuity with Old Testament covenant language that does not call merely for God to bring to mind what has been promised but rather pleased for God to act decisively so as to complete the work of salvation already begun in bringing in the kingdom through the *parousia*" (Freeman, *Contesting Catholicity*, 323).

134. Fiddes, *Tracks and Traces*, 170.

135. Perrin, "Sacraments and Sacramentality in the New Testament," 54.

those rightly concerned."[136] McClendon's description of communal discernment as an ecclesial practice helpfully articulates how it is informed by all three aspects of the *munus triplex*. As priests, believers begin by searching the Scriptures and interceding on behalf of one another in prayer. They then address one another in the meeting and commit to speaking the truth to one another as prophets. Finally, the goal is to better embody God's rule and walk in wisdom. Leeman writes, "Restoration to God means restoration to being ruled and to ruling. . . . Under the God of the Bible, the obedient action *is* authoritative action, which means that restoring a people to obedience *means* restoring them to office."[137] Out of every member's participation in Christ's threefold office, the entire church has the responsibility to live in accordance with the rule of Christ. In so doing, their lives become authoritative displays of the way of the kingdom.

I am aware that such an emphasis on the laity's participation in the kingly role of Christ can appear to negate the role of leadership or ordination. However, while it is beyond the scope of this present work to provide a robust argument for ordination or the role of elders within the local church, there is nothing in my argument that requires one to forgo ordination or the selection of elders and pastors within a local church.[138] John Colwell argues that ordination, properly understood, is "an attestation by the Church that the ordinand truly has been called by God to this ministry. The act of ordination occurs in response to the promise that what is done in the name of Christ upon earth will have been done by God."[139] If the church's act of ordaining pastors or selecting elders is rooted in the community's recognition that God has called certain members of his church to undertake unique tasks *in service of* that local congregation and is dependent upon the recognition and affirmation of that congregation, it does not appear incompatible with the above proposal. In fact, I would argue that for the Free Church both the ordination of pastors and the selection of elders can be rooted in an understanding of every member's participation in the kingship of Christ.[140]

136. McClendon, "Concept of Authority, 125.

137. Leeman, *Political Church*, 291, italics his.

138. In this paragraph and the next, I will focus predominantly on ordination and not on the selection of elders. This is not because I believe the ordination of a minister is somehow more appropriate for Free Church tradition than the act of selecting elders, but because any argument used to support the ordination of an individual to the pastoral office could conceivably be extended to defend the selection of elders as well.

139. Colwell, *Promise and Presence*, 222.

140. Nigel Wright writes, "The priesthood of all by no means excludes the calling of some to particular office and to leadership, since this is the way that those who are so called might make their particular contribution to the well-being of all in the shared priesthood of all believers" (Wright, "Inclusive Representation," 164). I believe the same

As Grenz observes, if Christ's authority is immediately present in the local congregation and every member participates in it, "it follows that ordination is in the final analysis a prerogative of the visible fellowship. As the local community ordains persons for pastoral ministry, they serve as the channel for Christ's ordaining through his Spirit."[141] This does require that we nuance our understanding of ordination in accordance with Free Church distinctives.[142] Yet as long as the entire local congregation participates in the act of ordaining leaders or selecting of elders, I do not believe that it is incompatible with my view of the church's participation in Christ's ministry.

Ordination and the appointment of elders can be viewed as analogous to the governor of a state selecting certain members of the community to serve as a task force to investigate or solve and monitor a certain problem. In so doing, the task force is called to a specific assignment and set of responsibilities that no longer directly belong to the governor. It is the task force's primary responsibility to interview members of the community, investigate potential root causes, and meet to brainstorm and research possible solutions. The governor, in contrast, has other responsibilities (i.e., granting pardons to prisoners and signing bills into law). Yet while the task force's assignment is in service of the governor, the governor still exercises a kind of responsibility and authority over the task force's effectiveness, the results of their investigation, and the manner in which they conduct it. Similarly, a local body may recognize a certain individual as called by God to preach God's Word or may identify a group of individuals who are then asked to serve that congregation in meeting material needs or exercising soul care. The local congregation may even delegate a certain kind of autonomy to this group of individuals so that they are enabled to make certain kinds of decisions, recognizing that these individuals are called by God to work in service of the body. Holmes writes, "The Church as a whole has a ministry, and individuals are occasionally set apart for individual tasks within that ministry."[143] However, while the congregation may delegate certain tasks to

---

logic could be applied to the kingship of all believers.

141. Grenz, *Theology for the Community of God*, 568.

142. Holmes helps articulate these nuances. He argues for a congregationalist ecclesiology on the following basis: "The primary location of ministry is the local fellowship of believers; the discerning and confirming of a 'call' to this ministry is properly done by such local fellowships; and this is properly done in church meeting" (Holmes, "Toward a Baptist Theology," 248).

143. Holmes, "Toward a Baptist Theology," 257. Holmes utilizes the Trinitarian concept of appropriation to describe how the performance of certain tasks or functions might belong both to the church as a whole and to particular leaders within the church. "We might argue that certain functions of the Church are appropriately performed by the particular people in the Church.... It would then be possible to locate certain tasks

some of its members, the congregation itself still ultimately retains a kind of authority over that individual's responsibilities or tasks.

Toward a Free Church Ecclesio-Anthropology

In the second section of this chapter I ventured to construct an ecclesiology rooted in the immediate lordship of Christ and the church's participation in a derivative form of his *munus triplex*. Ephesians 4–5 helped illustrate how the lordship of Christ orders the life of the local congregation. Sharing in Christ's prophethood and priesthood, the church is the means through which God mediates his promises and blessings through the agency of the Spirit. Sharing in Christ's kingship, the church is an embodiment of the kingdom of God in the present as the church awaits the future consummation of God's redemptive plan. I will now turn to focus on the primary goal of this chapter: the articulation of a Free Church ecclesio-anthropology. Here, I will argue for four distinctives of Free Church ecclesio-anthropology: a Spirit-ed account of identity, a Christotelic orientation to human formation, a interdependent and communal shape to human existence, and an embodied vocation where human creatures serve as the primary means through which God presents himself to his world.

A Spirit-ed Account of Identity

If the presence of the Spirit changes the way that human creatures relate to one another, to God's law, and to God, it stands to reason that his presence and work are vital to our understanding of human identity. It is the Spirit, after all, who shapes the Christian community and its members according to the rule of Christ, uniting them with Christ and initiating them into a community of disciples. This emerges as a particular point of emphasis in an ecclesiology that makes membership contingent upon the Spirit's work of regeneration.[144] Consequently, if members of the church are relating rightly

---

as appropriate to the ordained leadership of the Church, and preaching and liturgical presidency might fit here" (Holmes, "Toward a Baptist Theology," 259–60).

144. This is not to say Anglicans, Catholics, and Presbyterians cannot have a robust understanding of how the Spirit shapes human identity. I am simply arguing this particular emphasis in Free Church ecclesiology will give the proposal a unique shape. Other traditions within Christianity must account for the fact that the indwelling of the Spirit is not a *conditio sine qua non* of participation in the ecclesial community. This difference allows the Free Church to have a unique point of emphasis in its ecclesio-anthropology. Presbyterians may, for example, give covenant a more prominent role, while Anglicans and Catholics may want to view the Spirit's work vis-à-vis personal

to God, to his law, and to one another, it also stands to reason that the Spirit's work can meaningfully contribute to our understanding of those who are outside of the church as well. It is only in the Spirit that the human creature is able to possess a coherent sense of self.

Vanhoozer argues that when relational ontologies such as Zizioulas's grant logical priority to relations over substance, they fail to maintain the distinction between the concepts of personhood and personal identity. For Vanhoozer, persons are "basic particulars who have the capacity to relate to other persons in various and sundry ways."[145] However, a basic particular's personal identity is constituted by the way it relates to other persons.[146] Vanhoozer's observation helps us see what it means to objectively be this or that person. Furthermore, a coherent self-perception is realized when we subjectively perceive ourselves in light of who we objectively are.[147] Moreover, human persons exist in communities and these communities inform how we conceive of "relating" properly. Not only, then, is personal identity constituted by how one relates to other persons, but also by how we understand our personal histories (i.e., how we have related) and the ends we seek (i.e., what we hope to obtain in relating).[148] In other words, personal identity is constructed from how we understand our pasts, the "good life" we aspire to attain, and how we act (relate) in order to attain it. Yet the Free Church's emphasis on regenerate church membership and its understanding of its members as persons *in via* provide unique insights into how a coherent identity must be Spirit-ed.[149]

---

identity in light of confirmation. See Horton, "Post-Reformation Reformed Anthropology," 45–69.

145. Vanhoozer, *Remythologizing Theology*, 144.

146. Vanhoozer, *Remythologizing Theology*, 144.

147. This statement does not necessitate that the individual obtains a purely objective "view from nowhere," nor does it demand that our personal identity equates with our consciousness of our personal identity (Spaemann, *Persons*, 36). Rather, I am arguing the individual's understanding of their identity is coherent to the degree it corresponds to their actual identity.

148. James Smith provides a helpful description here. He writes, "We are *teleological* creatures. . . . In other words, what we love is a specific vision of the good life, an implicit picture of what we think human flourishing looks like" (Smith, *Desiring the Kingdom*, 52, italics his). This vision includes a vast swath of ideas ranging from recreational activities to the social relationships we seek to realize through our actions (Smith, *Desiring the Kingdom*, 52).

149. Additionally, my thesis regarding the mission of the church is helpful here. Mission, in many ways, is teleological. It identifies where our lives start and end, positioning them in relationship to God. Mission provides the overarching interpretive key for understanding the "who" of this pilgrim community of Spirited people, a community that is oriented teleologically toward a future with God.

The Spirit, as our ἀρραβών, tethers and unites the Christian community to a single conception of the good life: eschatological fellowship with God (cf. Eph 1:13–14). As a deposit of our future inheritance, the Spirit directs the ecclesial community to look forward to the day when God will "complete the transaction"—the day of redemption.[150] The Spirit serves as an eschatological marker of the ecclesial community's future inheritance. Indeed, the pilgrim community's "future" is eternal fellowship with God on the day of redemption, the day in which its members' identity as a holy and blameless people will be fully realized (cf. Eph 1:14; 4:30). While Christians may disagree about what precisely this fellowship entails, Christians together look forward to the resurrection of the dead and life in the world to come. The Spirit reveals to us that our "good life" is a life with God and that on that day we will finally be who we truly are.[151] The ecclesial person knows the end of their story, the telos to which they are intended, and the common hope they share with other Christians (cf. Eph 4:4).

Additionally, the Holy Spirit serves as the re-interpreter of the storied self. He shows us our own histories and their place within the greater story of God's redemption. Through the Spirit's illumination, the Christian confesses that their history, a life of sin and rebellion, was a result of their estrangement, alienation, and rebellion against God (cf. Eph 2:1–4, 11–13; 5:8). But now, believers are those who are being washed, whose blemishes are being removed, and who possess the hope that they will one day be resurrected to eternal life with God (cf. Eph 1:16–18). The re-interpreting work of the Spirit is illustrated in Paul's own transformed self-perception. In retrospect, Paul describes his personal history as consisting of wrongly persecuting Christ's church and sinning against God (cf. 1 Tim 1:13–15). Furthermore, he sees the vanity of this pursuit in comparison to the worth of Christ (cf. Phil 3:7–8). Yet after his conversion Paul rightly understands not only his past, but also his present. He is able to accurately perceive himself as a servant of God and God's church. This stands in contrast to how Paul would have interpreted these same actions *prior to* his conversion (cf. Acts 22:3–5; 24:14–15). In a sense, the Spirit provides corrective lenses that enable us to see ourselves rightly.

Moreover, the Spirit changes the nature and effect of our actions on ourselves and other human beings. If personal identity is dependent upon how we relate to other persons, we now begin to relate rightly within the ecclesial community. Christian action is distinctive in that it is done under

---

150. Thielman writes, "If we allow Paul's other use of the sealing metaphor in Ephesians to guide us to the proper meaning, then it seems to have a stronger orientation toward the future" (Thielman, *Ephesians*, 80–81).

151. So Webster, *Word and Church*, 259.

the guidance of the Spirit in response to the gift of God's grace for the purpose of formation in holiness. In Eph 4:11–16, it is only in virtue of Christ's gift that the members of the community are able to act in a way that leads to maturation and Christlikeness. While in the context of this passage Paul seems to describe how particular Christian vocations relate to Christian formation, these vocations are "Spirit-ed" vocations. Or, said differently, it is the Spirit's work in granting wisdom and enlightenment that enables any member of the Christian community to serve and minster rightly (cf. Eph 1:17). Since the Spirit enables human responses to divine grace and serves as the pedagogical guide for the human subject, his work ensures that members of the Christian community are rightly formed through Christian practice.

If this is indeed the case, how do we understand identity for those outside of the church? If the Spirit stabilizes our conception of the good life as eschatological fellowship with God, then he is essential to a coherent sense of self. Apart from his work, our perceived eschatological telos is transitory and unstable.[152] And if the only thing that provides an account for the individual's actions is the pursuit of perceived goods that lead to personal fulfillment, it seems that the individual's identity is only as stable as their commitment to a particular good. In other words, if a specific action (x) must be interpreted in a way that is consistent with story (y) in order to cohere with a particular idea of the good life (z), what happens when this ideal changes (e.g., from z to a)? All of the previous actions (x) must then be reinterpreted in light of this new conception of the good life (a). If this is the case, apart from the Spirit's work, we cannot fully understand "who" we are. Our self-perceptions are unstable.

Perhaps more importantly, even in the event that a human creature's perceived telos does not change, it still does not correspond to their *actual* telos unless they are recipients of the Spirit's illuminating work. The individual subjectively believes that they are pursuing a specific end, but they are actually striving in a different direction altogether. For example, Manasseh engages in "despicable practices" such as institutionalizing idolatry in the temple, consulting mediums and necromancers, and shedding innocent blood (2 Kgs 21:2–6). Yet presumably such actions were directed toward a specific end: either to secure the nation's deliverance from enemy forces or to procure divine favor for agricultural success. Similarly, Saul offers sacrifices in pursuit of God's favor and aid. However, the prophet Samuel reveals to the king that his actions are instead the very embodiment of rebellion (cf. 1

---

152. This is not to say that a non-Christian perceives rightly the end to which they are headed, but merely states that they do have an end in mind. It is a "perceived" *telos*, but not their actual *telos*.

Sam 13:8–13). Furthermore, Saul and Manasseh's engagement in despicable worship practices leads to deformation in both instances. Saul eventually becomes a king who seeks to destroy God's chosen ruler and suffers a string of military defeats (cf. 1 Sam 19:11; 31:6–7). Manasseh offers his own heirs as sacrifices and is forcibly removed from his kingdom, becoming the embodiment of Judah's wickedness (cf. 2 Chr 33:6, 11). These two examples are helpful illustrations as both individuals engage in liturgical practices that seem to deform them in fundamental ways. Both Manasseh and Saul fail to fulfill their designated vocation as king, pursuing a perceived telos in perverted ways. Their actions, actions intended to achieve this perceived telos, are both personally and socially destructive. In a sense, then, apart from the Spirit's work, we are being pulled in two directions, leading to fragmentation and deformation. It is only through the Spirit's illuminating work that one's subjectively perceived telos and absolute future can cohere.

In chapter 2, John Zizioulas challenged us to understand the true nature of humanity from its eschatological telos.[153] If the end informs our account of what it means for humans to act and to be rightly formed, then we can begin to see how there is a progressive sense in which humanity embodies the telos it pursues. Liturgical practices become the means through which we attain these perceived ends. Even when, as I would argue is the case for Manasseh and Saul, we envision our actions as pursuing a truly "good" end, if that end is devoid of God it is fundamentally perverse and idolatrous. Hauerwas has noted such a trajectory in his discussions of the rule of Caesar, using Caesar as a metonym for political leaders.[154] He argues that such rule must be sustained by violent practices in order to protect the ruler from their own terminality.[155] The end (immortality) is pursued in a perverse way (through violence) as it ultimately seeks a life bereft of God and refuses to acknowledge God's sovereignty over history.[156]

But does this emphasis on how human action and practices form the human subject necessarily lead to a functional or actualistic account of humanity that defines human beings primarily in terms of the roles, offices, and functions that they are called to perform? In many ways this

---

153. While there is a real danger in overrealizing the *eschaton* in Zizioulas's project, he still provides a helpful resource for Free Church anthropology in reminding us of humanity's teleological nature. With Zizioulas we can describe ways in which the church's *telos* informs its account of human identity and practices in the present. Yet we must also maintain that there is a degree of discontinuity between our present existence and our eschatological end.

154. Hauerwas and Willimon, *Resident Aliens*, 24–30.

155. Hauerwas, *Matthew*, 41.

156. Hauerwas, *Approaching the End*, 27.

can appear natural to a tradition that tends to construe baptism and the celebration of the Lord's Supper as arbitrary commands that Christ has given to his church.[157] However, I observed in chapter 5 that liturgy must be understood as Spirit-ed action that progressively forms human creatures in correspondence to their Lord. It is action performed by a community that has already been addressed by God and empowered by the Spirit. Zizioulas and Balthasar provide helpful resources for learning how to incorporate a more pneumatological approach to church practices and, consequently, the humans that engage in them. For both Zizioulas and Balthasar, it is the Spirit's activity within the church's liturgical life that makes ecclesial practices meaningful. Liturgy in and of itself does not guarantee proper formation. Rather, liturgical practices obtain their significance from the supervening work of the Spirit (cf. 1 Pet 2:5; Jude 20). The Spirit unmasks and reorders our desires so that we want the right things in the right ways. Additionally, he empowers our actions and practices so that they form us rightly. It is only in virtue of his work that we can desire the right ends, act in the right way, and become the people God has created us to be.

Christotelic Creatures: Prophets, Priests, and Kings

The statement that human creatures are Christotelic in nature is by no means novel.[158] One example in particular will suffice. Kathryn Tanner avers that there is a strong and weak sense in which humanity is in the image of God. In a weak sense, all of humanity is in the image of God in virtue of its participation in divine life.[159] Yet in a stronger sense, human beings image God through the Spirit's work of attaching us to the divine image, Christ. In so doing, "humanity gains a sort of natural connection to the divine comparable to the natural connection that the Word enjoys with other members of the trinity."[160] It is this latter state that remains the human creature's ultimate destiny in Christ.[161] But what does it mean for Christ to be the telos of humanity? Does Christlikeness consist of subsisting in a particular relationship or does it involve one's progressive development in virtue? Or does it also contain certain functional and political roles as well? I believe that the Free Church's unique emphasis on the entire church's

---

157. Freeman, *Contesting Catholicity*, 326; Lorrimar, "Church and Christ in the Work of Stanley Hauerwas," 319.

158. See Grenz, *Social God and the Relational Self*, 303; Liston, *Anointed Church*, 172.

159. Tanner, *Christ the Key*, 8.

160. Tanner, *Christ the Key*, 73.

161. Tanner, *Christ the Key*, 19.

participation in a derivative form of the priesthood, prophethood, and kingship of Christ provides a vital contribution to further develop this claim.[162]

The believer's participation in the threefold office is primarily an eschatological reality. Christians know and believe that one day they will reign with Christ in the resurrected state (cf. 2 Tim 2:12). On the day of our resurrection, we will fully and finally embody the redemption wrought in Christ (cf. 1 John 3:2–3). As prophets, believers bear witness to God's self-revelation in Christ with a testimony to redemption written on our very bodies. But as fallen and sinful creatures, our current acts of bearing witness are always imperfect and tainted. Because we merely "know in part" we can only "prophesy in part" until the day we see him "face to face" (cf. 1 Cor 13:9, 12).[163] If priesthood is predominantly about mediation and access to God, it too is ultimately an eschatological reality that is fully realized in the new creation. There, God will be present to his people in a new way and he will dwell in their midst as their God (cf. Rev 21:3–4).[164] Yet if all three of these categories are primarily eschatological, this could lead to an anthropology that is essentially apophatic. After all, we are not yet and do not quite know what we will be (1 John 3:2). However, since each of these roles is proleptically realized in the present on account of Christ's inauguration of the new creation in his death and resurrection, I believe that we have resources to discuss how they inform our understanding of humanity in the present.

As we saw in 2 Corinthians 5, the Christian shares in Christ's ministry of reconciliation. It is not merely that the church is a community that *will* participate in the threefold office, but, as I have argued above, the church and its members currently participate in Christ's ministry. Christians are currently being restored as prophets, priests, and kings.[165] Therefore, if the

162. Other traditions may indeed emphasize the Christotelic orientation of human creatures. However, it seems if this is tied to Christ's threefold office, then Free Church ecclesio-anthropology will be unique in that this *telos* is the end for every member. Additionally, priest and lay persons will not be formed in ontologically distinct ways as they both participate in the one ministry of Christ together.

163. On the one hand, 1 Corinthians 13 seems to indicate prophecy, or the prophetic office, is temporary for the believing community. However, on the other hand, there seems to be reason to believe that in the *eschaton* the church will continue to proclaim the revelation of God in Christ (cf. Rev 19:1–3, 5, 6–8). Additionally, to borrow from speech-act theory, insofar as their lives are permanently shaped by the revelation of God in Christ, they will serve as perlocutionary echoes of who God is and what he has done (cf. Rev 19:8, 22:4).

164. As Beale points out, in Revelation 22:4 believers are portrayed as "having reached their consummate access to God in the end-time temple; they are now in the position of the high priest, who had God's name written on the turban of his forehead" (Beale, *New Testament Biblical Theology*, 738–39).

165. It is worth noting that in 1 Peter 2:5 the priestly nature of the ecclesial

eschaton informs our account of human identity in the present and God's telos for the church involves a participation in Christ's threefold office, this end helps inform our understanding of what it looks like for human persons to live rightly in the present. While I still maintain that the resurrection of the body may drastically change the manner in which we share in Christ's *munus triplex*, this does not discount the fact that this inaugurated reality informs our understanding of the present. In other words, these eschatological roles are the particular end to which humanity was created vis-à-vis its relationship with the rest of creation and its relationship with the Creator. Humanity is ordered to be like Christ in particular kinds of ways, serving as the means through which God manifests his rule and mediates his presence and word in the world.

But if human creatures are teleological, how does this future telos relate to our understanding of humanity in the present? And what role does liturgical action play, if any, in achieving this telos? As I have noted in chapter 5, this is an issue that any ecclesio-anthropology will need to navigate. There, I demonstrated that my interlocutors present two ways of addressing the question of how liturgical practices relate to anthropology. Liturgical action can be viewed as either ontologically and metaphysically constitutive or progressively formative of human creatures.[166] Zizioulas's proposal represents the former. Yet, I have already demonstrated the ways in which his project appears to be problematic. The other option is to view liturgical action as formative of human subjects. Here, two ideas would need to be held in tension. On the one hand, we would posit that human nature is an issue of kind—that is, it is an all-or-nothing metaphysical property. On the other hand, we might argue that while all human creatures are fully human ontologically, all are not *being human* to the same extent. Here, the descriptor "being" is intended to communicate that there are ethical, intellectual, and vocational implications that are indicative of the role we have been cast in within the drama of redemption. To participate in inhumane liturgies on

---

community is described as a building that is still under construction. This seems to imply the priestly function of the believing community must also be understood eschatologically insofar as the completion of the "priestly project" is still future. As Elizabeth Newman writes, "We are to allow ourselves to be made a holy priesthood; this is not an inalienable right but a gift into which we grow" (Newman, "Priesthood of All Believers," 61).

166. As I discussed in chapter 5, the description of liturgical action as "ontologically constitutive" is intended to communicate the view that, for example, the creature transforms into a different kind of being while participating in the church's liturgy. In contrast, the description of liturgical action as "formative" is intended to communicate how liturgical action either progressively forms us so we better live as God intends his creatures to live, or, conceivably, gradually shapes the kind of being we are.

GATHERED UNDER THE RULE OF CHRIST 185

this latter account actively involves the rejection of one role and the demand to be recast in another.

Here, we venture in a direction similar to the distinction between image and likeness found in the work of figures such as Basil of Caesarea and Ireneaus of Lyons. In a certain sense, the category of "human" designates a kind of being. The description of the humanity's creation in Genesis 1 helps us move toward an understanding of the term humanity in this first sense. While human beings are not described as one of the types of creatures that God has created "according to their kinds," the singling out of their creation from the rest of the land-dwelling creatures accentuates the fact that they are one *kind* of being. Additionally, the call to "be fruitful and multiply" is given to all living creatures (Gen 1:22) and then repeated specifically for humanity (Gen 1:28), commissioning all members of the genus "creature" to perpetuate their specific species on the earth.[167] Furthermore, in Gen 2:23 the man awakens and notices with exclamation that God has at last created another creature like him—that is, like him in kind: bone of his bones and flesh of his flesh.[168] While there are similarities between human beings and the other living creatures, the human creature emerges as one distinct *kind* of being.

But how are we to make sense of this distinction? Roger Scruton avers that, contra Darwin and Fisher, humanity's creaturely distinction cannot be construed solely in biological or genetic terms. For Scruton, common human behaviors such as amusement and assigning blame are expressions of shared understandings among human creatures that are not reducible to the biological or genetic level. Instead, Scruton argues that human nature or humankind refers to the specific way that humans relate to one another—namely, relating to one another as subjects and not as mere objects.[169] For Scruton, this manner of relating defies Darwinian or Fisherian attempts to define human nature on a biological or genetic level and reveals humankind's psycho-social capacities.[170] Scruton avers that human nature describes how "we are the kind of thing that relates to members of its kind through interpersonal attitudes and through the self-predication of its own mental states."[171] This is a helpful description of what is intended by the phrase "human creature" in this first sense. The woman in Genesis 3 sees the tree of the knowledge of good and evil and evaluates it, determining

---

167. Westermann, *Genesis 1–11*, 1:158.
168. See Levering, *Engaging the Doctrine of Creation*, 185–86.
169. Scruton, *On Human Nature*, 34.
170. Scruton, *On Human Nature*, 46–47.
171. Scruton, *On Human Nature*, 45.

that the tree was "good for food and that it was a delight to the eyes, and . . . to be desired to make one wise" (Gen 3:6a). She then turns and gives some of its fruit to her husband, presuming that he too will arrive at the same conclusions (Gen 3:6b). To use Scruton's language, she "self-predicates" her judgments on her husband. In this thin sense, "human" refers to this kind of being.

Yet in another sense, the locution "being human" can be used to designates correspondence to Christ, the archetypal and perfect human, and thus can be thought of in degrees. In other words, being human is understood in terms of likeness to Christ. While Scruton's depiction seems to emphasize the rational and psycho-social capacities of the creature, Russell Reno argues that the creation of humanity in the image of God presupposes their present capacities to act in sundry ways and their future destiny as beings in fellowship with God.[172] Yet such an understanding of humanity seems to require us to understand humanity's telos in light of Christ. It is only in Christ and within those communities that form us "in Christ" that we are able to grow and perform in ways that accord with God's calling. In other words, the phrase "being human" in this sense is phenomenological, ethical, and covenantal, referring to the manner in which "creatures" who are being rightly formed through the church's liturgical action to correspond to the perfect humanity revealed in Christ. It is here that the teleological nature of the human creature emerges. To be human in this second sense is to learn to play our part to perfection, that is, to think, act, relate, believe, and perform in ways that accord with Christ.

In Ephesians 4:12–16, Paul begins by describing how particular "gifted" people have been equipped for the purpose of "building up the body of Christ" so that it might attain to maturity (4:12–13). The phrase εἰς ἄνδρα τέλειον refers to a fully mature human person.[173] Paul then parallels the concept of maturity with the standard of Christ.[174] Later, he will contrast it with the instability and immaturity of children who are quickly deceived and led astray by false teaching (4:14). Maturity, here, reflects a communal resoluteness in knowledge about the Son and the unity of faith. Yet, this

---

172. See Reno, *Genesis*, 53. Robert Spaemann avers that this future anticipation of transcendence is actually part of what characterizes human nature per se; see Spaemann, *Essays in Anthropology*, 18–22.

173. Hoehner, *Ephesians*, 555.

174. Thielman argues the references to fullness and growth in verses 13 and 14 communicate an architectural metaphor within the larger body metaphor where Paul "intends for his readers to think of the church, which is the body of Christ, as eventually attaining Christ's full height" (Thielman, *Ephesians*, 282). Arnold makes a similar observation regarding the phrase εἰς μέτρον ἡλικίας τοῦ πληρώματος τοῦ Χριστοῦ (Arnold, *Ephesians*, 266).

knowledge and unity cannot be construed as *merely* propositional. The maturity believe (4:4–6) and act in certain kinds of ways (5:1–2), indicating that this knowledge is Spirit-ed and covenantal. It seems that we can describe εἰς ἄνδρα τέλειον as living in ways that correspond to the revelation of God in Christ. While on the one hand maturity functions as a metaphor that communicates consistency in character, belief, and action, it also seems to intimate that the members of the Christian community to live in ways that accord with God's intention for human creatures living in his world: united to one another and in fellowship with God. In so doing, the Christian community is one that has been formed to live in ways that congruent with the perfect humanity of Christ.

Imagine for the sake of argument that human creatures possess the capacities to love and choose "freely" as essential properties. In this case, the ministry of the church is intended to form the manner in which we love one another and the character of our choices. However, this is not merely a quantitative difference. Christians, after all, are those who love one another with a Spirit-ed love (cf. Rom 5:5). Using the language of Ephesians 4, as our love increases in quality and reflects the perfect standard of the love of Christ (cf. 5:2), we are becoming more mature. And since maturation involves corporately growing in accordance with Christ (4:15), as Christians love, choose, and behave in ways that reflect the revelation of God in Christ they are becoming more human. To return to Scruton's definition, this would entail the ability to make the right kinds of judgments and to relate in the right kinds of ways. Yet while Scruton's definition may leave the character of these judgments and ways of relating nebulous, Ephesians 4 suggests that it is formation to the standard of Christ. In other words, "being human" in this second sense is understood as according with the perfect humanity revealed in Christ and to experience the kind of existence God has designed for his creatures. And it is this second sense of "being human" that we can speak in terms of degrees, a progression that is both teleological and eschatological.

But what is the value of speaking of "being human" as a degreed concept, albeit in a rather qualified sense, instead of using such language to describe the *imago Dei*? While exploring the image is beyond the scope of this project, this course of action is valuable on two fronts. First, as John Kilner has persuasively argued, the relationship between human dignity and the *imago Dei* should caution us against viewing the image as possessable in terms of degrees.[175] While the majority of the Christian tradition has tended

---

175. I am equally reticent to describe the term "person" as degreed for two reasons. First, "person," like the *imago*, is often used to ground human dignity in conversations involving Christian ethics or human rights. To become more or less of a "person" could

to adopt such a view of the *imago*, the Bible does not explicitly demand such an approach be taken. Instead, human beings are not described as possessing the image but are created *in* and *according to* God's image.[176] Additionally, as Kilner observes, historical propensities to denigrate or violate those who "possess" less of the image than others should caution us against such approaches to the image. Women and non-white minorities have typically been viewed as possessing a marred or broken image, which then decreases their dignity and justifies their maltreatment.[177] If this is the case, there is both biblical and historical-ethical precedent for refraining from speaking of the image as something that is possessed in degrees. Speaking of *being human* in degreed terms might help avoid this problem, especially if it is done in a qualified sense and if the relationship between humanity, dignity, and the image is rearticulated (see below).

Second, speaking of human existence from these two perspectives is useful in describing *how* liturgical action transforms the lives of its participants. Humans, in one sense, are being formed to become more human, in another sense. While it is possible to conceive of liturgical action in strictly existential terms, this is uncommon for most traditions. Consider, for example, the celebration of the Lord's Supper. The majority of Christian traditions argue that God is communicating some*thing* to his church that empowers them for his purposes.[178] Similarly, 2 Pet 1:4 seems to support such an understanding of the relationship between God's gift and human action. There, God's gift of divine power is portrayed as enabling human creatures to escape worldly corruption and live godly lives. However, it does not seem that this corruption can be construed as consisting of only moral impurity or false imaginations. Peter states that this corruption (φθορά) is caused by worldly desires. Here, the language of corruption refers to the decay and transitoriness brought about by sin.[179] This "corruption" results in

---

be construed as a way of increasing or decreasing the human subject's dignity. Second, there appears to be a lack of clarity in modern discussions about what we even mean by the term "person." If that is the case, there is no real way to say whether we can or should speak of personhood in degrees since we cannot agree on what personhood means in the first place. Furthermore, defining or exploring what ought to be intended by the term "person" is a complex discussion that is beyond the parameters of my present project.

176. See Kilner, *Dignity and Destiny*, 88–105.

177. See Kilner, *Dignity and Destiny*, 17–37.

178. See Billings, "Sacraments," 339–62; Durnbaugh, "Believers Church Perspectives on the Lord's Supper," 63–78; Morden, "Lord's Supper and the Spirituality of C. H. Spurgeon"; McFarland, *From Nothing*, 173–81.

179. Bauckham, *Jude, 2 Peter*, 182–83.

a certain kind of seeing, acting, and performing in God's world.[180] It seems, then, that we can say that sin affects our ability to be the type of creatures and enjoy the kind of existence God intends for us.

But does this really assuage the concern I raised in chapter 5 regarding Zizioulas's understanding of the image and the ethical concerns vis-à-vis non-Christians? It seems that a non-Christian is still understood as less human than a Christian, even if only in a qualified sense. This is very similar to the concern I raised against Zizioulas. Again, what governs the ethical interactions between the two groups? Furthermore, it seems that certain Christians would be *more human* than other Christians, depending on the frequency of their participation in formative practices. Would this not lend support to hierarchical forms of church polity or, at the very least, to paternalistic approaches to newer Christian communities? This is particularly important when we remember that many global church and minority figures have historically been viewed as inferior, regardless of their membership within ecclesial community.

Here, it may be helpful to rearticulate the relationship between humanity and the special dignity of image bearers. Humanity, in virtue of God's act of creation, is declared good and possesses a basic level of dignity insofar as they are God's creatures. Human beings care for their gardens and deal mercifully with their pets not because their pet or plant possesses an intrinsic value, but because it is valuable as a creature God cares for and sustains. God's continued providence for creation demonstrates that those who embody his rule cannot and must not sadistically exploit his creatures. Human creatures also possess this basic level of dignity insofar as they too are creatures enveloped in the providence of God. Here, they stand as one kind of creature among many.

Yet there is also stronger sense in which human creatures possess dignity insofar as they are a special kind of creature: one formed in the image of God. While exploring the *imago Dei* is beyond the scope of this project, it is important to note that we must approach it Christocentrically.[181] Kilner argues convincingly that all of humanity shares in the image as a status and standard that God has given to humanity.[182] Understood thusly, the image would appear to be an "un-degreed" gift, a status that God bestows upon the human creature out of the plentitude of his love and grace. As a gift, it designates human creatures with a unique status, requiring that we treat

---

180. Sylva, "Unified Field Picture of Second Peter 1.3–15," 101.

181. See Kilner, *Dignity and Destiny*, 40; Grenz, *Social God and the Relational Self*, 212–18.

182. Kilner, *Dignity and Destiny*, 104.

one another in particular ways. Both Jas 3:9 and Gen 9:6 seem to source a unique intra-human ethic in humanity's "image status." To mistreat a human creature is to do violence against not only them but the image of God itself. Or, to put the matter differently, to bless the Lord while cursing other human beings is contradictory.[183] Therefore, we treat human creatures in a unique manner because of the dignity that has been awarded to them by God. It is not significant for our purposes that humans possess the dignity that is common to all of creation. Rather, it is precisely because all of humanity is in the image of God that the human creature has special dignity and must be treated in a unique sense. If this is true, then becoming more or less rightly formed as a human creature does not increase or decrease one's dignity since human dignity is sourced in the image.[184] Therefore, it does not follow that becoming "rightly formed" as a human being increases the human creature's special dignity since this is awarded from God as a gift in virtue of his declaration that we are in his image. However, this does allow for a marginal level of discontinuity between Christians and non-Christian, while maintaining a strong degree of continuity as well. Additionally, we are able to alleviate some of our ethical concerns without denigrating the worth of non-Christians.

Interdependent and Communal Beings

Additionally, it seems then that we must conceive of the human creature as communal or social. However, this view of the human creature is not dependent upon certain understandings of the relationship between Trinitarian persons and the *imago Dei*. Rather, it emerges from an understanding of humanity's participation in Christ's threefold office. While other traditions may affirm the communal nature of the human creature, this emerges from a unique emphasis in the Free Church tradition.[185] In our discussion of

---

183. Blomberg and Kamell, *James*, 162.

184. While all of humanity is in the image of God, there are certain things about human beings we would not view as synonymous with the image (Kilner, *Dignity and Destiny*, 141). For example, as far as we know, all human creatures cannot survive without drinking water and breathing oxygen. Yet this dependency on oxygen and water is not synonymous with being in the image of God. It seems, then, if we can conceptually differentiate between humanity and the *imago*, the two are not synonymous. Yet this conceptual distinction does not require we deny all of humanity is in the image of God.

185. Here again, it is important to note Anglicans, Presbyterians, Methodists, and Catholics may all affirm the human creature is social. In fact, Zizioulas and Balthasar both make this a point of emphasis within their ecclesio-anthropology. However, as this section attempts to demonstrate, within the Free Church there is different motivation for affirming the social and interdependent nature of the human creature.

the priesthood, prophethood, and kingship of all believers, I noted that the Christian community participates in the threefold office together. It stands to reason, then, that human beings are fundamentally communal in nature. First, all three aspects of the *munus triplex* are received from God and, consequently, the recipient's identity is dependent upon a relationship with God. As I discussed above, the church is only able to engage in this vocation in virtue of its participation in Christ's ministry. So too, the individual is only able to mediate God's word, presence, and rule to the world on account of the church's sharing in the mission of Christ. Second, the very nature of these three vocations requires a relationship with other creatures to whom the believer can mediate the word, presence, and rule of God. Prophets mediate the word of God to the people of God. While non-human creatures may need to be reminded of their place in God's world, the scriptural point of emphasis seems to focus the prophet's task on mediating God's word to other human beings. Similarly, the priest mediates access to God to other created beings. This access includes the created order, but is primarily a gift given to *human* creatures. Christians gather *together* to discern the mind of Christ and embody his rule. It is not in the gathering of two or three creatures that Christ is present to instruct his church, but in the gathering of two or three human believers. The human creature is social because its vocation necessarily involves relating to God, other human creatures, and the rest of creation.

It is conceivable, however, within this schema that the blessings and presence of God are mediated to non-human creatures. In fact, this is an important aspect of the priesthood, kingship, and prophethood of all believers. But it is crucial to note that the church's participation in the *munus triplex* is a task of the gathered *community*. As I argued earlier, the locus classicus for Free Church ecclesiology is Matthew 18:20 and it is where two or three are gathered that Christ condescends and is present as king to rule his body (cf. Matthew 18:20). Haymes et al., give the following commentary on this passage: "In the same way that the Holy Spirit is the *sine qua non* of being a Christian (Rom. 8.9), it is the presence of the risen Christ among his people by his Spirit that constitutes the church."[186] They go on to state that "what *makes* us the church is not that we are baptized but that Christ is among us in and by his Spirit."[187]

Consequently, I believe that Free Church ecclesiological commitments are uniquely able to hold the tension between human autonomy and interdependence. As I have noted in my introduction, voluntary membership

---

186. Haymes et al., *On Being the Church*, 29.
187. Haymes et al., *On Being the Church*, 29, italics original.

is a pillar of Free Church ecclesiology.[188] However, Free Church commitments to voluntary membership are tethered to an understanding of the church as comprised of regenerate, baptized believers who are called to participate in Christ's ministry. Earlier I spoke of how humanity's personal identity is illuminated in light of the Spirit's work in reordering our actions and relationships. In Free Church ecclesiology, the covenantal call of Christ, regeneration by the Spirit, and inclusion into the new covenant all logically precede the choice of the individual to join the local church. It then seems that we must emphasize that the church is not merely the gathering of individuals, but a community of those gathered in Christ by the Spirit.[189] Here, the covenantal relationship between God and his people obtains primacy. As McClendon observes, the passive tense is an important one as it maintains "that it is not we who gather but God who gathers us."[190] For Geldbach, this emphasis on the covenant makes the community and the individual mutually dependent upon one another.[191]

Still, Free Church anthropology can tend to accentuate the individual over the community, possibly resulting from an emphasis on the individual's voluntary participation in the ecclesial community. Perhaps accenting the logical primacy of the covenantal call of Christ may help respond to the legitimate concern that is often raised vis-à-vis the voluntary nature of Free Church ecclesiology. Some worry that Free Church anthropology is inherently individualistic, relying too heavily on modernist and post-Enlightenment notions of autonomy. Hauerwas argues that such an approach to ecclesiology legitimizes secular commitments to individual autonomy, affirming the individual's logical primacy over the community.[192] Bebbington, for his part, seems to acknowledge that this is foundational for Free Church ecclesiology.[193] Hauerwas proposes that we must instead view the church as a set of practices or a communal story that determines the shape of our lives. However, the ecclesial community's qualification for discerning the mind of Christ is not primarily derived from Lockean conceptions of individual freedom, but it is derived from the community's covenantal relationship with God and one another as well as its participation in the *munus triplex*.[194]

188. Grenz, *Theology for the Community of God*, 469; Littell, "Historical Free Church Defined," 61; Niethammer, *Kirchenmitgliedschaft in der Freikirche*, 40.
189. Freeman, *Contesting Catholicity*, 246.
190. McClendon, "Voluntary Church in the Twenty-First Century," 155.
191. Geldbach, *Freikirchen*, 35.
192. Hauerwas, *In Good Company*, 71.
193. Bebbington, *Baptists through the Centuries*, 66–67.
194. Freeman, *Contesting Catholicity*, 278; Fiddes, *Tracks and Traces*, 42. See also Holmes, *Baptist Theology*, 101. David Bebbington notes this is one of John Smyth's

The church is a community where "each person stands in relation to each other a priori."[195] An individual Christian may choose to join a particular community, knowing that this community is comprised of those gathered by the call of Christ. Curtis Freeman and Paul Fiddes each argue that the Free Church commitment to the voluntary nature of church membership is tied to their covenantal ecclesiology and not to post-Enlightenment conceptions of individual autonomy. Fiddes avers that early Separatists viewed themselves as entering into a horizontal covenant with one another,[196] which was understood as a participation in the eternal covenant of grace.[197] Consequently, the church was not understood as a collection of autonomous monads gathering together, but as individuals gathered by grace and agreeing to walk together according to the appointment of Christ.[198] The gathering of Christ obtains logical primacy over the individual's free choice. As Freeman notes, the Free Church has traditionally understood itself as a gathered community of the new creation. Therefore, church is more than just a society of likeminded individuals. The Christian's freedom is realized in virtue of the fact that they stand together under Christ their king.[199] Furthermore, the believer's freedom is not rooted in the authority of their conscience, but in the gospel of Jesus Christ and the authorizing work of the Holy Spirit.[200]

Embodying God's Presence, Word, and Rule

Kelly Kapic has argued that theological anthropology must adopt both a protological and eschatological lens, focusing on the human as a creature

---

most distinctive contributions to Free Church ecclesiology as he located the polity of the local congregation in the immediate lordship of Christ. More specifically, Smyth articulated that Christ was present in the gathering of believers and that, insofar as they share in his kingly and priestly roles, no rule could be imposed on the congregation from without (Bebbington, *Baptists through the Centuries*, 33).

195. Spaemann, *Persons*, 38.
196. Fiddes, *Tracks and Traces*, 42.
197. Fiddes, *Tracks and Traces*, 39.
198. "The Orthodox Creed, 1678," in Lumpkin, *Baptist Confessions of Faith*, 318–19. Fiddes writes, "According to the covenant theology of the early Separatists, because the local church was under the direct rule of Christ all members shared in that ministry of 'kingship,' and so had the right to exercise judgment by watching over the spiritual health of each other and withdrawing from a church where the covenant was broken" (*Tracks and Traces*, 42).
199. Freeman, *Contesting Catholicity*, 72.
200. Freeman, *Contesting Catholicity*, 72.

as well as its telos of fellowship with God.²⁰¹ Yet ecclesio-anthropology adds a third component: insofar as the church exists in the present it also contributes significantly to our understanding of humanity *in via*. As the Free Church has consistently understood itself as a pilgrim or missionary community, this is especially pertinent.²⁰² Even now, as a community of yet-to-be-redeemed creatures, the church is given the particular task of mediating God's word and presence and embodying God's rule in the world through the agency of the Spirit. Paul hints at this in describing the effect of his preaching in 1 Thess 2:13. Regarding the content of Paul's preaching, Weima notes that Paul's combined use of παραλαμβάνω and δέχομαι in verse 13 refers to the traditional material of the gospel including ethical teachings, a confession regarding Jesus's death and resurrection, and Jesus's eucharistic sayings.²⁰³ This is reinforced by the previous verse where Paul recalls how he taught the church to correspond to the ways of the kingdom and the God who rules it (v. 12). As we saw in Ephesians 5, this injunction "to walk in a manner worthy of God" occurs frequently in Paul's letters and refers to "living in a way that corresponds to the character and demands of their God."²⁰⁴ Paul instructs the church to embody this eschatological reality of Christ's consummated reign over the created order.²⁰⁵ Here, we see that there is a degree of continuity between the church's present existence and the eschatological end to which they are oriented. In many ways, their lives are to reflect the to-be-consummated reign of God in Christ.

But perhaps of greater import for our purposes is how the Thessalonian church received Paul's preaching and what Paul's assessment of their reception implies. Returning to verse 13, Paul notes that the church received his preaching of the word of God as the word of God. He then affirms that their assessment of his preaching was accurate. On the one hand, this could communicate that the Thessalonian church recognized that Paul's preaching was of divine origin.²⁰⁶ On this reading the content of the gospel is not of

---

201. Kapic, "Anthropology," 170.

202. Cf. Littell, "Historical Free Church Defined," 59–60; McClendon, *Doctrine*, 2:343; Kärkkäinen, "Apostolicity of Free Churches," 483; Durnbaugh, *Believers' Church*, 33; Leer, "Which Future Church (Form)?," 45. It is worth noting other traditions may also affirm the "pilgrim nature" of the church. Yet this still remains a unique point of emphasis for the Free Church.

203. Weima, *1–2 Thessalonians*, 162.

204. Weima, *1–2 Thessalonians*, 157.

205. Shogren argues Paul's reference here to kingdom is eschatologically oriented. He writes, "The evidence points firmly toward the eschatological: 'glory' is a code for the future manifestation of God's reign" (Shogren, *1 and 2 Thessalonians*, 108).

206. Most commentators take τοῦ θεοῦ to be a genitive of origin or possession. See Wanamaker, *Epistles to the Thessalonians*, 111; Weima, *1–2 Thessalonians*, 163.

Paul's own making but comes from God himself. Such an exhortation could potentially encourage a persecuted church of the veracity of the gospel message.[207] But Balthasar would caution us against such a reductionistic account of divine revelation. For Balthasar, the Spirit transforms and elevates human preaching into an event of God's self-revelation.[208] If this is the case, God is speaking his word through Paul's preaching. Paul later describes this "same word" as active (ἐνεργεῖται) in the life of the church, leading to the church member's steadfastness and faithfullness (1:8), their desire to turn from idols and worship God (1:9b), and their willingness to show hospitality to Paul (1:8a). This would imply that the power and continued effects of the gospel are not simply the evidence of the gospel's truthfullness, but are the perlocutionary effect of the God who speaks through his prophets. This coheres well with Paul's description of the arrival of the word of God where he ties it to the power of the Holy Spirit (cf. 1 Thess 1:5). Paul's preaching ministry appears to be the means through which God communicates his word to his church.

Therefore, a fourth implication of our ecclesio-anthropology emerges: the instrumentality of the human person. If God has designed the church to be the means through which he manifests his presence, word, and rule in and to his creation, then it stands to reason that there is an instrumentality to the particulars that comprise the ecclesial community. While other traditions may affirm that God has assigned the church this task, the Free Church emphasizes every member's immediate participation in the ministry of Christ. This gives our understanding of instrumentality a unique shape. It is the task of every member to serve as the means through which God mediates his presence word and rule. This "state of life" is the telos and vocation of every member of the ecclesial community, not just those ordained in ministry, selected for the priesthood, or chosen to serve as representatives of the body.[209] Consequently, we can begin to develop an instrumental account of human personhood. While functional approaches to the *imago Dei* typically focus on how God has created human persons to act in particular ways within his world,[210] an instrumental account shifts the focus to divine action. The church, as a community of the new creation,

---

207. Wanamaker, *Epistles to the Thessalonians*, 111.

208. Balthasar, *TL III*, 328–29.

209. This statement does not deny it is possible to conceive of this "instrumentality" from other ecclesial locations. I am simply noting there will need to be conceptual nuances so as to allow for ontologically distinct roles between the priesthood and laity as well as different points of emphasis.

210. See Brueggemann, *Genesis*, 32–34; Westermann, *Genesis 1–11*, 1:137–59; Middleton, *Liberating Image*, 88–90.

shows us that God intends to manifest his presence in the world through his people. While Cortez argues that such an understanding can be attained through a pneumatological approach to the *imago*,[211] I would argue that the same conclusion can be reached and reinforced from Free Church ecclesiology. As a priesthood and prophethood, the local gathering becomes the means through which God manifests his presence and speaks his word. The gathering of believers does not force God to act and thereby compromise divine freedom. Rather, Christ promises to meet with his people and does so in virtue of fidelity to his promise. God has commanded and created the church to be about a certain *kind* of task, one that he initiates through them.

But if God presents himself to the church in a unique sense when they gather, it seems that I have left the Free Church vulnerable to the same critique I raised against Zizioulas regarding ethics and the Eucharist. In Zizioulas's schema, the human being experiences a punctiliar, ontological transformation during the celebration of the Eucharist. I was worried that in this framework once the liturgical rite has concluded the human creature no longer subsists in the Son-Father relationship and is no longer capable of exhibiting an eschatological ethic. Similarly, I have argued that the church serves as the embodiment of Christ's rule and that, in the gathering of two or three believers, Christ comes to meet them as Lord of his church to order their life. Is this not also a punctiliar experience? I think that we can avoid my critique of Zizioulas's eucharistic ethics for two reasons. First, I am not arguing that the members of the church are *ontologically* constituted in the event of encountering their Lord. For Zizioulas, recall that the members of the ecclesial community are switching between different modes of being: from biological hypostases to ecclesial hypostases to eucharistic hypostases. Contra Zizioulas, I am merely noting that the church's gathering informs the lives of its members. To return to our discussion of Ephesians 4, as the church gathers to "learn Christ" this necessarily involves an ethical transformation and the abandonment of false forms of worship. Second, just as Moses beheld the face of God and radiated his glory, so too as the human creature encounters the *autobasileia* they progressively radiate the kingdom, being changed from "one degree of glory to the next" (2 Cor 3:18).[212]

Yet while I have avoided the problem of ethics and the Eucharist, have we not also returned to Balthasar's portrayal of the human person as the instrumental means to God's own self-fulfillment? In the previous chapter, I

---

211. See Cortez, "Idols, Images, and a Spirit-ed Anthropology," 267–82.

212. Paul makes this point explicitly when elucidating the difference between the old and new covenants. Harris argues the usage of the phrase ἀπὸ δόξης εἰς δόξαν communicates a progressive transformation in the believer's life (Harris, *Second Epistle to the Corinthians*, 316–17).

noted that Tina Beattie, Agnetta Sutton, and Barabara Sain have voiced concerns vis-à-vis Balthasar's reliance on nuptial imagery. Beattie in particular was concerned that Balthasar does not give women their own subjectivity as they become the means for masculine (divine) self-fulfillment.[213] I extended this concern to Balthasar's view of all human rational subjects, both men and women. Since the Marian *disponsibilité* is the true form of humanity, in order to attain it human beings must hand themselves over completely to the will of God in an act of self-abnegation.[214] If my analysis is correct, this would mean that in Balthasar's schema every human creature lacks its own subjectivity. This is indeed troubling. Not only does it appear to require human creatures to divest themselves of aspects of their creatureliness, but, as I noted in chapter 5, Balthasar's male/female polarity also appears to make the creature necessary to God's self-actualization. If women are the means through which men find their fulfillment and all creatures must adopt this disposition in relationship to God, it seems that the creature becomes essential to God's self-fulfillment. How then can we construe the human creature as the means through which God manifests his presence in the world without falling into this same error? Two statements might be helpful in this regard. First, the human creature *is* essential to God's purposes in the world insofar as God has chosen to manifest his presence through them. For reasons that are beyond our knowing, God does not choose to appear to his creatures as a *disembodied* being but uses material realities to communicate his promise and presence. But this does not entail that God is self-actualizing when he commissions his creatures to accomplish his purposes. Second, it is not necessarily the case that God's commissioning of the human creature decreases their dignity unless we draw a strict link between certain kinds of human action and human dignity. Consider the following analogy. Imagine that a highly decorated golfer is training for the British Open, yet one thing she lacks: a caddy. While there are many qualified candidates, each with no shortage of experience, she instead chooses a young, inexperienced college student to carry her bags, clean her clubs, and assess the slopes and breaks of the course's greens. However, if the caddy is to be competent, he must learn from the golfer, watching the manner in which she approaches the green, the irons she prefers to use on the fairway, and the specific techniques for alleviating the hitch in her backswing. And if the college student is to be effective, in many ways his subjectivity is now placed in service of and ordered to the subjectivity of the golfer. Yet the invitation to serve as a caddy does not degrade the college student's worth. In fact, it

---

213. Beattie, *New Catholic Feminism*, 108.
214. Sutton, "Complementarity and Symbolism of the Two Sexes," 423.

could be argued that the offer from the master golfer as well as the resources she provides *confers* greater dignity upon the college student.

While recognizing the limits of this analogy, the church's status as a community of witnesses to the redemption wrought in Christ does not necessitate the abnegation of its members' subjectivity. It is the proper reorientation of their subjectivity in service of God. But does this denigrate the dignity of the creature? This would only seem to be the case if the creature's dignity is tied to the autonomy of their subjectivity. Perhaps one would respond to my proposal by arguing that every creature has some sense of autonomy and that it is this freedom that grants the creature its dignity. However, as Hans Schwartz has convincingly demonstrated, this would be to misconstrue the very nature of human freedom.[215] Humanity is only free within certain contexts. Moreover, as I have already argued, human dignity is not grounded in human autonomy, but is grounded in humanity's status as an image bearer of God.

Furthermore, this approach to anthropology reinforces a commitment to the goodness of human embodiment and creatureliness, for it is precisely as embodied creatures that humans are able to participate in the *munus triplex* and thereby serve as the means through which God mediates his presence in and to the world. This responds to a concern I raised in the previous chapter that Zizioulas, Balthasar, and Hauerwas each tended to blur the distinction between Creator and creature, leading to a devaluing of human creatureliness. But I would submit that a disembodied person cannot truly mediate God's blessings as priest by the agency of the Spirit, God's word as prophet, nor can they embody God's rule as king in and to the created world. It is important to note that David and Hezekiah both pray for God's deliverance from death, emphasizing the inability of the dead to worship and serve God rightly in the land (cf. Ps 30:8–10; Isa 38:18–19).[216] John Oswalt argues that this is a consistent theme throughout the Old Testament.[217] This is particularly relevant given the fact that both David and Hezekiah are kings, tasked with the embodiment of God's rule.[218] A similar pattern

---

215. Schwarz, *Human Being*, 135.

216. Brueggemann argues these types of prayer indicate God has warded off death "because the dead do not thank or praise or hope or witness to God's faithfullness" (Brueggemann, *Isaiah*, 1:307).

217. Oswalt notes other passages such as Job 10:21–22; Psalm 6:6; 30:30; and 115:17. Furthermore, he notes the righteous dead and unrighteous dead are depicted in a similar light, neither of which includes praising God (Oswalt, *Book of Isaiah*, 1:687–88).

218. Goldingay argues that in Israel "the king [had] a broader responsibility before God for honest dealings in the community. . . . He can act to punish evil and encourage good or to put down faithful people and encourage faithlessness" (Goldingay, *Israel's Life*, 3:736). In other words, the king served as a sort of delegated authority and was

GATHERED UNDER THE RULE OF CHRIST 199

holds true for Elijah,[219] Paul (cf. Phil 1:23-25), and Peter (cf. 2 Pet 1:13-14). Each figure views their ministry as coming to a close upon their death and Peter explicitly connects this to the "putting off of [his] body" (2 Pet 1:14). Remaining "in the flesh" is essential for the ministry God desires to enact through his creatures (Phil 1:24). Physical death, at minimum, separates the individual from the local, ecclesial community and makes them unable to serve in that capacity any longer. Disembodiment leaves the human subject unable to fully bear witness, mediate access, or discern and embody the rule of Christ with that community. That particular ministerial function has been suspended. Knowing, as I have already articulated, that when believers are "re-embodied" in the kingdom's consummation they will continue to serve as prophets, priests, and kings, I would argue that there is something about disembodiment that prevents the individual from serving in these functions.[220]

---

responsible for ensuring the law of God was clearly communicated to his people. "It is the king who fights; they are the awesome deeds of his right hand. But God works with him and through him. His victories reflect the fact that he sits on God's throne, ruling Israel on God's behalf and destined to rule the world on God's behalf" (Goldingay, *Israel's Life*, 3:737).

219. Nicholas Lunn convincingly notes both Elisha and Elijah are closely connected with divine presence, as there are both conceptual and linguistic parallels between their two ministries that are closely associated with the temple and right worship of Yahweh. He avers that both figures are linguistically identified with the concept of standing before God, address God in the first-person singular contra the other prophets, call down fire from heaven in a manner evocative of the Sinai events, and are uniquely related to the divine vehicle of theophanic manifestation: chariots of fire (Lunn, "Prophetic Representations of the Divine Presence," 53–55). Furthermore, Lunn notes both figures receive obeisance and make miraculous crossings of the Jordan (Lunn, "Prophetic Representations of the Divine Presence," 57). Lunn argues, given the separation of the people from the temple in the Northern Kingdom, Elijah and Elisha almost serve in a surrogate role, functioning as a representation of divine presence (Lunn, "Prophetic Representations of the Divine Presence," 61). If Lunn is right, then a strong connection is being made between the two prophets and the communication of divine presence. Yet, in the death of both, a transition is noted: neither Elijah nor Elisha will serve in this capacity any longer. The phrase "my father, my father! The chariots of Israel and its horsemen!" is exclaimed by Elisha as Elijah departs in 2 Kings 2:9 and is later echoed by King Joash upon the death of Elisha. At minimum, it connotes a continuity between the ministries of Elijah and Elisha, one which suggests Elijah's ministry is passed on to Elisha. This suggestion is bolstered by how 2 Kings portrays Elisha's ministry immediately after Elijah's departure. For our purposes, this is important insofar as it suggests the prophetic ministries of both Elijah and Elisha stand in continuity with one another and come to a close at their respective deaths.

220. This does not necessitate a physicalist or materialist interpretation of the human person, but simply affirms God presents himself to the world in and through material realities.

But how does the human creature's participation in the *munus triplex* change in the intermediate state? If these particular ministerial functions are tied to embodiment as I have argued, then we cannot perform them adequately when we are disembodied. Priesthood involves the task of mediating access to God to other embodied, human creatures through the agency of the Spirit. But an essential element of the priestly task also involves the vocation of mediating the relationship between God and the rest of creation. Additionally, kingship seems to require ruling in a particular place over other created things. Revelation 5 itself seems to make this clear as the work of Christ results in making human agents reign "on the earth" (Rev 5:10). Yet it is precisely our bodies that tether us to this earth. Of the three ministries, it seems that only mediating God's word could be construed as a disembodied ministry. But even here it seems that the task of bearing witness is tethered to embodiment. I have argued that humanity's prophetic vocation of bearing witness is tied to both speech *and* action in God's world, the latter of which seems to require a body. While disembodied human creatures still exist in community and in relationship with one another, a disembodied being does not exist in the right kind of relationship with the created world. Therefore, it cannot mediate God's presence, word, and rule on the earth to God's creatures. Furthermore, if human beings were created for these purposes and we cannot fulfill them, it seems that in the intermediate state as disembodied persons we are *less* than what we were created to be. While this coheres with the church's traditional commitment to the bodily resurrection of believers, it also provides insight into how embodiment is a good thing. The human person can only fully achieve the end to which God has oriented them as a resurrected, embodied being.

Conclusion

In this chapter, I have ventured to put forth a Free Church ecclesio-anthropology that is rooted in the immediate lordship of Christ. In so doing, I argued that the church participates in a derivative form of Christ's *munus triplex* in virtue of the Spirit's work in the new covenant. As prophets and priests, the church serves as the means through which God manifests his word and presence to the created world. As kings, the church embodies the rule of Christ insofar as they gather to discern his will and order their lives accordingly.

How then does this inform our account of anthropology? In what way does Free Church ecclesiology robustly contribute to our understanding of humanity? I noted four points of emphasis in particular: a Spirit-ed account of identity, a Christotelic orientation, an intrinsically interdependent and communal nature, and an uniquely embodied vocation wherein human beings serve as the means through which God manifests his presence and rule. The Spirit's work provides the framework for understanding a coherent sense of human identity as he re-interprets our stories, tethers our conception of the good life to eternal fellowship with God, and enables us to act in accordance with that eschatological vision in the present. The Christotelic orientation of humanity demonstrates how conformity to Christ involves being proleptically formed as prophets, priests, and kings who mediate God's word and presence to his creatures through the agency of the Spirit. Additionally, humanity is thoroughly interdependent and communal. Such an observation is not dependent upon a social understanding of the Trinity or of the *imago Dei*. Rather, it is derived from the observation that maturation into Christlikeness occurs in a community of mutually *in*-forming members that strive to attain our true telos in Christ. Next, we identified that there is an instrumentality to the human person as they serve as the means through which God manifests his presence in and to the created world. Finally, I argued that Free Church ecclesio-anthropology reinforces a commitment to the goodness of human bodily existence, as it is only embodied humans who are privileged to serve in such a capacity.

John Zizioulas, Hans Urs von Balthasar, and Stanley Hauerwas each presented us with compelling portrayals of the ecclesio-anthropology, demonstrating how the doctrine of the church might play a constitutive role in our understanding of the human creature. In this chapter I have used insights from their work to argue that the church is a community of those gathered by the Spirit. Authorized by the Son who rules them as their Lord, its members are placed on the road to eternal fellowship with God. As a prophetic, priestly, and kingly community, it is the means through which God mediates his word and the blessings of the new covenant as they embody the rule of God in Christ. As we will see in the following chapter, there are clear limitations to ecclesio-anthropology. Yet for now, suffice it to say that Christ is present in the gathering of his people—a people who gather to hear his will, embody his wisdom, and proclaim his light to a world in darkness (cf. Eph 5:7–10).

7

Conclusion

Patrick Franklin writes, "Our understanding of community is intimately linked with our understanding of what it means to be human."[1] Franklin makes this statement as he ventures to demonstrate how the relational, rational, and eschatological characteristics of human beings ground our understanding of the nature and identity of the church. While not denying the fact that anthropology may in fact inform ecclesiology, I have argued ecclesiology robustly shapes and makes unique contributions to our understanding of anthropology. This is particularly true for the Free Church where commitments to voluntary adult membership, freedom from state and provincial governance, congregationalist forms of polity, and an emphasis on the priesthood of all believers contain clear anthropological implications. Viewing itself as a "pilgrim people," the Free Church is a community *in via*—that is, it is a community of those gathered under their Lord and King as he orders their lives and worship, while leading them to a place of eschatological rest. To a certain extent, the articulation of these implications is the goal of ecclesio-anthropology. Put positively, ecclesio-anthropology seeks to discern how ecclesiological claims are germane to anthropological concerns. But while ecclesiology and anthropology may be dialogically related loci, my project has involved a stronger aim: to demonstrate how Free Church ecclesiology robustly informs and uniquely contributes to our understanding of anthropology. In this final section, I will begin with

1. Franklin, *Being Human, Being Church*, 51.

a review of the work covered thus far. Next, I will examine some of the key ways ecclesio-anthropology contributes to our understanding of humanity, as well as some of the ways it is limited. Finally, I will return to my definition of ecclesio-anthropology from the introduction and refine it in light of some conclusions that have been reached in the preceding work.

SUMMARIZING THE WORK THUS FAR

In the previous chapters, I have attempted to present three clear examples of ecclesio-anthropology. Interacting with John Zizioulas, Hans Urs von Balthasar, and Stanley Hauerwas, I demonstrated that ecclesiology plays a constitutive role in each figure's understanding of the human person. For Zizioulas, the church is a eucharistic community, subsisting in the Son-Father relationship. Its mission is to offer the gift of communion to the world, bringing all of creation into eucharistic fellowship with God. The practice of baptism and the celebration of the Eucharist are viewed in ontological terms—that is, they are ontologically and existentially constitutive of human persons. In baptism, the individual undergoes an ontological transformation, changing from a biological to an ecclesial hypostasis. However, in many ways, baptism prepares the way for the Eucharist. During the celebration of the Eucharist, the Spirit realizes the *eschaton* in the present, allowing the members of the church to temporarily experience a foretaste of *theosis* and fulfill their ecstatic vocation of referring creation back to God. *Theosis*, then, emerges as the true *telos* to which this community is oriented. Consequently, I argued that Zizioulas's ecclesio-anthropology articulates an account of human personhood that is ontologically constituted through the church's liturgy and experienced in a punctiliar fashion. It is also oriented toward theotic and ecstatic communion with God.

For Balthasar, the church perpetuates the eucharistic mission of Christ for the sake of the world's redemption. Typified by Mary's *disponsibilité*, the church is grounded in the kenotic descent of Christ. The church's mission, in many ways, is to perpetuate *his* mission—that is, Christ's act of self-surrender and his readiness to suffer for the sake of the world. The sacramental and liturgical practices of the church are the means through which the members of the ecclesial community receive the mission of Christ and are progressively formed as theological persons. In baptism, the individual receives their ecclesial identity and is given a particular role in the mission Christ has given to his Church. Through the reception of the Eucharist, ecclesial members are continually formed by the mission of Christ as they find their identity in their divinely assigned role. Finally, the church's *telos* involves a participation in the theotic life of God. For Balthasar, God creates space within his own life for the creature, ensuring their particularity even as they surrender themselves in service to his will. I then identified five characteristics of Balthasar's ecclesio-anthropology: personhood is ecclesially received, sacramentally formed, and vocationally embodied, culminating in kenotic love and receptivity to the divine.

According to Hauerwas, the church is grounded in the story of Jesus. The narrative of God's peaceful reign provides the church with its form, marking it as a distinct political institution that is organized around the rule of God. The mission of the church is primarily one of bearing witness to the kingdom of God through the ecclesial community's life together. The practices of the church, ranging from the celebration of the Eucharist to forgiveness and marriage, carry a twofold purpose. On the one hand, these practices merely are what it means to live faithfully to the Christian story. Yet on the other hand, these practices are formative. As the Christian community embodies the story of Jesus in concrete, ecclesial practices, its members are formed to be a people who possess a character that bears witness to the inauguration of the kingdom of God in Christ. While Hauerwas does not equate the church with the kingdom, he repeatedly argues that the church is a community whose outlook is reoriented by the revelation of God's peaceful, eschatological reign. Hauerwas's ecclesio-anthropology contains four particular distinctives: the narrative shape of the self, the political nature of human action, the eschatological orientation of human identity, and the peaceable nature of humanity's telos as *homo pacem*.

In the next chapter, I placed these three theologians in dialogue with one another in order to learn how to go about the process of *doing* ecclesio-anthropology. As I articulated in the introduction, ecclesio-anthropology seeks to understand how the nature, mission, liturgical practices, and telos of the church inform our account of humanity. Over the course of this dialogue, four helpful theses emerged that helped guide the project as I moved forward. Regarding the nature of the church, I learned that the church must be understood as a contingent community, constituted by God's acts in history. Yet the church's divine grounding cannot blur the distinction between the church's members and the God who constitutes it. Mission, then, provides the larger interpretive key for understanding the trajectory of the church and its life, involving the task of bearing witness to God's revelation in Christ and rightly relating to the world as God's redeemed creatures through the work of the Spirit. Additionally, I saw that human creatures are rightly and progressively formed through their covenantal participation in the Spirit-ed, liturgical action of the church so as to become the type of people ready for eternal fellowship with God. Finally, regarding the church's telos, I observed that the church's proleptic nature, subsisting in the time between the kingdom's inauguration and consummation, must inform our understanding of anthropology while maintaining the importance of the resurrection of the body as essential to human fulfillment and formation. These four theses serve as the guardrails or guiding principles that emerged from interacting with my interlocutors and are to be used to shape ecclesio-anthropology on a general level.

However, the specific goal of my project was to develop a Free Church ecclesio-anthropology. This was the task of the sixth chapter. First, I attempted to articulate a Free Church ecclesiology that was grounded in the church's derivative participation in Christ's *munus triplex*. There, I engaged Ephesians 4–5 and argued that the lordship of Christ provides the local church with its form, as the church gathers to hear the Lord's voice, grow in maturity together, and learn to live in ways that rightly reflect the confession that Jesus Christ is Lord. The church's mission involves a derivative participation in Christ's threefold office. The liturgical practices of baptism, the Eucharist, and communal discernment are the primary means through which the church bears witness as prophets, mediates access to God through the agency of the Spirit as priests, and discerns and embodies his rule as kings. From there, I articulated four distinctives of Free Church ecclesio-anthropology: a Spirit-ed account of identity, a Christotelic orientation, an intrinsically interdependent and communal nature, and a uniquely embodied vocation wherein human beings serve as the means through which God manifests his presence and rule in the world.

RETURNING TO THE QUESTION

At the beginning of this project I asked two questions: How do the ecclesio-anthropologies of John Zizioulas, Hans Urs von Balthasar, and Stanley Hauerwas assist in the development of a Free Church ecclesio-anthropology? And how *should* ecclesiology inform anthropology? I have already answered the first question, showing that these figures present vibrant examples of how to go about the process of *doing* ecclesio-anthropology. Additionally, after interacting with the ecclesio-anthropologies of these three figures in my fifth chapter, I was placed in a better position to construct a Free Church ecclesio-anthropology. These three figures raise necessary questions that must be addressed, concerns that must be navigated, and tensions that must be maintained. In so doing, Zizioulas, Hauerwas, and Balthasar provided necessary resources for understanding how a Free Church ecclesiology should, for example, construe the relationship between God and his church as well as the consequences that arise from certain decisions.

It is now time to move toward answering the second question: How *should* ecclesiology inform anthropology? I will begin by articulating some of the key contributions that ecclesio-anthropology provides to the study of humanity before moving on to discuss some of its limitations. Here, I will argue that Free Church ecclesio-anthropology helpfully provides insight into questions involving the nature of liturgical action, the goodness of human embodiment, and human teleology. However, the effective utilization of ecclesio-anthropology is limited by the need to supplement it with other approaches to theological anthropology and my use of the term to exclusively focus on the "ideal" church.

The Key Contributions of Free Church Ecclesio-Anthropology

Human Action and Christian Liturgy

While the Free Church firmly believes that its gathered members are disciples who have come to know and serve their Lord, the Free Church has not been immune to some the historical failures and shortcomings that have seemed to mark the church since its inception. Baptism has been forced upon some while denied to others. The Lord's Table is divided across traditions and often segregated across demographics. The Lord's will has been sought while some members of the community are actively excluded or silenced. Furthermore, the history of the Free Church is one marked by persecution. As Siegrist makes clear, fratricide is a crime against the body of which the entire body is guilty and of which the entire body must grieve. He writes, "We must address the question stretched through time, asking not just how *a* community of Jesus' followers might constitute God's ongoing presence but how *this* community—the Christian community as Anabaptists have known it—can be said to do the same."[2] How can such communities claim to rightly form their members with such a stained history? Any approach to the human person that begins with ecclesiology cannot but help to recognize the many ways in which Christian practices have been practiced insufficiently or destructively, often resulting in communal *de*formation.

Barth's approach to liturgical action seems to avoid this problem altogether. This is perhaps most clearly illustrated in Barth's view of baptism. Barth disentangles the concepts of Spirit baptism and water baptism. For Barth, Spirit baptism is described as an act that is an "effective, causative,

---

2. Siegrist, *Participating Witness*, 109, italics his.

even creative action on man and in man. It is, indeed, divinely effective, divinely causative, divinely creative."[3] While Spirit baptism can be viewed in a sacramental sense, water baptism is understood as a truly human act of obedience and hope.[4] For Barth, "The crux of a correct answer to the question of the meaning of baptism lies in a strict correlation and a no less strict distinction between the human action as such and the divine action from which it springs, on whose basis it is possible, and towards which it moves."[5] For Barth, water baptism is a response to God's summons, a prayer offered in reply to God's declaration in Christ.[6] Consequently, water baptism and the Lord's Supper are acts of Christian witness.[7] If Barth is right, then deficient or malicious practices might be construed as *improper* responses to divine grace or malformed prayers. Deficient practices, then, are acts that bear witness to divine revelation improperly or that fail to bear witness altogether. But since water baptism does not shape the human person per se and only asks God to do so,[8] it does not result in the human creature's formation or deformation.

However, in the course of the past few chapters I have sought to articulate a description of liturgical practices that emphasizes their Spirit-ed nature even as these practices are performed by human creatures. This seems to go against Barth's desire to separate divine and human action.[9] As Cross notes, "Fundamental to Barth's separation of Spirit- and water-baptism is his belief that no action can be at the same time both divine *and* human, but this has been rightly criticized on both theological and exegetical grounds."[10] While it is beyond the scope of this present project to exhaustively explain the relationship between divine and human action, it seems that God does choose to proclaim his message of reconciliation *through* his people, even in the face of their limitations and failures.[11] And in so doing, the Spirit is some-

3. Barth, *CD* IV/4, 34.
4. Barth, *CD* IV/4, 134.
5. Barth, *CD* IV/4, 34.
6. Barth, *CD* IV/4, 210–11. See Cocksworth, "Revisiting Karl Barth's Doctrine of Baptism," 255–72.
7. Barth, *CD* IV/4, 147. See Hunsinger, "Karl Barth on the Lord's Supper," 152.
8. Barth, *CD* IV/4, 212. For a larger treatments of Barth's view of baptism, see Hunsinger, "Baptism and the Soteriology of Forgiveness"; Bok, "Barth on Baptism,"135–51; Stout, *Fellowship of Baptism*, 15–48; McMaken, "Definitive, Defective or Deft?," 89–114.
9. John Webster sees in Barth a desire to maintain the Chalcedonian formula when discussing divine and human action, keeping the two unconfused. See Webster, *Barth's Ethics of Reconciliation*, 170–72.
10. Cross, *Recovering the Evangelical Sacrament*, 168, italics his.
11. See Colwell, *Promise and Presence*, 118.

how capable of rightly forming the members of the ecclesial community as they gather together, hear the proclamation of God's word, partake of the elements of the Lord's Supper, and welcome new initiates through baptism. This ought not minimize the way in which performing Christian practices poorly is destructive to the purposes for which God has created us and is fundamentally destructive to the communities in which we exist. However, God's freedom is not bound by the motives or prejudices of his creatures. The Spirit is still capable of confronting the church with the revelation of God in Christ even as God's people live in a manner that does violence to the very gospel they preach.

The Goodness of Human Embodiment

As I have mentioned in the previous chapter, the locus classicus for Free Church is Matthew 18:20. There, Christ promises to come and dwell with those "two or three" believers who gather for the purpose of submitting to his reign. Volf comments on this passage: "According to this text, Christ's presence is promised not to the believing individual directly, but rather to the entire congregation, and only through the latter to the individual. This is why no one can come to faith alone and no one can live in faith alone."[12] If it is in the gathering of two or three believers that Christ is present, then the gathering of embodied believers seems to be a prerequisite for the human creature's ability to participate in the *munus triplex*. Human embodiment, then, becomes necessary for our enjoyment of the kind of existence God has intended for us and the fulfillment of God's purposes for us. It seems, then, that a Free Church ecclesio-anthropology necessarily affirms and emphasizes the goodness of human bodies. There is something about the gathering of embodied beings in a particular space that is necessary for properly performing the church's practices and participating in the threefold office of Christ. Baptism, the celebration of the Lord's Supper, and communal discernment are practices that occur among individuals-in-community. Furthermore, they are practices practiced by *embodied* individuals-in-community. If substance dualism can express a proclivity to view embodied existence as unessential to the creature's life and flourishing, explicitly developing anthropology within the context of ecclesiology may help temper that inclination.

For Ola Sigurdson, the church's life together conditions the way we experience and exist in the world. According to Sigurdson, the church's life together transforms our bodily experience of the world, training us in

12. Volf, *After Our Likeness*, 162.

certain practices and realizing our participation in the Christian drama.[13] While my goal here is certainly not to create a theology of the body per se and my task is not phenomenological in focus, I do believe that Free Church ecclesio-anthropology in particular has the potential to focus on human creatures' life together as embodied beings. In the rhythms of gathering and dispersing, the members of the church are formed and re-formed in accordance with the standard of Christ (cf. Eph 4:16). This then challenges us to recognize the goodness of human bodies since it is only in their *embodied life together* that human creatures are able to live, function, and imagine rightly. Again, it is not in the gathering of two or three disembodied spirits that Christ promises to come and dwell. Rather, he promises to come and meet his embodied, human creatures as they gather in his name.

Teleology, Ecclesiology, and the Human Person

Additionally, I believe that ecclesio-anthropology provides a way of affirming a teleological account of the human creature that is not dependent upon natural theology. Each of my interlocutors, regardless of their philosophical commitments, has articulated a teleological understanding of the church and, by extension, those who comprise it. Zizioulas, despite his reticence to adopt philosophical commitments vis-à-vis his understanding of the church, argued that the church's telos is *theosis*—that is, ecstatic participation in the life of God. Consequently, its members possess an ecstatic orientation and a theotic destiny. Similarly, both Hauerwas and Balthasar, despite their differing philosophical starting points, each view the church as a community destined for a particular end. For Hauerwas, this end is the realization of the peaceable kingdom where God and his people dwell together in harmony. While Hauerwas is reluctant to explicate the details of what our eschatological life with God entails, it is this knowledge of the Christian story's *end* that enables human creatures to live peaceably in the present. For Balthasar, after the Son has been sent forth into the world, he returns and creates space within God's own life for the creature. The church lives and acts in light of this eschatological promise of fellowship with God. In each case, the church itself is understood on teleological terms. Since the doctrine of the church informs our understanding of the human creatures that comprise it, the church's teleological nature provides unique insight into how teleology shapes our understanding of the human person.

Since the Free Church has historically understood itself as a "pilgrim church," teleology also shapes its ecclesio-anthropology. The church is a

13. Sigurdson, *Heavenly Bodies*, 417.

community headed in a particular direction and the Scriptures make it clear that God elects the church for a specific end. Ephesians emphasizes that the body of Christ was elected for holiness (1:4) and will stand before its Savior purified and spotless (5:26) to dwell with him on the earth. Regardless of whether election is understood as corporate or individual, the church is a community with a definite destiny: holiness. If this is the case—that is, if the church itself is teleological—then it stands to reason that those who comprise it are as well. Unfortunately, this does little to mitigate questions involving the relationship between nature and grace, and space does not permit me to engage in a robust discussion at the present moment. However, if the church is teleological, it seems that we can begin by questioning how human creatures achieve or reach their telos and work backward from there. In other words, does the human person *become* teleologically oriented through its inclusion into the church? Or does inclusion into the ecclesial community reorient one's telos? This seems to return to our question of the nature of liturgical action from the previous chapter. While I will not reiterate those developments here, it seems that ecclesio-anthropology opens up room to explore the human creature's teleological nature.

The Limits of Ecclesio-Anthropology

However, while ecclesio-anthropology makes some key contributions to our investigation into the nature of the human person, I believe that there are limits to the extent that ecclesiology can adequately inform theological anthropology. First, I believe that Free Church ecclesio-anthropology must be supplemented by other approaches to theological anthropology due to its emphasis on the Spirit's work in establishing identity and the Christotelic orientation to humanity. Second, viewing the church in abstraction from concrete settings can potentially result in an idealized ecclesiology and, by extension, an unrealistic account of the human person.

Supplementing Ecclesio-Anthropology

First, ecclesio-anthropology may need to be supplemented by, for example, christological or pneumatological approaches to theological anthropology. In my introduction, I asked if ecclesio-anthropology was exclusive or if other approaches to theological anthropology might be legitimate. In light of the above study, it seems that we must acknowledge that ecclesio-anthropology is not the dogmatic location of theological anthropology nor is it to be viewed over against a christological, pneumatological, or Trinitarian approach to understanding humanity. This sentiment seems to be reinforced by the fact that Free Church ecclesio-anthropology is Christotelic in orientation. The Scriptures appear to affirm this destiny. Although "what we will be has not yet appeared," the Christian community believes and confesses "that when he appears we shall be like him, because we shall see him as he is" (1 John 3:2). Therefore, if the liturgical practices of the Christian community are intended to form the Christian community to live and flourish in a particular kind of way that accords with the perfect revelation of God in Christ, it seems that we must begin to explore how Jesus Christ reveals humanity and calibrate our actions accordingly. While we are currently being formed through our worship and re-oriented in the Spirit, our telos is to be like Christ and all that this entails. Earlier in the introduction, I asked how the liturgical practices of the church elucidate the nature of humanity. In response, I have argued that the Spirit-ed liturgical practices of the church form us toward the end of existing, relating, loving, and acting in a manner that corresponds to Christ. In fact, I have claimed that this is what it means to be human in the fullest sense. Yet this answer seems to only raise another question: What does the perfect humanity revealed in Christ "look" like? It is here that christological approaches to theological anthropology provide what might be a necessary supplement to ecclesio-anthropology.

A similar sentiment may be true for "Third Article" theological anthropology—that is, an approach to theological anthropology that begins with the Spirit. As I have outlined above, a Free Church emphasis on regenerate church membership seems to require that the Holy Spirit plays a constitutive role in establishing human identity. Yet the questions of if or how this relates to the *imago Dei* as well as the Spirit's presence and work in human creatures outside of the church remain unanswered. While there may be a need to maintain a degree of apophaticism when discussing the relationship between human action and the Spirit, my project has left plenty of room to explore how the Spirit contributes to our understanding of the human creature per se.

Relatedly, we must be cautious when attempting to articulate which elements emerge distinctly from ecclesiology per se, especially when considering the strong overlap that often exists in some understandings of the relationship between Christology and ecclesiology. There are strong christological elements in both Hauerwas's and Zizioulas's theological anthropologies while both Christology and Mariology play a prominent role in Balthasar's conceptualization of the human creature. Furthermore, Balthasar appeals to Buber's dialogical philosophy and Hauerwas, at times, appropriates MacIntyre's articulation of the narrative shape of particular communities and Wittgenstein's philosophy of language. This requires us to maintain a level of caution as differences in ecclesiology may reflect disagreements over philosophical or hermeneutical approaches. However, this does not mean that the ecclesio-anthropologies presented above are necessarily incompatible. Yes, for example, Zizioulas's punctiliar account of human personhood does seem incongruous with Balthasar's and Hauerwas's view of human identity and formation. Yet, there may be common *questions* and *concerns* that all three figures are asking and addressing. And insofar as Christology, Mariology, ecclesiology, and anthropology remain distinct loci of theological investigation, there remains a place to examine the manner in which they interrelate.

Ecclesio-Anthropology and Ecclesiological Ethnography

Additionally, the majority of my interaction with ecclesiology has focused on the "ideal" church to the neglect of how such ecclesiological commitments manifest themselves in concrete, local congregations. My interlocutors come from traditions that possess liturgical forms that tend to be relatively more static than those of the Free Church. Consequently, Zizioulas can, in theory, reflect on the epiclesis of Greek Orthodox eucharistic practice with the knowledge that this is a fairly ubiquitous practice among churches of his tradition. But this can hardly be a viable option when examining Free Churches in light of their commitment to the local church's freedom in regard to its liturgical life. Furthermore, Nicholas Healy warns that approaches to ecclesiology that focus on the church in abstraction fail to properly take into account the church's sinfulness and failures.[14] Healy argues that ethnographic research ought to serve as a helpful supplement to ecclesiological inquiry and calls for the development of an ecclesiological ethnography that gives attention to how the practices and beliefs of concrete congregations and the worldwide church change over time.[15] "Ecclesiological ethnography within a theo-dramatic horizon must be critical, carefully assessing our ecclesial culture and the cultural patterns of other traditions of inquiry in an effort to render the church's witness and discipleship more truthful."[16] Healy is reluctant to supplement theological inquiry with sociology due to some of the agnostic or atheistic philosophical commitments this may entail.[17] However, Healy is hopeful that ecclesiological ethnography may prove

---

14. Healy, *Church, World, and the Christian Life*, 9.
15. Healy, *Church, World, and the Christian Life*, 180.
16. Healy, *Church, World, and the Christian Life*, 174.
17. Healy, *Church, World, and the Christian Life*, 166–67.

vital in providing self-critical analysis of church forms and practices.[18] If Healy is right, it seems that ecclesiology must be supplemented with the critical examination of concrete congregations. However, as is evident from the above chapters, this project has not engaged in ethnographic inquiry. If there is a disconnect between the "ideal" and "concrete" manifestations of Free Churches, this project is not positioned to adequately address or articulate it.[19] Additionally, incorporating ethnographic research could add an important element in analyzing the worship and liturgical practices of particular congregations. What songs are sung? How is the Lord's Supper practiced? How does the congregation respond or participate in the baptism of initiates? How does the community seek to discern the will of its Lord and what does this entail?

James Smith gives an example of what ethnographic ecclesiology may involve in his discussion of liturgical anthropology. In *Desiring the Kingdom*, Smith gives a liturgical analysis of a shopping mall in order to demonstrate how the event of going to the mall is intended to shape our loves and perceptions of the good life, ultimately forming us in certain kinds of ways.[20] Smith takes time to describe a trip to the mall as a religious event in order to elucidate the relationship between ritual practice and the formation of desires. He writes, "The pedagogy of the mall does not primarily take hold of the head, so to speak; it aims for the heart, for our guts, our *kardia*."[21] While in many ways Smith's description is an imaginative exercise and not ethnography qua ethnography, Smith's approach could prove fruitful in examining the ways that ecclesial communities live together. For example, an examination of the ways that services are ordered, the prominence given to certain elements of liturgy, the choice of various songs, and the words that are spoken in service all may prove vital in understanding the role of how the church imagines itself. This may prove to be particularly important for Free Churches where the freedom of conscience and freedom of liturgy play such a prominent role.

Sarah Coakley's project, *God, Sexuality, and the Self*, involves a similar undertaking, albeit from a more sociological perspective. Coakley's work seeks to demonstrates how "the questions of right contemplation of God, right speech about God, and right ordering of desire all hang together."[22]

18. Healy, *Church, World, and the Christian Life*, 184.

19. James Smith makes a similar call for ecclesiological ethnography, arguing it allows us to account for the empirical witness of the church and the manner in which it forms its parishioners. See. Smith, *Awaiting the King*, 188–92.

20. Smith, *Desiring the Kingdom*, 19–27.

21. Smith, *Desiring the Kingdom*, 24.

22. Coakley, *God, Sexuality, and the Self*, 2.

In the center of her project, Coakley examines the Trinitarian beliefs, understandings of gender, and approach to erotic desire in two concrete gatherings of Christians: an Anglican parish and a smaller fellowship group. Borrowing sociological insights from Ernst Troeltsch's discussion of sectarian typology, Coakley was able to identify parallels between charismatic and contemplative modes of "church."[23] In Coakley's estimation, there was a greater propensity in sectarian "forms of social organization" to "go along with a non-trinitarian pneumatology," expecting movements of the Spirit to correspond with "*particular* ecstatic manifestations and 'high' feeling states."[24] Coakley's sociological fieldwork is then later brought into the larger dialogue of her work in order to help show the primacy of place that must be given to contemplation and the Spirit in Trinitarian theology.[25]

I am not necessarily endorsing either of these two projects in toto. Furthermore, I understand the limitations of integrative approaches to theological inquiry. Still, Smith's and Coakley's projects serve as examples of fruitful work that lies ahead in our investigation into how the doctrine of the church informs our understanding of humanity. Additionally, they both highlight the limitations of my own project and the fruitful space that remains for the examination of particular human communities and their liturgical practices. This also represents an opportunity for future research.

Reassessing Our Definition of Ecclesio-Anthropology

In the introduction, I presented a minimal definition of ecclesio-anthropology. There, I argued that an ecclesio-anthropology seeks to articulate how the nature, mission, practices, and telos of the church robustly inform our understanding of the human creature. This description seeks to explore how each of these important aspects of ecclesiology distinctly contributes to our investigation into the human creature. To a large degree, my three interlocutors seem to confirm this minimal definition. Each figure articulated key ways in which ecclesiology helps us to understand both who the human creature *is* and also who they will *become*.

However, on second glance, it appears that more must be said beyond this minimal definition. For example, in chapter 5 we saw that Christian liturgy is not merely a description of what Christians do together, but is intended to form Christians and their communities rightly through the empowering work of the Spirit. Additionally, each of my interlocutors seemed

---

23. Coakley, *God, Sexuality, and the Self*, 175.
24. Coakley, *God, Sexuality, and the Self*, 181, italics hers.
25. Coakley, *God, Sexuality, and the Self*, 340–44.

to describe the church as essential to understanding humanity's vocation. For Zizioulas and Balthasar, human creatures were created to serve as either priests (Zizioulas) or theological persons (Balthasar) who bring creation back into fellowship with God. For Hauerwas, the rightly formed human exists in a community of subversive witnesses whose peaceable life together provides the world with a foretaste of the kingdom. In each case, participation in the church's vocation provides *vital* insight into what it means for human creatures to live or behave rightly with respect to creation and other human creatures. Moreover, if the church is a community of the new creation inaugurated in Jesus, it provides a foretaste of God's future eschatological plan for his creatures. These insights seem to require that we take seriously how the Christian community is called to live together if we are to see humanity's telos.

It appears, then, that we are able to arrive at a more maximal definition of ecclesio-anthropology. While my minimal definition seeks to describe the different ways that ecclesiology uniquely and distinctly informs anthropology, from the above discussion it seems that there are in fact certain ways in which ecclesiology serves as a *necessary* resource for theological anthropology. Therefore, we can say that, maximally, ecclesio-anthropology seeks to articulate how ecclesiology—that is, the nature, mission, practices, and telos of the church—provides *necessary* insight into our study of human imagination, vocation, formation, and flourishing. Here the addition of the term "necessary" does not demand that ecclesiology explains anthropology *comprehensively* or *exhaustively*. Such a claim could potentially exclude the insights from other approaches to theological anthropology. Rather the term "necessary" is intended to communicate that human imagination, vocation, formation and flourishing are rightly understood and experienced within the ecclesial community. Furthermore, it seeks to stipulate that insights from ecclesiology are essential for understanding those four categories correctly. Finally, in this maximal definition I have begun to clarify the ways that ecclesiology informs anthropology, particularly as it relates to the construction of a coherent identity, the divinely assigned vocation God has given to his creatures, the manner in which human creatures are rightly formed, and the nature of their flourishing. While these four categories emerged as particular points of emphasis in Free Church ecclesio-anthropology, they were also present in the work of my interlocutors.

Conclusion

In this chapter, I have attempted to demonstrate some of the key contributions and limitations of ecclesio-anthropology. I have argued that ecclesio-anthropology uniquely contributes to our understanding of theological anthropology by providing an important emphasis and insight into the nature of human action, the goodness of human embodiment, and the teleological nature of human creatures. However, I have also noted that ecclesio-anthropology is limited by its need to be supplemented by other approaches to theological anthropology and highlighted the possible role that ecclesiological ethnography might serve as a potentially helpful resource in complimenting Free Church ecclesiological reflection. The appropriation of ecclesiological ethnography is particularly important given the manner in which the Free Church's commitment to freedom of liturgy results in a variety of liturgical practices across churches of this tradition. Additionally, I argued that ecclesio-anthropology is not exclusive and will need to be supplemented by other approaches to theological anthropology, including but not limited to christological and pneumatological approaches to theological anthropology. Finally, I revisited the preliminary definition that I had presented in the introduction. Acknowledging that ecclesiology does in fact provide helpful insight into the human person, I identified specific ways in which ecclesio-anthropology is a necessary resource for theological anthropology by adding a maximal definition. Maximally, ecclesio-anthropology seeks to articulate how ecclesiology—that is, the nature, mission, practices, and telos of the church—provides *necessary* insight into our study of human imagination, vocation, formation, and flourishing. While ecclesio-anthropology is not an exhaustive or exclusive approach to understanding the human person, it is a helpful and necessary tool that makes a unique contribution to our understanding of who we are and what God has created us to do.

Bibliography

Allik, Tiina. "Narrative Approaches to Human Personhood: Agency, Grace, and Innocent Suffering." *Philosophy and Theology* 1.4 (1987) 305–33.
Allison, Gregg R. *Sojourners and Strangers: The Doctrine of the Church*. Foundations of Evangelical Theology. Wheaton, IL: Crossway, 2012.
Anizor, Uche, and Hank Voss. *Representing Christ: A Vision for the Priesthood of All Believers*. Downers Grove, IL: IVP Academic, 2016.
Aquinas, Thomas. *Summa Theologica*. Translated by the Fathers of the English Dominican Province. New York: Ave Maria, 1948.
Arnold, Clinton E. *Ephesians*. Zondervan Exegetical Commentary on the New Testament. Grand Rapids: Zondervan, 2010.
Ashley, Benedict M. "The Priesthood of Christ, the Baptized, and the Ordained." In *The Theology of Priesthood*, edited by Donald J. Goergen and Ann Garrido, 139–64. Collegeville, MN: Liturgical, 2000.
Athanasius of Alexandria. *On the Incarnation of the Word*. Translated by and revised by David Nutt. In *St. Athanasius: Select Works and Letters*, edited by Archibald Robertson, 31–67. NPNF2 4. 1891. Reprint. Grand Rapids: Eerdmans, 1975.
Ayres, Lewis. *Nicaea and its Legacy: An Approach to Fourth-Century Trinitarian Theology*. Oxford: Oxford University Press, 2004.
Baan, Ariaan. *The Necessity of Witness: Stanley Hauerwas's Contribution to Systematic Theology*. Eugene, OR: Pickwick, 2015.
———. "Stanley Hauerwas and the Necessity of Witness: A Research Report." *Zeitschrift für Dialektische Theologie* 29.2 (2013) 34–49.
Backus, Isaac. *Isaac Backus on Church, State, and Calvinism: Pamphlets, 1754–1789*. Edited by William G. McLoughlin. Cambridge: Belknap Press of Harvard University Press, 1968.
Baillargeon, Gaëtan. *Perspectives orthodoxes sur l'Église-Communion: L'oeuvre de Jean Zizioulas*. Montréal: Paulines, 1989.
Baker, Kimberly F. "Augustine's Doctrine of the *Totus Christus*: Reflecting on the Church as Sacrament of Unity." *Horizons* 37.1 (2010) 7–24.
Balthasar, Hans Urs von. *The Christian State of Life*. Translated by Mary Francis McCarthy. San Francisco: Ignatius, 1983.
———. *Church and World*. Translated by A. V. Littledale with Alexander Dru. Montreal: Palm, 1967.

———. *Dare We Hope That All Men Be Saved? With a Short Discourse on Hell*. Edited by David Kipp and Lothar Krauth. 2nd ed. San Francisco: Ignatius, 2014.

———. *Dramatis Personae: Persons in Christ*. Vol. 3 of *Theo-Drama: Theological Dramatic Theory*. 5 vols. Translated by Graham Harrison. San Francisco: Ignatius, 1992.

———. *Engagement with God: The Drama of Christian Discipleship*. Translated by John Halliburton. 2nd ed. San Francisco: Ignatius, 2008.

———. *Epilogue*. Translated by Edward T. Oakes. San Francisco: Ignatius, 1991.

———. *Love Alone is Credible*. Translated by David C. Schindler. San Francisco: Ignatius, 2004.

———. *Man is Created*. Translated by Adrian Walker. Explorations in Theology 5. San Francisco: Ignatius, 2014.

———. *Mysterium Paschale: The Mystery of Easter*. Translated by Aidan Nichols. San Francisco: Ignatius, 2005.

———. *New Elucidations*. Translated by Mary Theresilde Skerry. San Francisco: Ignatius, 1986.

———. "On the Concept of Person." Translated by Peter Verhalen. *Communio* 13.1 (1986) 18–26.

———. *Seeing the Form*. Translated by Erasmo Leiva-Merikakis. Vol. 1 of *The Glory of the Lord: A Theological Aesthetics*. 5 vols. San Francisco: Ignatius, 1982.

———. *Spirit and Institution*. Translated by Edward T. Oakes. Explorations in Theology 4. San Francisco: Ignatius, 1995.

———. *Spouse of the Word*. Translated by A. V. Littledale. Explorations in Theology 2. San Francisco: Ignatius, 1991.

———. *Theo-Drama: Theological Dramatic Theory*. Translated by Graham Harrison. 5 vols. San Francisco: Ignatius, 1988–2003.

———. *Theo-Logic*. Translated by Adrian Walker. 3 vols. San Francisco: Ignatius, 2001–5.

———. *A Theological Anthropology*. Translated by Benziger Verlag. New York: Sheed and Ward, 1967.

———. *Theology: The New Covenant*. Edited by John Riches. Translated by Brian McNeil. Vol. 3 of *The Glory of the Lord: A Theological Aesthetics*. 7 vols. San Francisco: Ignatius, 1990.

———. *Truth of the World*. Vol. 1 of *Theo-Logic*. 3 vols. Translated by Adrian J. Walker. San Francisco: 2000.

———. *The Word Made Flesh*. Translated by A. V. Littledale. Explorations in Theology 1. San Francisco: Ignatius, 1989.

Barnett, Paul. *The Second Epistle to the Corinthians*. The New International Commentary on the New Testament. Grand Rapids: Eerdmans, 1997.

Barth, Karl. *The Church and the Churches*. Grand Rapids: Eerdmans, 2005.

———. *Church Dogmatics: The Doctrine of Reconciliation*. Vol. IV/1. Edited by G. W. Bromiley and T. F. Torrance. Translated by G. W. Bromiley. Edinburgh: T. & T. Clark, 1957.

———. *Church Dogmatics: The Doctrine of Reconciliation*. Vol. IV/2. Edited by G. W. Bromiley and T. F. Torrance. Translated by G. W. Bromiley. Edinburgh: T. & T. Clark, 1957.

———. *Church Dogmatics: The Doctrine of Reconciliation.* Vol. IV/3.1. Edited by G. W. Bromiley and T. F. Torrance. Translated by G. W. Bromiley. Edinburgh: T. & T. Clark, 1961.

———. *Church Dogmatics: The Doctrine of Reconciliation.* Vol. IV/4. Edited by G. W. Bromiley and T. F. Torrance. Translated by G. W. Bromiley. Edinburgh: T. & T. Clark, 1975.

Barth, Markus. *Ephesians.* 2 vols. Anchor Bible 34–34A. Garden City, NY: Doubleday, 1974.

Bartholomä, Philipp F. "The Self and the Collapsed Other: Towards Defining Free Church Identity and Mission in a Post-Christian Age." *Baptistic Theologies* 6.2 (2014) 53–73.

Bauckham, Richard. *Jude, 2 Peter.* Word Biblical Commentary 50. Waco, TX: Word, 1983.

Beale, G. K. *John's Use of the Old Testament in Revelation.* Sheffield: Sheffield Academic Press, 1998.

———. *A New Testament Biblical Theology: The Unfolding of the Old Testament in the New.* Grand Rapids: Baker Academic, 2011.

Beattie, Tina. *New Catholic Feminism: Theology and Theory.* London: Routledge, 2006.

Bebbington, David. *Baptists through the Centuries: A History of a Global People.* Waco, TX: Baylor University Press, 2010.

Behr, John. *Becoming Human: Meditations on Christian Anthropology in Word and Image.* Crestwood, NY: St. Vladimir's Seminary Press, 2013.

Belcher, Richard P. *Prophet, Priest, and King: The Roles of Christ in the Bible and Our Roles Today.* Phillipsburg, NJ: P&R, 2016.

Bell, Catherine M. *Ritual Theory, Ritual Practice.* Oxford: Oxford University Press, 2009.

Bell, Daniel M. "The Way of God with the World: Hauerwas on War." In *Unsettling Arguments: A Festschrift on the Occasion of Stanley Hauerwas's 70th Birthday*, edited by Kelly S. Johnson et al., 112–31. Eugene, OR: Cascade, 2010.

Bender, Kimlyn J. *Karl Barth's Christological Ecclesiology.* Aldershot, UK: Ashgate, 2005.

Best, Ernest. *A Critical and Exegetical Commentary on Ephesians.* International Critical Commentary on the Holy Scriptures in the Old and New Testaments. Edinburgh: T. & T. Clark, 1998.

Billings, J. Todd. "Sacraments." In *Christian Dogmatics: Reformed Theology for the Church Catholic*, edited by Michael Allen and Scott R. Swain, 339–62. Grand Rapids: Baker Academic, 2016.

Block, Daniel. *For the Glory of God: Recovering a Biblical Theology of Worship.* Grand Rapids: Baker Academic, 2014.

Blomberg, Craig L., and Mariam J. Kamell. *James.* Zondervan Exegetical Commentary on the New Testament. Grand Rapids: Zondervan, 2008.

Bok, Nico den. "Barth on Baptism: Concerning a Crucial Dimension of Ecclesiology." *Zeitschrift für Dialektische Theologie* 5 (2011) 135–51.

Bortnyk, Sergii. *Kommunion und Person: Die Theologie von John Zizioulas in systematischer Betrachtung.* Forum Orthodoxe Theologie 13. Munster: LIT, 2014.

Boyd, Stephen B. "Community as Sacrament in the Theology of Hans Schlaffer." In *Anabaptism Revisited: Essays on Anabaptist/Mennonite Studies in Honor of C. J. Dyck*, edited by Walter Klaassen, 50–64. Scottdale, PA: Herald, 1992.

Bray, Gerald. *The Church: A Theological and Historical Account.* Grand Rapids: Baker Academic, 2016.

Brink, Gijsbert van den. "Social Trinitarianism: A Discussion of Some Recent Theological Criticisms." *International Journal of Systematic Theology* 16.3 (2014) 331–50.

Brock, Brian, and Stanley Hauerwas. *Beginnings: Interrogating Hauerwas*. Edited by Kevin Hargaden. T. & T. Clark Enquiries in Theological Ethics. London: Bloomsbury, 2017.

Brom, Luco Johan van den. "Church on its Way to Community in the Image of God: Calling, Practising and Looking for Fulfilment of Hope." *Zeitschrift für Dialektische Theologie* 5 (2011) 27–44.

Brown, Alan. "On the Criticism of Being as Communion." In *The Theology of John Zizioulas: Personhood and the Church*, edited by Douglas H. Knight, 35–78. Burlington, VT: Ashgate, 2007.

Brown, Raymond E. *An Introduction to the New Testament*. Anchor Yale Bible Reference Library. New York: Doubleday, 1997.

Brueggemann, Walter. *Genesis*. Interpretation: A Bible Commentary for Teaching and Preaching. Atlanta: John Knox, 1982.

———. *Isaiah: Chapters 1–39*. 2 vols. Westminster Bible Companion. Louisville: Westminster John Knox, 1998.

———. *Theology of the Old Testament: Testimony, Dispute, Advocacy*. Minneapolis: Fortress, 1997.

Butner, D. Glenn. "For and against de Régnon: Trinitarianism East and West." *International Journal of Systematic Theology* 17.4 (2015) 399–412.

Calvin, John. *Institutes of the Christian Religion*. Edited by John T. McNeil. Translated by Ford Lewis Battles. 2 vols. Library of Christian Classics. Philadelphia: Westminster, 1960.

Cary, Jeffrey W. *Free Churches and the Body of Christ: Authority, Unity, and Truthfulness*. Free Church, Catholic Tradition. Eugene, OR: Cascade, 2012.

Catholic Church. *Catechism of the Catholic Church: Revised in Accordance with the Official Latin Text Promulgated by Pope John Paul II*. Vatican City: Libreria Editrice Vaticana, 1997.

Chan, Simon. *Liturgical Theology: The Church as a Worshipping Community*. Downers Grove, IL: InterVarsity, 2006.

Chute, Anthony L., et al. *The Baptist Story: From English Sect to Global Movement*. Nashville: B&H Academic, 2015.

Ciraulo, Jonathan Martin. "Sacraments and Personhood: John Zizioulas' Impasse and a Way Forward." *Heythrop Journal* 53.6 (2012) 993–1004.

Clowney, Edmund P. *The Church*. Contours of Christian Theology. Downers Grove, IL: InterVarsity, 1995.

Coakley, Sarah. *God, Sexuality, and the Self: An Essay "On the Trinity."* Cambridge: Cambridge University Press, 2013.

Cocksworth, Ashley. "Revisiting Karl Barth's Doctrine of Baptism from a Perspective on Prayer." *Scottish Journal of Theology* 68.3 (2015) 255–72.

Colwell, John E. "The Church as Sacrament: A Mediating Presence." In *Baptist Sacramentalism 2*, edited by Anthony R. Cross and Philip E. Thompson, 48–60. Studies in Baptist History and Thought 25. Carlisle: Paternoster, 2008.

———. *Promise and Presence: An Exploration of Sacramental Theology*. Milton Keynes: Paternoster, 2005.

Congar, Yves. "Sur la trilogie: Prophète-roi-prêtre." *Revue des sciences philosophiques et théologiques* 67.1 (1983) 97–115.
Copeland, M. Shawn. *Enfleshing Freedom: Body, Race, and Being*. Minneapolis: Fortress, 2010.
Cortez, Marc. *Christological Anthropology in Historical Perspective: Ancient and Contemporary Approaches to Theological Anthropology*. Grand Rapids: Zondervan, 2016.
———. "Idols, Images, and a Spirit-ed Anthropology: A Pneumatological Account of the *Imago Dei*." In *Third Article Theology: A Pneumatological Dogmatics*, edited by Myk Habets, 267–82. Minneapolis: Fortress, 2016.
Crammer, Corinne. "One Sex or Two? Balthasar's Theology of the Sexes." In *The Cambridge Companion to Hans Urs von Balthasar*, edited by David Moss and Edward T. Oakes, 93–111. Cambridge: Cambridge University Press, 2004.
Crawford, David S. "Love, Action, and Vows as 'Inner Form' of the Moral Life." In *Love Alone is Credible: Hans Urs von Balthasar as Interpreter of the Catholic Tradition*, edited by David L. Schindler, 243–60. Grand Rapids: Eerdmans, 2008.
Cross, Anthony R. *Recovering the Evangelical Sacrament: Baptisma Semper Reformandum*. Eugene, OR: Pickwick, 2013.
Cumin, Paul. "Looking for Personal Space in the Theology of John Zizioulas." *International Journal of Systematic Theology* 8.4 (2006) 356–70.
Cuneo, Terence. *Ritualized Faith: Essays on the Philosophy of Liturgy*. Oxford Studies in Analytic Theology. Oxford: Oxford University Press, 2016.
Darko, Daniel K. *No Longer Living as the Gentiles: Differentiation and Shared Ethical Values in Ephesians 4.17—6.9*. Library of New Testament Studies 375. London: T. & T. Clark, 2008.
Dean, Robert J. *For the Life of the World: Jesus Christ and the Church in the Theologies of Dietrich Bonhoeffer and Stanley Hauerwas*. Eugene, OR: Pickwick, 2016.
Deane-Drummond, Celia E. "The Breadth of Glory: A Trinitarian Eschatology for the Earth through Critical Engagement with Hans Urs von Balthasar." *International Journal of Systematic Theology* 12.1 (2010) 46–64.
Dermange, François. "Église et communautarisme: Une interrogation à partir de Karl Barth et Stanley Hauerwas." *Théophilyon* 11.1 (2006) 97–122.
Dieser, Helmut. *Der gottähnliche Mensch und die Gottlosigkeit der Sünde: Zur Theologie des Descensus Christi bei Hans Urs von Balthasar*. Trierer theologische Studien 62. Trier, Germany: Paulinus, 1998.
Doyle, Dennis M. *Communion Ecclesiology: Vision and Versions*. Maryknoll, NY: Orbis, 2000.
Durand, Emmanuel. "La variété des langues dans le *Christus totus* selon saint Augustin: L'universalité chrétienne en voie d'accomplissement." *Epherides Theologicae Lovanienses* 86.1 (2010) 1–25.
Durić, Grigorije. "Constitutiveness of Otherness for Person and Church." *Philotheos* 14 (2014) 248–53.
Durnbaugh, Donald F. *The Believers' Church: The History and Character of Radical Protestantism*. 2nd ed. Scottdale, PA: Herald, 1985.
———. "Believers Church Perspectives on the Lord's Supper." In *The Lord's Supper: Believers Church Perspectives*, edited by Dale R. Stoffer, 63–78. Scottdale, PA: Herald, 1997.

Dykstra, Craig R. *Growing in the Life of Faith: Education and Christian Practices*. 2nd ed. Louisville: Westminster John Knox, 2005.

Dykstra, Craig R., and Dorothy Bass. "A Theological Understanding of Christian Practices." In *Practicing Theology: Beliefs and Practices in Christian Life*, edited by Miroslav Volf and Dorothy Bass, 13–32. Grand Rapids: Eerdmans, 2002.

Erickson, Millard J. *Christian Theology*. 3rd ed. Grand Rapids: Baker Academic, 2013.

Farrow, Douglas. "Person and Nature: The Neccessity-Freedom Dialectic in John Zizioulas." In *The Theology of John Zizioulas: Personhood and the Church*, edited by Douglas H. Knight, 109–23. Burlington, VT: Ashgate, 2007.

Fiddes, Paul S. *Tracks and Traces: Baptist Identity in Church and Theology*. Studies in Baptist History and Thought 13. Carlisle: Paternoster, 2003.

Fiddes, Paul S., et al. *Baptists and the Communion of Saints: A Theology of Covenanted Disciples*. Waco, TX: Baylor University Press, 2014.

Finger, Thomas N. *A Contemporary Anabaptist Theology: Biblical, Historical, Constructive*. Downers Grove, IL: InterVarsity, 2004.

Fox, Patricia. *God as Communion: John Zizioulas, Elizabeth Johnson, and the Retrieval of the Symbol of the Triune God*. Collegeville, MN: Liturgical, 2001.

Franklin, Patrick S. *Being Human, Being Church: The Significance of Theological Anthropology for Ecclesiology*. Paternoster Theological Monographs. Carlisle: Paternoster, 2016.

Freeman, Curtis W. *Contesting Catholicity: Theology for Other Baptists*. Waco, TX: Baylor University Press, 2014.

———. "Mediating Ministry and the Renewal of the Church." *American Baptist Quarterly* 31.4 (2012) 392–409.

———. "'To Feed Upon by Faith': Nourishment at the Lord's Table." In *Baptist Sacramentalism*, edited by Anthony R. Cross and Philip E. Thompson, 194–210. Studies in Baptist History and Thought 5. Carlisle: Paternoster, 2003.

Gandolfo, Elizabeth O'Donnell. *The Power and Vulnerability of Love: A Theological Anthropology*. Minneapolis: Fortress, 2015.

Gardner, Lucy. "Balthasar and the Figure of Mary." In *The Cambridge Companion to Hans Urs von Balthasar*, edited by David Moss and Edward T. Oakes, 64–78. Cambridge: Cambridge University Press, 2004.

Garland, David E. *1 Corinthians*. Baker Exegetical Commentary on the New Testament. Grand Rapids: Baker Academic, 2003.

Gawronski, Raymond. *Word and Silence: Hans Urs von Balthasar and the Spiritual Encounter between East and West*. Grand Rapids: Eerdmans, 1995.

Geldbach, Erich. *Freikirchen: Erbe, Gestalt und Wirkung*. Bensheimer Hefte 70. Göttingen: Vandenhoeck & Ruprecht, 1989.

George, Timothy. "The Priesthood of All Believers and the Quest for Theological Integrity." *Criswell Theological Review* 3 (1989) 283–94.

Gerber, Christine. "Die alte Braut und Christi Leib: Zum ekklesiologischen Entwurf des Epheserbriefs." *New Testament Studies* 59.2 (2013) 192–221.

Gingerich, Mark. "The Church as Kingdom: The Kingdom of God in the Writings of Stanley Hauerwas and John Howard Yoder." *Didaskalia* 19.1 (2008) 129–43.

Goergen, Donald J. "Priest, Prophet, King: The Ministry of Jesus Christ." In *The Theology of Priesthood*, edited by Donald J. Goergen and Ann Garrido, 187–209. Collegeville, MN: Liturgical, 2000.

Goldingay, John. *Israel's Life*. Vol. 3 of *Old Testament Theology*. 3 vols. Downers Grove, IL: InterVarsity, 2009.
Gombis, Timothy G. *The Drama of Ephesians: Participating in the Triumph of God*. Downers Grove, IL: IVP Academic, 2010.
Gourges, Michel. "'Réveille-toi . . .' (Ep 5,14): De l'évocation de la Pâque baptismale à la motivation parénétique." *Science et Esprit* 63.3 (2011) 367–83.
Greene, Joseph R. "The Spirit in the Temple: Bridging the Gap between Old Testament Absence and New Testament Assumption." *Journal of the Evangelical Theological Society* 55.4 (2012) 717–42.
Greggs, Tom. "The Priesthood of No Believer: On the Priesthood of Christ and His Church." *International Journal of Systematic Theology* 17.4 (2015) 374–98.
Grenz, Stanley J. "Ecclesiology." In *The Cambridge Companion to Postmodern Theology*, edited by Kevin J. Vanhoozer, 252–68. Cambridge: Cambridge University Press, 2003.
———. *The Named God and the Question of Being: A Trinitarian Theo-Ontology*. Louisville: Westminster John Knox, 2005.
———. *Rediscovering the Triune God: The Trinity in Contemporary Theology*. Minneapolis: Fortress, 2004.
———. *Renewing the Center: Evangelical Theology in a Post-Theological Era*. Grand Rapids: Baker, 2000.
———. *Revisioning Evangelical Theology: A Fresh Agenda for the 21st Century*. Downers Grove, IL: InterVarsity, 1993.
———. *The Social God and the Relational Self: A Trinitarian Theology of the* imago Dei. Louisville: Westminster John Knox, 2001.
———. *Theology for the Community of God*. 2nd ed. Grand Rapids: Eerdmans, 2000.
Grimsrud, Ted. "Reflections from a Chagrined 'Yoderian' in Face of His Sexual Violence." In *John Howard Yoder: Radical Theologian*, edited by J. Denny Weaver, 334–50. Eugene, OR: Cascade, 2014.
Gunton, Colin. "The Church as a School of Virtue? Human Formation in Trinitarian Framework." In *Faithfulness and Fortitude: In Conversation with the Theological Ethics of Stanley Hauerwas*, edited by Mark Nation and Samuel Wells, 211–31. Edinburgh: T. & T. Clark, 2000.
———. "Persons and Particularity." In *The Theology of John Zizioulas: Personhood and the Church*, edited by Douglas H. Knight, 97–107. Burlington, VT: Ashgate, 2007.
Gunton, Colin E., and Daniel W. Hardy. "The Church on Earth: The Roots of Community." In *On Being the Church: Essays on the Christian Community*, edited by Colin E. Gunton, 48–80. Edinburgh: T. & T. Clark, 1989.
Guth, Karen V. "Doing Justice to the Complex Legacy of John Howard Yoder: Restorative Justice Resources in Witness and Feminist Ethics." *Journal for the Society of Christian Ethics* 35.2 (2015) 119–39.
Guthrie, George H. *2 Corinthians*. Baker Exegetical Commentary on the New Testament. Grand Rapids: Baker Academic, 2015.
Hamilton, Victor P. *The Book of Genesis*. 2 vols. The New International Commentary on the Old Testament. Grand Rapids: Eerdmans, 1995.
Harmon, Steven R. "Free Church Theology, the Pilgrim Church, and the Ecumenical Future." *Journal of Ecumenical Studies* 49.3 (2014) 420–42.
———. *Towards Baptist Catholicity: Essays on Tradition and the Baptist Vision*. Studies in Baptist History and Thought 27. Carlisle: Paternoster, 2006.

Harper, Brad, and Paul Louis Metzger. *Exploring Ecclesiology: An Evangelical and Ecumenical Introduction*. Grand Rapids: Brazos, 2009.

Harris, Murray J. *The Second Epistle to the Corinthians: A Commentary on the Greek Text*. The New International Greek Testament Commentary. Grand Rapids: Eerdmans, 2005.

Harrison, Nonna Verna. "Zizioulas on Communion and Otherness." *St. Vladimir's Theological Quarterly* 42.3-4 (1998) 273–300.

Hauerwas, Stanley. *Against the Nations: War and Survival in a Liberal Society*. Minneapolis: Winston, 1985.

———. *Approaching the End: Eschatological Reflection on Church, Politics and Life*. London: SCM, 2013.

———. *A Better Hope: Resources for a Church Confronting Capitalism, Democracy, and Postmodernity*. Grand Rapids: Brazos, 2000.

———. *Character and the Christian Life: A Study in Theological Ethics*. 2nd ed. San Antonio: Trinity University Press, 1985.

———. *Christian Existence Today: Essays on Church, World, and Living in Between*. Grand Rapids: Brazos, 2001.

———. *A Community of Character: Toward a Constructive Christian Social Ethic*. Notre Dame: University of Notre Dame Press, 1981.

———. *A Cross-Shattered Church: Reclaiming the Theological Heart of Preaching*. Grand Rapids: Brazos, 2009.

———. *Hannah's Child: A Theologian's Memoir*. Grand Rapids: Eerdmans, 2010.

———. "Hooks: Random Thoughts by Way of a Response to Griffiths and Ochs." *Modern Theology* 19.1 (2003) 89–101.

———. "How to 'Remember the Poor.'" In *The Work of Theology*, by Stanley Hauerwas, 208–28. Grand Rapids: Eerdmans, 2015.

———. *In Good Company: The Church as Polis*. Notre Dame: University of Notre Dame Press, 1995.

———. *Matthew*. Brazos Theological Commentary on the Bible. Grand Rapids: Brazos, 2006.

———. "Must a Patient Be a Person to Be a Patient? Or, My Uncle Charlie is Not Much of a Person, but He is Still My Uncle Charlie." In *The Hauerwas Reader*, edited by John Berkman and Michael Cartwright, 596–602. Durham, NC: Duke University Press, 2001.

———. "On Surviving Justly: An Ethical Analysis of Nuclear Disarmament." *Central Journal* 3.1 (1983) 123–52.

———. *The Peaceable Kingdom: A Primer in Christian Ethics*. Notre Dame: University of Notre Dame Press, 1983.

———. *Sanctify Them in the Truth: Holiness Exemplified*. Nashville: Abingdon, 1998.

———. *Suffering Presence: Theological Reflections on Medicine, the Mentally Handicapped, and the Church*. Notre Dame, IN: Notre Dame University Press, 1986.

———. *Without Apology: Sermons for Christ's Church*. New York: Seabury, 2013.

———. *With the Grain of the Universe: The Church's Witness and Natural Theology*. 2002. Reprint. Grand Rapids: Baker Academic, 2013.

———. *Working with Words: On Learning to Speak Christian*. Eugene, OR: Cascade, 2011.

———. *The Work of Theology*. Grand Rapids: Eerdmans, 2015.

Hauerwas, Stanley, and John Berkman. "The Chief End of All Flesh." *Theology Today* 49.2 (1992) 196–208.
Hauerwas, Stanley, and Richard Bondi. "Memory, Community and the Reasons for Living: Theological and Ethical Reflections on Suicide and Euthanasia." *Journal of the American Academy of Religion* 44.3 (1976) 439–52.
Hauerwas, Stanley, and Samuel Wells. "The Gift of the Church and the Gifts God Gives it." In *The Blackwell Companion to Christian Ethics*, edited by Stanley Hauerwas and Samuel Wells, 13–27. Malden, MA: Blackwell, 2004.
Hauerwas, Stanley, and William H. Willimon. *Resident Aliens: Life in the Christian Colony; a Provocative Christian Assessment of Culture and Ministry for People Who Know That Something is Wrong*. Expanded 25th anniversary ed. Nashville: Abingdon, 2014.
Haykin, Michael A. G. "'His Soul-Refreshing Presence': The Lord's Supper in Calvinistic Baptist Thought and Experience in the 'Long' Eighteenth Century." In *Baptist Sacramentalism*, edited by Anthony R. Cross and Philip E. Thompson, 177–93. Studies in Baptist History and Thought 5. Carlisle: Paternoster, 2003.
Haymes, Brian, et al. *On Being the Church: Revisioning Baptist Identity*. 2008. Reprint, Eugene, OR: Wipf & Stock, 2009.
Healy, Nicholas J. *The Eschatology of Hans Urs von Balthasar: Being as Communion*. Oxford: Oxford University Press, 2005.
Healy, Nicholas J., and David Schindler. "For the Life of the World: Hans Urs von Balthasar on the Church as Eucharist." In *The Cambridge Companion to Hans Urs von Balthasar*, edited by David Moss and Edward T. Oakes, 51–63. Cambridge: Cambridge University Press, 2004.
Healy, Nicholas M. *Church, World, and the Christian Life: Practical-Prophetic Ecclesiology*. Cambridge Studies in Christian Doctrine. Cambridge: Cambridge University Press, 2000.
———. *Hauerwas: A (Very) Critical Introduction*. Grand Rapids: Eerdmans, 2014.
Helwys, Thomas. *A Short Declaration of the Mystery of Iniquity (1611/1612)*. Classics of Religious Liberty 1. Edited by Richard Groves. Mercer, GA: Mercer University Press, 1998.
Herdt, Jennifer A. "Hauerwas among the Virtues." *Journal of Religious Ethics* 40.2 (2012) 202–27.
Hill, Daniel L. "'Breathe on Us, O Breath of God': The Pneumatological Grounding of Ecclesial Identity." *Southeastern Theological Review* 11.1 (2020) 79–98.
Hoehner, Harold W. *Ephesians: An Exegetical Commentary*. Grand Rapids: Baker Academic, 2002.
Holmes, Stephen R. *Baptist Theology*. London: T. & T. Clark, 2012.
———. "Toward a Baptist Theology of Ordained Ministry." In *Baptist Sacramentalism*, edited by Anthony R. Cross and Philip E. Thompson, 247–62. Studies in Baptist History and Thought 5. Carlisle: Paternoster, 2003.
Holzer, Vincent. "La kenose christologique dans la pensée de Hans Urs von Balthasar: Une kénose christologique étendue à l'être de Dieu." *Théophilyon* 9.1 (2004) 207–36.
Horton, Michael S. *The Christian Faith: A Systematic Theology for Pilgrims on the Way*. Grand Rapids: Zondervan, 2011.
———. *Lord and Servant: A Covenant Christology*. Louisville: Westminster John Knox, 2005.

———. *People and Place: A Covenant Ecclesiology*. Louisville: Westminster John Knox, 2008.

———. "Post-Reformation Reformed Anthropology." In *Personal Identity in Theological Perspective*, edited by Richard Lints et al., 45–69. Grand Rapids: Eerdmans, 2006.

Howsare, Rodney A. *Balthasar: A Guide for the Perplexed*. London: T. & T. Clark, 2009.

———. '. London: T. & T. Clark, 2005.

Hubmaier, Balthasar. *Balthasar Hubmaier: Theologian of Anabaptism*. Edited by H. Wayne Pipkin and John Howard Yoder. Classics of the Radical Reformation 5. Scottdale, PA: Herald, 1989.

Hunsinger, George. "Baptism and the Soteriology of Forgiveness." *International Journal of Systematic Theology* 2.3 (2000) 247–69.

———. "Karl Barth on the Lord's Supper: An Ecumenical Appraisal." *Zeitschrift für Dialektische Theologie* 5 (2011) 152–74.

Ide, Pascal. *Une théologie de l'amour: L'amour, centre de la Trilogie de Hans Urs von Balthasar*. Donner Raison 37. Brussels: Lessius, 2012.

Jenson, Matt, and David Wilhite. *The Church: A Guide for the Perplexed*. London: T. & T. Clark, 2010.

Jobes, Karen H. *1 Peter*. Baker Exegetical Commentary on the New Testament. Grand Rapids: Baker Academic, 2005.

Johnson, Kelly S. "Worshipping in Spirit and in Truth." In *Unsettling Arguments: A Festschrift on the Occasion of Stanley Hauerwas's 70th Birthday*, edited by Charles Pinches et al., 300–14. Eugene, OR: Cascade, 2011.

Johnson, Luke Timothy. *The Writings of the New Testament: An Interpretation*. Philadelphia: Fortress, 1999.

Jones, Joe R. *A Grammar of Christian Faith: Systematic Explorations in Christian Life and Doctrine*. 2 vols. Lanham, MD: Rowman & Littlefield, 2002.

Kammler, Hans-Christian. "Die Wahrheit des Evangeliums und die Einheit der Kirche: Exegetische Überlegungen zu ihrem sachlichen Verhältnis." *Kerygma und Dogma* 60.2 (2014) 126–52.

Kapic, Kelly M. "Anthropology." In *Christian Dogmatics: Reformed Theology for the Church Catholic*, edited by Michael Allen and Scott R. Swain, 165–93. Grand Rapids: Baker Academic, 2016.

Kärkkäinen, Veli-Matti. "The Apostolicity of Free Churches." *Pro Ecclesia* 10.4 (2001) 475–86.

Kereszty, Roch. "The Eucharist and Mission in the Theology of Hans Urs von Balthasar." In *Love Alone is Credible: Hans Urs von Balthasar as Interpreter of the Catholic Tradition*, edited by David L. Schindler, 3–15. Grand Rapids: Eerdmans, 2008.

Keener, Craig S. *Acts: An Exegetical Commentary*. 4 vols. Grand Rapids: Baker Academic, 2015.

Kerr, Fergus. *Twentieth-Century Catholic Theologians: From Neoscholasticism to Nuptial Mysticism*. Malden, MA: Blackwell, 2007.

Kerr, Nathan R. *Christ, History and Apocalyptic: The Politics of Christian Mission*. Eugene, OR: Cascade, 2009.

Kilby, Karen. *Balthasar: A (Very) Critical Introduction*. Interventions. Grand Rapids: Eerdmans, 2012.

Kilner, John F. *Dignity and Destiny: Humanity in the Image of God*. Grand Rapids: Eerdmans, 2015.

Kinghorn, Joseph. *The Life and Works of Joseph Kinghorn*. 3 vols. Edited by Terry Wolever. Springfield, MO: Particular Baptist, 2005.

Kirchner, Hurbert. "Einführung: Was ist eine Freikirche? Ein Versuch zur Verständigung." In *Freikirchen und konfessionelle Minderheitskirchen: Ein Handbuch*, edited by Hubert Kirchner, 9–18. Berlin: Evangelische Verlagsantalt, 1987.

Klaghofer-Treitler, Wolfgang. *Gotteswort im Menschenwort: Inhalt und Form von Theologie nach Hans Urs von Balthasar*. Innsbruck, Austria: Tyrolia-Verlag, 1992.

Koerpel, Robert C. "The Form and Drama of the Church: Hans Urs von Balthasar on Mary, Peter, and the Eucharist." *Logos* 11.1 (2008) 70–99.

Koopman, Nico. "The Role of Pneumatology in the Ethics of Stanley Hauerwas." *Scriptura* 79 (2002) 33–40.

Körner, Bernhard. "Fundamentaltheologie bei Hans Urs von Balthasar." *Zeitschrift für katholische Theologie* 109.2 (1987) 129–52.

Küng, Hans. *The Church*. Translated by Ray Ockenden and Rosaleen Ockenden. New York: Sheed & Ward, 1968.

Larsen, Sean. "How I Think Hauerwas Thinks about Theology." *Scottish Journal of Theology* 69.1 (2016) 20–38.

Lawson, James Barry. "Theological Formation in the Church of 'the Last Men and Women.'" *Ecclesiology* 9.3 (2013) 335–46.

Leeman, Jonathan. *Political Church: The Local Assembly as Embassy of Christ's Rule*. Studies in Christian Doctrine and Scripture. Downers Grove, IL: IVP Academic, 2016.

Leer, Teun van der. "Which Future Church (Form)? A Plea for a 'Believers Church' Ecclesiology." *Journal of European Baptist Studies* 9.3 (2009) 40–51.

Lehenbauer, Joel D. "The Theology of Stanley Hauerwas." *Concordia Theological Quarterly* 76.1–2 (2012) 157–74.

Leonard, Bill. *Baptists in America*. Columbia Contemporary American Religion Series. New York: Columbia University Press, 2005.

Levering, Matthew. *Engaging the Doctrine of Creation: Cosmos, Creatures, and the Wise and Good Creator*. Grand Rapids: Baker Academic, 2017.

Liston, Gregory J. *The Anointed Church: Toward a Third Article Ecclesiology*. Minneapolis: Fortress, 2015.

Littell, Franklin H. "The Historical Free Church Defined." *Brethren Life and Thought* 50.3–4 (2005) 51–65.

Lorrimar, Victoria. "Church and Christ in the Work of Stanley Hauerwas." *Ecclesiology* 11.3 (2015) 306–26.

Lösel, Steffen. *Kreuzwege: Ein ökumenisches Gespräch mit Hans Urs von Balthasar*. Paderborn, Germany: Schöningh, 2001.

———. "A Plain Account of Christian Salvation? Balthasar on Sacrifice, Solidarity, and Substitution." *Pro Ecclesia* 13.2 (2004) 141–71.

Loudovikos, Nicholas. "Person Instead of Grace and Dictated Otherness: John Zizioulas' Final Theological Position." *Heythrop Journal* 52.4 (2011) 684–99.

Lumpkin, William L., ed. *Baptist Confessions of Faith*. Rev. ed. Valley Forge, PA: Judson, 1980.

Lüning, Peter. *Der Mensch im Angesicht des Gekreuzigten: Untersuchungen zum Kreuzesverständnis von Erich Przywara, Karl Rahner, Jon Sobrino und Hans Urs von Balthasar*. Münster: Aschendorff Verlag, 2007.

Lunn, Nicholas P. "Prophetic Representations of the Divine Presence: The Theological Interpretation of the Elijah-Elisha Cycles." *Journal of Theological Interpretation* 9.1 (2015) 49–63.

Luther, Martin. *Luther's Works*. Edited by Jaroslav Pelikan (vols. 1–30) and Helmut T. Lehmann (vols. 31–55). Philadelphia: Muhlenberg; St. Louis: Concordia, 1955–86.

Lyons, Greg. "Church and Holiness in Ephesians." In *Holiness and Ecclesiology in the New Testament*, edited by Kent E. Brower and Andy Johnson, 219–38. Grand Rapids: Eerdmans, 2007.

Macaskill, Grant. *Union with Christ in the New Testament*. Oxford: Oxford University Press, 2013.

MacDougall, Scott. *More than Communion: Imagining an Eschatological Ecclesiology*. London: Bloomsbury, 2015.

MacIntyre, Alasdair C. *After Virtue: A Study in Moral Theory*. 3rd ed. Notre Dame: University of Notre Dame Press, 2007.

———. *Whose Justice? Which Rationality?* Notre Dame: University of Notre Dame Press, 1988.

MacKinnon, Donald M. "Some Reflections on Hans Urs von Balthasar's Christology with Special Reference to Theodramatik II/2 and III." In *Analogy of Beauty: The Theology of Hans Urs von Balthasar*, edited by John Riches, 164–79. Edinburgh: T. & T. Clark, 1986.

Marpeck, Pilgram. *The Writings of Pilgram Marpeck*. Edited by William Klassen and Walter Klassen. Classics of the Radical Reformation. Scottdale, PA: Herald, 1978.

Martin, Jennifer Newsome. "The 'Whence' and the 'Whither' of Balthasar's Gendered Theology: Rehabilitating Kenosis for Feminist Theology." *Modern Theology* 31.2 (2015) 211–34.

Matera, Frank J. *II Corinthians: A Commentary*. The New Testament Library. Louisville: Westminster John Knox, 2003.

Materne, Pierre-Yves. *La condition du disciple: Éthique et politique chez J. B. Metz et S. Hauerwas*. Cogitatio fidei 289. Paris: Cerf, 2013.

McClendon, James Wm, Jr. "The Concept of Authority: A Baptist View (1988)." In *The Collected Works of James Wm. McClendon, Jr.*, vol. 2, edited by Ryan Anderson Newson and Andrew C. Wright, 120–25. 3 vols. Waco, TX: Baylor University Press, 2014.

———. *Systematic Theology*, volume 1: *Ethics*. 3 vols. 1994–2002. Reprint. Waco, TX: Baylor University Press, 2012.

———. *Systematic Theology*, volume 2: *Doctrine*. 3 vols. 1994–2002. Reprint. Waco, TX: Baylor University Press, 2012.

———. *Systematic Theology*, volume 3: *Witness*. 3 vols. Nashville: Abingdon, 1994–2002. Reprint. Waco, TX: Baylor University Press, 2012.

———. "The Voluntary Church in the Twenty-First Century (1998)." In *The Collected Works of James Wm. McClendon, Jr.*, vol. 1, edited by Ryan Anderson Newson and Andrew C. Wright, 151–69. 3 vols. Waco, TX: Baylor University Press, 2014.

McFarland, Ian A. *From Nothing: A Theology of Creation*. Louisville: Westminster John Knox, 2014.

McIntosh, Mark A. "Christology." In *The Cambridge Companion to Hans Urs von Balthasar*, edited by David Moss and Edward T. Oakes, 24–36. Cambridge: Cambridge University Press, 2004.

———. *Christology from Within: Spirituality and the Incarnation in Hans Urs von Balthasar*. Notre Dame: Notre Dame University Press, 1996.
McMaken, W. Travis. "Definitive, Defective or Deft? Reassessing Barth's Doctrine of Baptism in Church Dogmatics IV/4." *International Journal of Systematic Theology* 17.1 (2015) 89–114.
McPartlan, Paul. *The Eucharist Makes the Church: Henri de Lubac and John Zizioulas in Dialogue*. Edinburgh: T. & T. Clark, 1993.
Mead, Sidney Earl. *The Lively Experiment: The Shaping of Christianity in America*. 1st ed. New York: Harper & Row, 1963.
Middleton, J. Richard. *The Liberating Image: The imago Dei in Genesis 1*. Grand Rapids: Brazos, 2005.
Mong, Ambrose Ih-Ren. "The One and Many: An Examination of John Zizioulas' Ecclesiology." *The Canadian Journal of Orthodox Christianity* 9.3 (2014) 44–59.
Morden, Peter J. "The Lord's Supper and the Spirituality of C. H. Spurgeon." In *Baptist Sacramentalism 2*, edited by Anthony R. Cross and Philip E. Thompson, 175–96. Studies in Baptist History and Thought 25. Carlisle: Paternoster, 2008.
Moser, Matthew A. Rothaus. *Love Itself is Understanding: Hans Urs von Balthasar's Theology of the Saints*. Minneapolis: Fortress, 2016.
Muddiman, John. *The Epistle to the Ephesians*. Black's New Testament Commentaries. London: Continuum, 2001.
Munteanu, Daniel. "Anthropologie der Freiheit: Grundlagen des trinitarischen und ekklesiologischen Freiheitsverständnisses von Johannes Zizioulas." *Ökumenische Rundschau* 62.1 (2013) 64–77.
———. "Homo eucharisticus—Die anthropologische und kosmische Dimension der Eucharistie." *International Journal of Orthodox Theology* 2.3 (2011) 188–202.
Nagel, Norman E. "Luther and the Priesthood of All Believers." *Concordia Theological Quarterly* 61.4 (1997) 277–98.
Newman, Elizabeth. "The Priesthood of All Believers and the Necessity of the Church." In *Recycling the Past or Researching History? Studies in Baptist Historiography and Myths*, edited by Philip E. Thompson and Anthony R. Cross, 50–66. Studies in Baptist History and Thought 11. Carlisle: Paternoster, 2005.
Newson, Ryan Andrew. "Ethics as Improvisation: Anabaptist Communal Discernment as Method." *The Mennonite Quarterly Review* 87.2 (2013) 187–205.
Nichols, Aidan. "Marian Co-Redemption: A Balthasarian Perspective." *New Blackfriars* 95.1057 (2014) 249–62.
Niethammer, Hans-Martin. *Kirchenmitgliedschaft in der Freikirche: Kirchensoziologische Studie aufgrund einer empirischen Befragung unter Methodisten*. Kirche und Konfession 37. Göttingen: Vandenhoeck & Ruprecht, 1995.
Nutt, Aurica. "Das 'Leib Christi'-Verständnis Hans Urs von Balthasars: Eine geschlechtersensible Analyse seiner Christologie und Ekklesiologie." *Theologische Quartalschrift* 197.2 (2017) 133–54.
Oakes, Edward T. "'He Descended into Hell': The Depth of God's Self-Emptying Love on Holy Saturday in the Thought of Hans Urs von Balthasar." In *Exploring Kenotic Christology: The Self-Emptying of God*, edited by C. Stephen Evans, 218–45. Oxford: Oxford University Press, 2006.
———. *Pattern of Redemption: The Theology of Hans Urs von Balthasar*. New York: Continuum, 1994.

Ochs, Peter. "On Hauerwas' *With the Grain of the Universe.*" *Modern Theology* 19.1 (2003) 77–88.

O'Donnell, John. "Hans Urs von Balthasar: The Form of His Theology." In *Hans Urs von Balthasar: His Life and Work*, edited by David L. Schindler, 207–20. San Francisco: Ignatius, 1991.

Olsen, Cyrus P. "Act and Event in Rahner and von Balthasar: A Case Study in Catholic Systematics." *New Blackfriars* 89.1019 (2008) 3–21.

Osborne, Grant R. *Revelation*. Baker Exegetical Commentary on the New Testament. Grand Rapids: Baker Academic, 2002.

Oswalt, John N. *The Book of Isaiah: Chapters 1–39*. 2 vols. The New International Commentary on the Old Testament. Grand Rapids: Eerdmans, 1986.

Papanikolaou, Aristotle. *Being with God: Trinity, Apophaticism, and Divine-Human Communion*. Notre Dame: Notre Dame University Press, 2006.

———. "Is John Zizioulas an Existentialist in Disguise? Response to Lucian Turcescu." *Modern Theology* 20.4 (2004) 601–7.

———. "Person, Kenosis and Abuse: Hans Urs von Balthasar and Feminist Theologies in Conversation." *Modern Theology* 19.1 (2003) 41–65.

Paul, Herman. "Stanley Hauerwas: Against Secularization in the Church." *Zeitschrift für Dialektische Theologie* 29.2 (2013) 12–33.

Perrin, Nicholas. "Sacraments and Sacramentality in the New Testament." In *The Oxford Handbook of Sacramental Theology*, edited by Matthew Levering and Hans Boersma, 52–67. Oxford: Oxford University Press, 2015.

Peterson, Paul Silas. "Fortschritt und Untergang: Die antimoderne Moderne in Hans Urs von Balthasars frühen Schriften." *Kirchliche Zeitgeschichte* 24.1 (2011) 225–47.

Pinches, Charles. "Considering Stanley Hauerwas." *Journal of Religious Ethics* 40.2 (2012) 193–201.

Pitstick, Alyssa Lyra. *Light in Darkness: Hans Urs von Balthasar and the Catholic Doctrine of Christ's Descent into Hell*. Grand Rapids: Eerdmans, 2007.

Pitts, Jamie. "Anabaptist Re-Vision: On John Howard Yoder's Misrecognized Sexual Politics." *Mennonite Quarterly Review* 89.1 (2015) 153–71.

Puffer, Matthew W. "Human Dignity after Augustine's *imago Dei*: On the Sources and Uses of Two Ethical Terms." *Journal of the Society of Christian Ethics* 37.1 (2017) 65–82.

Rad, Gerhard von. *The Message of the Prophets*. New York: Harper & Row, 1967.

Rahner, Karl, et al. *Karl Rahner in Dialogue: Conversations and Interviews, 1965–1982*. New York: Crossroad, 1986.

Rasmusson, Arne. *The Church as Polis: From Political Theology to Theological Politics as Exemplified by Jürgen Moltmann and Stanley Hauerwas*. Notre Dame: University of Notre Dame Press, 1995.

Rempel, John D. *The Lord's Supper in Anabaptism: A Study in the Christology of Balthasar Hubmaier, Pilgram Marpeck, and Dirk Philips*. Studies in Anabaptist and Mennonite History 33. Scottdale, PA: Herald, 1993.

Reno, Russell R. *Genesis*. Brazos Theological Commentary on the Bible. Grand Rapids: Brazos, 2010.

———. "Stanley Hauerwas and the Liberal Protestant Project." *Modern Theology* 28.2 (2012) 320–26.

Rivera, Joseph. "Human Nature and the Limits of Plasticity: Revisiting the Debate Concerning the Supernatural." *Neue Zeitschrift für systematische Theologie und Religionsphilosophie* 59.1 (2017) 34–53.

Robinson, Dominic. *Understanding the "imago Dei": The Thought of Barth, von Balthasar and Moltmann*. Burlington, VT: Ashgate, 2010.

Rommel, Birgit. *Ekklesiologie und Ethik bei Stanley Hauerwas: Von der Bedeutung der Kirche für die Rede von Gott*. Entwürfe zur christlichen Gesellschaftswissenschaft 14. Münster: LIT, 2003.

Rostock, Nigel. "Two Different Gods or Two Types of Unity? A Critical Response to Zizioulas' Presentation of 'The Father as Cause' with Reference to the Cappadocian Fathers and Augustine." *New Blackfriars* 91.1033 (2010) 321–34.

Roten, Johann. "Marian Light on Our Human Mystery." In *The Beauty of Christ: An Introduction to the Theology of Hans Urs von Balthasar*, edited by Bede McGregor and Thomas Norris, 112–39. Edinburgh: T. & T. Clark, 1994.

Rothmann, Bernhard. "Restitution." In *Anabaptism in Outline: Selected Primary Sources*, edited by Walter Klaassen, 106–7. Classics of the Radical Reformation 3. Scottdale, PA: Herald, 1981.

Russell, Edward. "Reconsidering Relational Anthropology: A Critical Assessment of John Zizioulas's Theological Anthropology." *International Journal of Systematic Theology* 5.2 (2003) 168–86.

Ryan, Mark. *The Politics of Practical Reason: Why Theological Ethics Must Change Your Life*. Eugene, OR: Cascade, 2011.

Sain, Barbara K. "Through a Different Lens: Rethinking the Role of Sexual Difference in the Theology of Hans Urs von Balthasar." *Modern Theology* 25.1 (2009) 71–96.

Saracino, Michele. *Christian Anthropology: An Introduction to the Human Person*. New York: Paulist, 2015.

Sass, Hartmut von. "Politik des Pazifismus: Eine theologische Verteidigung." *Zeitschrift für Evangelische Ethik* 60 (2016) 41–47.

Saward, John. "Mary and Peter in the Christological Constellation: Balthasar's Ecclesiology." In *Analogy of Beauty: The Theology of Hans Urs von Balthasar*, edited by John Riches, 105–33. Edinburgh: T. & T. Clark, 1986.

Scharen, Christian. *Public Worship and Public Work: Character and Commitment in Local Congregational Life*. Virgil Michel Series. Collegeville, MN: Liturgical, 2004.

Schlabach, Gerald W. "Continuity and Sacrament, or Not: Hauerwas, Yoder, and Their Deep Difference." *Journal of the Society of Christian Ethics* 27.2 (2007) 171–207.

Schnackenburg, Rudolf. *Ephesians: A Commentary*. Black's New Testament Commentaries. Edinburgh: T. & T. Clark, 1991.

———. *God's Rule and Kingdom*. New York: Herder & Herder, 1963.

Schrijver, Georges de. "Hans Urs von Balthasars Christologie in der Theodramatik." *Bijdragen* 59.2 (1998) 141–53.

Schuele, Andreas. "Uniquely Human: The Ethics of the *imago Dei* in Genesis 1–11." *Toronto Journal of Theology* 27.1 (2011) 5–16.

Schwarz, Hans. *The Human Being: A Theological Anthropology*. Grand Rapids: Eerdmans, 2013.

Scruton, Roger. *On Human Nature*. Princeton: Princeton University Press, 2017.

Sesboüé, Bernard. "Comment sortir de la néo-scolastique? La genèse de deux pensées." *Gregorianum* 86.2 (2005) 257–75.

Sexton, Jason S. *The Trinitarian Theology of Stanley J. Grenz*. London: T. & T. Clark, 2013.
Sherman, Robert. *Covenant, Community, and the Spirit: A Trinitarian Theology of Church*. Grand Rapids: Baker Academic, 2015.
Shogren, Gary Steven. *1 and 2 Thessalonians*. Zondervan Exegetical Commentary on the New Testament. Grand Rapids: Zondervan, 2012.
Shults, F. LeRon. *Reforming Theological Anthropology: After the Philosophical Turn to Relationality*. Grand Rapids: Eerdmans, 2003.
Siegrist, Anthony G. *Participating Witness: An Anabaptist Theology of Baptism and the Sacramental Character of the Church*. Eugene, OR: Pickwick, 2013.
Sigurdson, Ola. *Heavenly Bodies: Incarnation, the Gaze, and Embodiment in Christian Theology*. Translated by Carl Olsen. Grand Rapids: Eerdmans, 2016.
Simons, Menno. *The Complete Writings of Menno Simons: c.1496–1561*. Edited by John C. Wenger. Translated by Leonard Verduin. Scottdale, PA: Herald, 1986.
Smith, David I., and James K. A. Smith. "Introduction: Faith, Practices, and Pedagogy." In *Teaching and Christian Practices: Reshaping Faith and Learning*, edited by David I. Smith and James K. A. Smith, 1–23. Grand Rapids: Eerdmans, 2011.
Smith, James K. A. *Awaiting the King: Reforming Public Theology*. Cultural Liturgies 3. Grand Rapids: Baker Academic, 2017.
———. *Desiring the Kingdom: Worship, Worldview, and Cultural Formation*. Cultural Liturgies 1. Grand Rapids: Baker Academic, 2009.
———. *Imagining the Kingdom: How Worship Works*. Cultural Liturgies 2. Grand Rapids: Baker Academic, 2013.
Smyth, John. *The Works of John Smyth: Fellow of Christ's College, 1594-8*. Edited by William Thomas Whitley. 2 vols. Cambridge: Cambridge University Press, 1915.
Snyder, C. Arnold. *Following in the Footsteps of Christ: The Anabaptist Tradition*. Traditions of Christian Spirituality. Maryknoll, NY: Orbis, 2004.
Sonderegger, Katherine. "The Life of Christ, the Life of the Church." *Zeitschrift für Dialektische Theologie* 5 (2011) 191–206.
Spaemann, Robert. *Essays in Anthropology: Variations on a Theme*. Translated by Guido de Graaff and James Mumford. Eugene, OR: Cascade, 2010.
———. *Persons: The Difference between "Someone" and "Something."* Oxford: Oxford University Press, 2006.
Stout, Tracey Mark. *A Fellowship of Baptism: Karl Barth's Ecclesiology in Light of His Understanding of Baptism*. Princeton Theological Monograph Series 139. Eugene, OR: Pickwick, 2010.
Sutton, Agneta. "The Complementarity and Symbolism of the Two Sexes: Karl Barth, Hans Urs von Balthasar and John Paul II." *New Blackfriars* 87.1010 (2006) 418–33.
Sylva, Dennis D. "A Unified Field Picture of Second Peter 1.3–15: Making Rhetorical Sense Out of Individual Images." In *Reading First Peter with New Eyes: Methodological Reassessments of the Letter of First Peter*, edited by Robert Lloyd Webb and Duane F. Watson, 91–118. Library of New Testament Studies 364. London: T. & T. Clark, 2007.
Talbert, Charles H. *Ephesians and Colossians*. Paideia Commentaries on the New Testament. Grand Rapids: Baker Academic, 2007.
Tanner, Kathryn. *Christ the Key*. Current Issues in Theology. Cambridge: Cambridge University Press, 2010.

Thielman, Frank. "Ephesians." In *Commentary on the New Testament Use of the Old*, edited by G. K. Beale and D. A. Carson, 813–34. Grand Rapids: Baker Academic, 2007.

———. *Ephesians*. Baker Exegetical Commentary. Grand Rapids: Baker Academic, 2010.

Thomson, John B. *The Ecclesiology of Stanley Hauerwas: A Christian Theology of Liberation*. Ashgate New Critical Thinking in Religion, Theology and Biblical Studies. Burlington, VT: Ashgate, 2003.

Torrance, Alexis. "Personhood and Patristics in Orthodox Theology: Reassessing the Debate." *Heythrop Journal* 52.4 (2011) 700–7.

Torrance, T. F. *Royal Priesthood: A Theology of Ordained Ministry*. 2nd ed. Edinburgh: T. & T. Clark, 1993.

Tull, James E. *High-Church Baptists in the South: The Origin, Nature, and Influence of Landmarkism*. Edited by Morris Ashcraft. Macon, GA: Mercer University Press, 2000.

Turcescu, Lucian. "'Person' versus 'Individual,' and Other Modern Misreadings of Gregory of Nyssa." *Modern Theology* 18.4 (2002) 527–39.

Turner, Robert. "Eschatology and Truth." In *The Theology of John Zizioulas: Personhood and the Church*, edited by Douglas H. Knight, 15–34. Burlington, VT: Ashgate, 2007.

Ulrich, Hans Günter. "Ethos als Zeugnis: Konturen christlichen Lebens mit Gott in der 'Welt' bei Stanley Hauerwas und Karl Barth." *Zeitschrift für Dialektische Theologie* 29.2 (2013) 50–73.

Vanhoozer, Kevin J. *Biblical Authority after Babel: Retrieving the Solas in the Spirit of Mere Protestant Christianity*. Grand Rapids: Brazos, 2016.

———. *Remythologizing Theology: Divine Action, Passion, and Authorship*. Cambridge: Cambridge University Press, 2010.

———. "Three (or More) Ways of Triangulating Theology: On the Very Idea of a Trinitarian System." In *Revisioning, Renewing, Rediscovering the Triune Center: Essays in Honor of Stanley J. Grenz*, edited by Derek J. Tidball et al., 31–58. Eugene, OR: Cascade, 2014.

Villegas, Isaac Samuel. "The Ecclesial Ethics of John Howard Yoder's Abuse." *Modern Theology* 37.1 (2021) 191–214.

Volf, Miroslav. *After Our Likeness: The Church as the Image of the Trinity*. Grand Rapids: Eerdmans, 1997.

———. "Being as God is: Trinity and Generosity." In *God's Life in Trinity*, edited by Miroslav Volf and Michael Welker, 3–12. Minneapolis: Fortress, 2006.

———. "Community Formation as an Image of the Triune God: A Congregational Model of Church Order and Life." In *Community Formation in the Early Church and in the Church Today*, 213–37. Peabody, MA: Hendrickson, 2002.

———. "'The Trinity is Our Social Program': The Doctrine of the Trinity and the Shape of Social Engagement." *Modern Theology* 14.3 (1998) 403–23.

Wanamaker, Charles A. *The Epistles to the Thessalonians: A Commentary on the Greek Text*. The New International Greek Testament Commentary. Grand Rapids: Eerdmans, 1990.

Webster, John. *Barth's Ethics of Reconciliation*. Cambridge: Cambridge University Press, 1995.

———. *Word and Church: Essays in Christian Dogmatics*. Cornerstones. London: Bloomsbury, 2016.
Weima, Jeffrey A. D. *1–2 Thessalonians*. Baker Exegetical Commentary on the New Testament. Grand Rapids: Baker Academic, 2014.
Weiss, Daniel H. "Direct Divine Sanction, the Prohibition of Bloodshed, and the Individual as Image of God in Classical Rabbinic Literature." *Journal of the Society of Christian Ethics* 32.2 (2012) 23–38.
Wells, Samuel. *Transforming Fate into Destiny: The Theological Ethics of Stanley Hauerwas*. Carlisle: Paternoster, 1998.
Westermann, Claus. *Genesis 1–11: A Continental Commentary*. 3 vols. Translated by John J. Scullion. Minneapolis: Fortress, 1984.
Wilks, John G. F. "The Trinitarian Ontology of John Zizioulas." *Vox Evangelica* 25 (1995) 63–88.
Wolterstorff, Nicholas. *The God We Worship: An Exploration of Liturgical Theology*. Grand Rapids: Eerdmans, 2015.
Wright, Nigel. *Free Church, Free State: The Positive Baptist Vision*. Milton Keynes: Paternoster, 2005.
———. "Inclusive Representation: Towards a Doctrine of Christian Ministry." *The Baptist Quarterly* 39.4 (2001) 159–74.
Yarnell, Malcolm B. *The Formation of Christian Doctrine*. Nashville: B&H Academic, 2007.
Yoder, John Howard. *Body Politics: Five Practices of the Christian Community before the Watching World*. Nashville: Discipleship Resources, 1992.
———. "A 'Free Church' Perspective on Baptism, Eucharist, and Ministry." *Mid-Stream* 23.3 (1984) 270–77.
———. *The Royal Priesthood: Essays Ecclesiastical and Ecumenical*. Edited by Michael G. Cartwright. Rev. ed. Scottdale, PA: Herald, 1994.
Zimmerman, Earl. "Church and Empire: Free-Church Ecclesiology in a Global Era." *Political Theology* 10.3 (2009) 471–95.
Zizioulas, John D. *Being as Communion: Studies in Personhood and the Church*. Crestwood, NY: St. Vladimir's Seminary Press, 1993.
———. "The Church as Communion." *St. Vladimir's Theological Quarterly* 38.1 (1994) 3–16.
———. *Communion and Otherness*. Edited by Paul McPartlan. New York: Continuum, 2006.
———. *Eucharist, Bishop, Church: The Unity of the Church in the Divine Eucharist and the Bishop during the First Three Centuries*. Brookline, MA: Holy Cross Orthodox Press, 2001.
———. *The Eucharistic Communion and the World*. Edited by Luke Ben Tallon. London: Bloomsbury, 2011.
———. *Lectures in Christian Dogmatics*. Edited by Douglas H. Knight. London: T. & T. Clark, 2008.
———. *The One and the Many: Studies on God, Man, the Church, and the World Today*. Edited by Gregory Edwards. Alhambra, CA: Sebastian, 2010.
Zwank, Rudolf. *Geschlechteranthropologie in theologischer Perspektive? Zur Phänomenologie des Geschlechtlichen in Hans Urs von Balthasars "Theodramatik."* Regensburger Studien zur Theologie 50. Frankfurt: Peter Lang, 1996.

Topic Index

baptism, 4, 8–10, 12, 21, 26, 30, 33–34, 36, 39–42, 47, 50, 53, 56, 63–64, 70, 72, 76, 79, 83, 95–96, 108, 114, 129, 130–31, 132, 150, 159, 164, 171, 172–73, 182, 191, 203, 205, 206–8
biological hypostasis, 21, 30–33, 40–41, 46, 47–48, 50, 121, 126, 130–31, 140, 196, 203

communal discernment, 8, 9, 164, 167, 171, 172, 174–77, 205, 208
communion, 15, 16, 21, 25–47, 49–50, 54, 71, 77, 78, 80, 113–14, 121–22, 126, 130–31, 136, 146, 203
creatureliness, 59, 102, 115, 123, 125, 197–98

ecclesial hypostasis, 31–35, 36, 38, 40–41, 46, 46–50, 114, 126, 196, 203
ecclesial identity, 61, 81n1, 129, 146, 203
ecclesial vocation, 67, 73
ecstasis, 21, 29, 31 36, 37, 39, 45, 47–49, 50, 53, 61, 76–77, 203, 209, 214
ethnography, 212–14, 216
eucharist, 4, 6, 21, 25–26, 30, 35–39, 41–47, 49–50, 64–66, 70, 72, 76, 96, 107, 113, 126–31, 135, 137, 139–41, 146–47, 173–74, 196, 203–5

eucharistic hypostasis, 127

Free Church, ix–x, 2–3, 7–12, 15–16, 19–23, 111, 147–52, 168–72, 174–78, 182, 190–94, 196, 200–2, 205–6, 208–13, 215–216
freedom, 2, 8, 11, 27–29, 33–34, 47, 63, 67, 75, 77–78, 114–15, 121–22, 127, 130–31, 146, 192–93, 196, 198, 202, 208, 212–13, 216

Holy Spirit, 5, 8, 10, 13–14, 16, 23, 27–30
human identity, 14, 17, 40, 42, 65, 67, 74, 76, 100, 102, 105, 107, 137–40, 142, 145–46, 177, 184, 201, 204, 211–12
Human nature 16, 23, 55, 184–85

imago Dei (image of God), ix, 13, 27, 30–32, 37–38, 40, 44, 70, 76, 95, 98, 101, 104–05, 109, 112, 130–33, 137, 146, 182, 186–87, 189–90, 195, 198, 201, 211
individualism, 16, 24, 26, 30–33, 35, 36, 39, 41, 45, 48, 50, 52, 55, 100, 192

kenosis, 51–66, 67, 71, 72, 76–80, 102, 112, 113, 118–19, 121, 125, 129, 203

235

kingdom of God, 4, 6, 17, 18, 22–23, 25, 26, 34–35, 37, 44–45, 78, 82, 84–89, 90–98, 101–102, 104–6, 108–10, 112, 116, 122, 132–33, 140–41, 143, 145, 147, 150, 152, 154–55, 160, 161, 163, 167, 171, 175, 177, 181, 194, 196, 199, 204–5, 209, 215

liturgy, 5, 8, 11, 16–17, 21, 25, 35–39, 42–49, 50, 62, 83, 94, 104, 107–8, 128–30, 134, 136–37, 139, 141, 146, 182, 203, 206, 213–214, 216
liturgical practices, 4–5, 26, 38, 88, 95–96, 107, 135, 172, 181–82, 184, 203–5, 207, 211, 213–14, 216
Lord's Supper, 1, 4, 6, 9, 164, 168, 172, 173–74, 182, 188, 207, 208, 213
lordship ecclesiology, 149, 150–152, 168, 170, 177

Mary, 22, 52, 59–61, 69, 72–73, 118–19, 122, 124, 139, 203
Marian *disponsibilité*, 73, 197
munus triplex (threefold office), 10–11, 18, 23, 155–57, 168–77, 182–93, 198, 200, 205, 208

narrative, 9–10, 13, 16–17, 22, 81–84, 88, 90, 93–96, 97–100, 102–110, 112–13, 116–17, 120, 127, 129, 133–35, 144, 146, 153, 204

otherness, 27–29, 31–32, 35–36, 38, 41–42, 44, 46–47
ontological necessity, 30, 33, 40, 42, 57, 113–15, 122

pacifism, 94, 104
participation, 10–11, 14, 31–32, 34, 36–39, 42, 47, 49–50, 60, 65–66, 68, 70–71, 73, 75, 79–80, 107–8, 118, 120, 122, 128–29, 137, 139, 146, 161, 168–73, 175–77, 182–84, 189, 190–93, 195, 200, 204, 205, 209

particularity, 5, 29, 114–15, 117, 120, 146, 161, 204
personhood, 13, 15–16, 20–22, 25–33, 35–44, 46–48, 50, 52, 67–71, 73, 76–77, 79–80, 107, 109, 113–14, 118, 126–32, 137, 146, 178, 195, 203–4, 212, 217
polis, 22, 82–84, 89–90, 96–97, 101, 107–9, 112, 116–17, 142
prolepsis, 14, 15, 37, 86, 138, 144–45, 147, 158, 183, 201, 205

relationality, 14, 18, 114
rule of Christ, 6, 10, 11–12, 82–85, 86, 89, 90, 102, 112, 116, 118, 132, 135, 143, 149–52, 153–63, 167–71, 174–77, 181, 189, 191, 193–201, 204, 205

self-abnegation, 54, 55, 66, 72, 78, 79–80, 122, 123–25, 197, 198
substance, 24, 27, 65, 67, 115, 178, 208

telos of the church, 2–3, 6, 19, 22, 38, 94, 97, 128, 138, 145, 184, 203–5, 209, 214, 215–16
theosis, 6, 21, 26, 32, 34–35, 37, 39, 41–44, 46, 49–50, 115, 126, 138, 140–41, 165, 203, 209
Trinity, 13–15, 24, 27–29, 35, 40, 53, 112, 116, 121, 145, 182, 201

virtue, 22, 55, 82, 92–94, 96–97, 99, 104–9, 122, 134, 139, 142, 155–56, 166, 171, 180, 182, 189–91, 193, 196, 200
vocation, ix, 18, 20–21, 23, 37, 49–50, 60, 65, 67, 69–70, 73–75, 77–78, 80, 91, 93, 98, 101, 113, 121, 132, 161, 164, 169–71, 174, 177, 181, 191, 195, 200–1, 203, 205, 215–16

witness, 4, 82–91, 96–99, 105–6, 108–9, 122, 127–28, 136, 146, 160, 164–66, 172, 183, 199–200, 204–5, 207, 212

www.ingramcontent.com/pod-product-compliance
Lightning Source LLC
Chambersburg PA
CBHW051053230426
43667CB00013B/2274